D0924709

THE
BEST
SHORT
PLAYS 1988

edited and introduced by
RAMON DELGADO

Best Short Plays Series

THEATRE BOOK PUBLISHERS
211 West 71 Street, New York, NY 10023

Copyright © 1988 by Ramon Delgado
All Rights Reserved
Published in New York, by Applause Theatre Books Publishers
Library of Congress Catalog Card No. 38-8006
ISBN 1-55783-026-6 (paper)
ISBN 1-55783-025-8 (cloth)
ISSN: 0067-6284
Manufactured in the United States of America

For Paul Baker

Contents

Introduction

HORTON FOOTE
Blind Date 1

TIMOTHY MASON
Bearclaw 23

LAURENCE HOLDER
When the Chickens Came Home to Roost 71

JACK HEIFNER
Bargains 101

DAVID KRANES
Cantrell 143

SHEILA WALSH
Molly and James 175

HUGH LEONARD
Pizzazz 193

KATHARINE HOUGHTON
Buddha 237

DEBORAH PRYOR
The Love Talker 255

PAUL SELIG
Terminal Bar 281

BOOKS AND PLAYS BY RAMON DELGADO

The Best Short Plays 1981 (with Stanley Richards)
The Best Short Plays 1982
The Best Short Plays 1983
The Best Short Plays 1984
The Best Short Plays 1985
The Best Short Plays 1986
The Best Short Plays 1987
Acting With Both Sides of Your Brain

The Youngest Child of Pablo Peco
Waiting for the Bus
The Little Toy Dog
Once Below A Lighthouse
Sparrows of the Field
The Knight-Mare's Nest
Omega's Ninth
Listen, My Children
A Little Holy Water
The Fabulous Jeromes
The Jerusalem Thorn
Stones

INTRODUCTION

Within the past year and a half, feature articles on the short play have appeared in the *Dramatists Guild Quarterly*, the *American Theatre* magazine, and the *New York Times*—all testifying to the interest in the one-act form among playwrights, critics, and audiences. Reasons for this popularity are more frequently artistic than commercial. Playwrights find the short play an exciting challenge. For example, Israel Horovitz, author of about thirty short plays (seven published in this series), participating on a panel for the Dramatists Guild, observes, "I don't think there's anything like the one-act play if you're working with a strongly dramatic subject and you put the audience, as they say, on the edge of their seats. There's no way that they can escape your world; it's so contained. I think it's an enormously challenging form." Horton Foote (whose *Blind Date* appears in this edition) concurs: "There is, of course, a great challenge in fitting a complex character or situation into one act. It demands concentration, great clarity and economy."

Anne Cattaneo, dramaturg of New York City's Second Stage, writing in the *American Theatre* magazine, points out the value the form has for both the established professional playwright and the beginning writer: "...the one-act can be a place for non-naturalistic experimentation as well as consolidation of the techniques and themes that have made their professional reputations. Just as the young writer may feel freed working within the limitations of a swifter and more concentrated form, a well-known writer with a large following can use the 'smallness' of the one-act to explore new territory without the same burden of expectation a new full-length would entail."

Theatre reviewer Mel Gussow featured the short play in an article for the *New York Times,* declaring that "...the one-act is a vital—and even a necessary—theatrical form, one with special artistic demands. It challenges playwrights to say more with less and in many cases, it brings out their strength."

The selections for this volume of *Best Short Plays* demonstrate how the challenge of the form has been fulfilled as once again the selected playwrights convey the universal concerns of our common humanity through the specific issues and varied facets of our culture. In *Blind Date* Horton Foote examines the conflict between changing behavior and traditional values in the poignant yet humorous problem of finding a suitable suitor for an overly critical visiting niece. Timothy Mason's *Bearclaw* poses the problem of whether or not an elderly parent is better off in a nursing home.

Black playwright Laurence Holder examines the morality of leadership in the struggle for power between two black politicians in *When the Chickens Came Home to Roost*. Jack Heifner's comedy, *Bargains*, reckons with the value of experience against authority in a small town variety store, while David Kranes's *Cantrell* raises an issue on the possible reformation of a hit man. *Pizzazz* by Hugh Leonard presents a Pirandellian puzzle of relationships which tests the nature of love and loyalty, and Sheila Walsh's *Molly and James* examines the monetary value of literary observations from the viewpoint of the observed. Katharine Houghton offers a Zen consideration of erotic attraction between a middle-aged man and woman in *Buddha*, and Deborah Pryor's *The Love Talker* presents a fantastic folk tale that validates superstitions while it questions them, exposing the repressions that may be responsible for their existence. And, lastly, Paul Selig's vision of the future in *Terminal Bar* speculates with the survivors of a devastating plague while he evokes the terror of AIDS.

Though most of the plays in this volume are written in a traditional realistic style, there are a couple of exceptions, demonstrating the versatility of the form and confirming the lyrical description of the short play offered by Louis Catron, professor of theater at the College of William and Mary and author of the excellent text *Writing, Producing, and Selling Your Play*. In his chapter on the short play, "The One-Act Play: Theatre's Iconoclast," Professor Catron rhapsodizes on the form: "Bold and brassy like a circus band or gentle like a sea breeze with the sunset; rebellious and stubborn like a kid brother or conservative to the point of being reactionary; irritably didactic with the subtlety of an aroused porcupine intent upon proving the righteousness of its beliefs, or wide-eyed and innocent as in the hearts of children the week before Christmas—the one-act play is all of these, and more. It deliberately defies all literary descriptions: As soon as it appears to be securely walled up inside a neat definition, it bursts free into new territory with a triumphant leap. The one-act is theatre's iconoclast, and damn proud of it." (The last two plays in this collection are the most iconoclastic and are undoubtedly the most controversial.)

Finally, a note about the dedication of this year's volume. While recently in Texas to give an acting workshop and a lecture on short plays, I was once again reminded of the influence Paul Baker has had on the development of theater creativity—particularly in that state, but also upon performers, writers, and directors throughout the country. During his twenty-five years as artistic director of the Dallas Theater Center, he and his creative staff—especially Mary Sue Jones and Eugene McKinney—helped to develop scores of new plays and playwrights. As one of his students some twenty-eight years ago who still values the joy of his creative influence, I take this opportunity to thank him and sing his praises.

Horton Foote

BLIND DATE

Horton Foote

Horton Foote is the dean of American dramatic writers. In both length and breadth of experience in writing for stage, television, and film, he has few equals. His work returns to this series after a hiatus of thirty-five years; his last appearance was with *John Turner Davis* in *The Best Short Plays 1953-54*, then edited by Margaret Mayorga.

The source of Mr. Foote's success is his careful examination of human experiences in the specific culture he knew best from growing up in a small Texas town. As he wrote a few years ago: "From the beginning most of my plays have taken place in the imaginary town of Harrison, Texas, and it seems to me a more unlikely subject could not be found in these days of Broadway and world theatre, than this attempt of mine to recreate a small Southern town and its people. But I did not choose this task, this place, or these people to write about so much as they chose me, and I try to write of them with honesty."

In *Blind Date*, originally produced in Manhattan at the HB Playwrights Foundation in 1985 and then at Curt Dempster's Ensemble Studio Theatre in Marathon '86, Mr. Foote continues his exploration of the humorous and poignant moments in the lives of a small town Texas family. The reviewer for the *New York Times*, Frank Rich, called the play "perfect of its kind . . . a gem." And *New York* magazine reviewer John Simon concurred: "Foote writes with intelligence, sensitivity, humor, and compassion . . . *Blind Date*, understatedly funny and uninsistently touching, is full of lived humanity."

In a recent article for the *New York Times*, Mr. Foote explained his reasons for writing in the one-act play form: "I realized that the one-act play was as important to me, and what I was trying to do as a writer, as the short story form is to some novelists. The form allows me to flesh out and explore facets of what has become for me an attempt to create a moral and social history of a particular idea over a period of time."

To list all of Mr. Foote's distinguished works—well documented in standard reference works—is beyond the scope of this introduction. But his highest achievements should be noted. Among his honors for screenplays: *On Valentine's Day*, the official American entry for the Venice Film Festival in 1986; an Academy

Award nomination for the Best Screenplay for *Trip to Bountiful* in 1985; Academy Award winner and Writers Guild Award for Best Original Screenplay for *Tender Mercies* in 1983; Academy Award for Best Screenplay and Writers Guild Award for adaptation of Harper Lee's *To Kill A Mockingbird* in 1962.

Mr. Foote's contributions to television drama are numerous, starting with work written in the "Golden Days" of the 1950s for Playhouse 90, Studio One, the Philco-Goodyear Playhouse, and Omnibus, and continuing through 1987 with *Story of A Marriage*, a 5-part series for the PBS American Playhouse. Among his additional notable works for television is the *Harrison, Texas* collection, published in 1956, and produced on stage by HB Studio in 1976.

Mr. Foote's produced plays go back as far as 1944 with *Only the Heart*, which starred Mildred Dunnock and June Walker, and continue through the present. During the 1986-87 theatre season, New York theatergoers also could see two other plays with Mr. Foote's Texas portraits, *The Widow Claire* and *Lily Dale*. It is a privilege to welcome back Mr. Foote and his work to the pages of *Best Short Plays*.

Characters:
ROBERT
SARAH NANCY
DOLORES
FELIX

Setting:

The living room of Robert and Dolores Henry. It is empty. Robert comes in. He is a lawyer and has a brief case, several newspapers, a package of purchases from the drug store. He drops all these on the sofa, takes his coat off, throwing that over a chair. He calls:"Dolores." There is no answer. He kicks his shoes off and calls: "Children." Again no answer. He goes to the radio and turns it on. He gets one of the newspapers and spreads it around the rooms as he looks through it. He calls again: "Dolores, I am home." A voice calls back: "She's not here."

ROBERT: *(Calling)* Where is she?
SARAH NANCY: *(The voice—calling)* Yes.
ROBERT: Where?
SARAH NANCY: She took the children to a friend's to spend the night.
ROBERT: Where are you?
SARAH NANCY: In my room.
ROBERT: Did your aunt say when we were having supper?
SARAH NANCY: We've had supper. We ate with the children.
ROBERT: What did you have?
SARAH NANCY: Peanut butter and jelly sandwiches. *(He is depressed by that. He goes to the window and looks out. He goes to the radio and turns it off. He sees two college yearbooks on a table. He goes and picks them up to look at them when his wife Dolores comes in)*
ROBERT: Where is my supper?
DOLORES: What?
ROBERT: Where is my supper? Do you know what time it is? I'm starved. I have been here at least half an hour.
DOLORES: Have you forgotten our conversation at breakfast?
ROBERT: What conversation?
DOLORES: Oh, Robert. I told you to eat uptown tonight.

ROBERT: I don't remember that.

DOLORES: I told you I was not going to fix supper tonight.

ROBERT: I don't remember a single word of that.

DOLORES: You were looking right at me when I told you. I said I was giving the children peanut butter and jelly sandwiches at five thirty and at six thirty after their baths I was taking them over to Hannah's to spend the night so they would not be running in and out of here while Sarah Nancy was entertaining her date.

ROBERT: Does Sarah Nancy have another date?

DOLORES: Yes. Thank God. I told you that too this morning.

ROBERT: If you did I don't remember.

DOLORES: Of course not. You never listen to a word I say. Oh, if I live through this I'll live through anything. *(Whispering)* Don't you remember my telling you this morning that at last I had arranged another date for her? After trying desperately for three days?

ROBERT: No.

DOLORES: Well, I did. And I hope this one turns out better than the last time. I talked to Sister late this afternoon. She is just beside herself. You know suppose, she said, she takes it into her head to insult this date too. Sister, I said, I refuse to get discouraged. I did not get on the beauty pages of the University of Texas and the Texas A. & M. yearbooks on my looks alone. It was on my personality. And that can be acquired. Don't you agree?

ROBERT: I guess.

DOLORES: I wasn't born a conversationalist, you know. I can remember being as shy as the next one, but I gritted my teeth and forced myself to converse, and so can Sarah Nancy. Don't you agree?

ROBERT: I guess. Who did you get her a date with?

DOLORES: Felix.

ROBERT: Felix who?

DOLORES: Felix Robertson.

ROBERT: Is that the best you could do? My God.

DOLORES: My God, yourself. I have been calling all over town all week trying to arrange dates for the poor little thing, and you know very well I had absolutely no luck. Not a one wanted to come over here until I called Felix Robertson. I finally called Sister two days ago I was so depressed and had a frank talk with her. I explained the situation to her and she said it was nothing new. She said every time a boy has come around they don't stay long, because Sarah Nancy either won't talk or is very sarcastic. She wants me to have a frank talk with her before Felix gets here and try and help her improve her disposition and I said I would. But it's not so easy to do, you know. I have been worrying over how to talk to her about all this all afternoon. And I almost have a sick headache.

ROBERT: What about supper?

DOLORES: What about your supper? What about it?

ROBERT: I forgot about eating uptown and I'm tired and I don't want to go back out. Is there anything to eat in the kitchen?

DOLORES: My God, Robert. I don't know what's in the kitchen. I feel this is a crisis in my niece's life and I really haven't had time to worry about what is in the kitchen. (*A pause*) And don't start pouting, Robert.

ROBERT: I'm not pouting.

DOLORES: Yes, you are. I know you very well.

ROBERT: Well, my God, how much longer is this going on? Ever since your niece has been here all you've done is worry about her.

DOLORES: I tried to explain to you. (*She looks at the room*) Oh, look at this room. I spent all afternoon cleaning it. (*She starts to pick up his shoes, his coat, etc.*)

ROBERT: I'll do that.

DOLORES: Just take them all out. I need to be alone now with Sarah Nancy. (*He goes. She fixes pillows on the couch, rearranges a few chairs about the room all the while singing in a bright, happy manner. After a moment she calls:* "Sarah Nancy." *She gets no answer and she calls again:* "Sarah Nancy, Sarah Nancy, I don't want to hurry you, but it's almost time for your date to be here." *Again, no response from Sarah Nancy and she is about to leave the room when Sarah Nancy appears. She is as doleful looking as Dolores Henry is cheerful. Dolores gives her a bright, determined smile, which Sarah Nancy does not return*) Well, you do look sweet. Is that a new dress?

SARAH NANCY: Oh, no.

DOLORES: Well, it's new to me. It's very becoming. It has a lot of style. That's what I always look for first in my clothes, style. (*Sarah Nancy gives no reaction*) Now, precious lamb, let me tell you a little bit about the young man who is coming to see you tonight. I don't know whether you remember meeting him or not, but he says he met you at Louise Davis' swim party as you were the only one that didn't want to swim. He is Felix Robertson. (*Sarah Nancy groans*) What's the matter dear? Do you remember him?

SARAH NANCY: I remember him.

DOLORES: That's nice. He felt sure you would. Why do you remember him?

SARAH NANCY: Because he kept slapping me on the back and asking me how I was.

DOLORES: He is a very sensitive boy. He was just trying to make you feel at home. And he is, as I'm sure you could tell, from a lovely family. His mother and your dear mother were girlhood friends. Now, difficult as it is for me to do, I feel I have to discuss a few things with you, Sarah Nancy, before Felix arrives. I think, dear, you have to learn to be a little more gracious to the young men that come to see you. Now, I am extremely puzzled why my phone hasn't been rung off the wall since you've been my guest, but I think last night I was given a clue. Sam and Ned, those two boys that called last week, told their mother you were extremely hard to converse with. Boys, you know, need someone peppy to talk to. (*Sarah Nancy rolls her eyes*) Now, don't roll your eyes, darling. You know I have your best interest at heart. I want you to be just as popular as any girl here. But to accomplish that you have to learn to converse.

SARAH NANCY: I don't know what to talk about.

DOLORES: I know. I know. I called up your mother this very morning and told her all this, and she said that always seemed to be your trouble. When boys come around, you can't think of things to say. (*She goes to the desk and opens a drawer and takes out a list*) So I sat down and made a list of topics to talk about. And I thought before Felix got here, you and I could go over it, and you could memorize them and then you would always be sure of making conversation. All right, dear? (*Sarah Nancy doesn't answer. Robert enters*)

ROBERT: Excuse me.

DOLORES: Robert?

ROBERT: How much longer are you going to be?

DOLORES: Why?

ROBERT: Because I am starving, that's why.

DOLORES: Did you look in the icebox?

ROBERT: I looked in the icebox.

DOLORES: Well...

ROBERT: The ice has all melted.

DOLORES: Well, maybe you had better ride over to the icehouse and get a block of ice.

ROBERT: I will after I've eaten. I'm hungry.

DOLORES: All right. Just be patient. I won't be long with Sarah Nancy.

ROBERT: Honey, I'm starved.

DOLORES: I know you are starved. You have told us that a thousand times. Honestly, I'm not deaf. And I'll be out there as soon as I can, but Felix will be here any minute and Sarah Nancy and I have to go over some things first. Now excuse us please. (*He goes*) Now where were we. Oh, yes. I was going over my list of things to talk about. (*Dolores picks up her list and begins reading*) One: Who is going to win the football game next Friday? Two: Do you think we have had enough rain for the cotton yet? Three: I hear you were a football player in high school. What position did you play? Do you miss football? Four: I hear you are an insurance salesman. What kind of insurance do you sell? Five: What is the best car on the market today do you think? Six: What church do you belong to? Seven: Do you enjoy dancing? Eight: Do you enjoy bridge? (*She puts the list down*) All right, that will do for a start. Now, let's practice. I'll be Felix. Now. Hello, Sarah Nancy. (*A pause, Sarah Nancy looks at her like she thinks she's crazy*) Now, what do you say, Sarah Nancy.

SARAH NANCY: About what?

DOLORES: About what? About what you say when someone says hello to you, Sarah Nancy. Now, let's start again. Hello, Sarah Nancy.

SARAH NANCY: Hello.

DOLORES: Honey, don't just say hello and above all don't scowl and say hello. Smile. Hello, how very nice to see you. Let me feel your warmth. Now, will you remember that? Of course you will. All right, let's start on our questions. Begin with your first question. (*A pause*) I'm waiting, honey.

SARAH NANCY: I forget.

DOLORES: Well, don't be discouraged. I'll go over the list carefully and slowly again. One: Who is going to win the football game next Friday? Two: Do you think we have enough rain for the cotton yet? Three: I hear you were a football player in high school. What position did you play? Do you miss football? Four: I hear you are an insurance salesman. What kind of insurance do you sell?

Five: What is the best car out on the market today, do you think?
Six: What church do you belong to? Seven: Do you enjoy dancing?
Eight: Do you enjoy bridge? Now, we won't be rigid about the
questions, of course. You can ask the last question first if you want
to.

SARAH NANCY: What's the last question again?

DOLORES: Do you enjoy bridge?

SARAH NANCY: I hate bridge.

DOLORES: Well, then, sweetness, just substitute another
question. Say, do you enjoy dancing?

SARAH NANCY: I hate dancing.

DOLORES: Now, you don't hate dancing. You couldn't hate
dancing. It is in your blood. Your mother and daddy are both
beautiful dancers. You just need to practice is all. Now . . .

SARAH NANCY: Why didn't you get me a date with Arch Leon? I
think he's the cute one.

DOLORES: He's going steady, honey, I explained that.

SARAH NANCY: Who is he going steady with?

DOLORES: Alberta Jackson.

SARAH NANCY: Is she cute?

DOLORES: I think she's right cute, a little common looking and
acting for my taste.

SARAH NANCY: He sure is cute.

DOLORES: Well, Felix Robertson is a lovely boy.

SARAH NANCY: I think he's about as cute as a warthog.

DOLORES: Sarah Nancy.

SARAH NANCY: I think he looks just like a warthog.

DOLORES: Sarah Nancy, precious . . .

SARAH NANCY: That's the question I'd like to ask him. How is
the hog pen, warthog?

DOLORES: Precious, precious.

SARAH NANCY: Anyway, they are all stupid.

DOLORES: Who, honey?

SARAH NANCY: Boys.

DOLORES: Precious, darling.

SARAH NANCY: Dumb and stupid. (*She starts away*)

DOLORES: Sarah Nancy, where in the world are you going?

SARAH NANCY: I'm going to bed.

DOLORES: Sarah Nancy, what is possessing you to say a thing
like that. You're just trying to tease me.

SARAH NANCY: Oh, no, I'm not. (*She starts away*)

DOLORES: Sarah Nancy, you can't go to bed. You have a young man coming to call on you at any moment. You have to be gracious...

SARAH NANCY: I don't feel like being gracious. I'm sleepy. I'm going to bed.

DOLORES: Sarah Nancy, you can't. Do you want to put me in my grave? The son of one of your mother's dearest friends will be here at any moment to call on you, and you cannot be so rude as to go to bed and refuse to receive him. Sarah Nancy, I beg you. I implore you.

SARAH NANCY: Oh, all right. (*She sits down*) Ask me some questions.

DOLORES: No, dear. You ask me some questions.

SARAH NANCY: What church do you attend?

DOLORES: That's lovely. That's a lovely question to begin with. Now I'll answer as Felix will. Methodist.

SARAH NANCY: That's a dumb church.

DOLORES: Sarah Nancy.

SARAH NANCY: I think it's a dumb church. It's got no style. We used to be Methodist but we left for the Episcopal. They don't rant and rave in the Episcopal Church.

DOLORES: And they don't rant and rave in the Methodist Church either, honey. Not here. Not in Harrison.

SARAH NANCY: Last time I was here they did.

DOLORES: Well, things have changed. Anyway, you're not supposed to comment when he answers the questions, you're just supposed to sit back and listen to the answers as if you're fascinated and find it all very interesting.

SARAH NANCY: Why?

DOLORES: Because that's how you entertain young men, graciously. You make them feel you are interested in whatever they have to say.

SARAH NANCY: Suppose I'm not.

DOLORES: Well, it is not important if you are or not, you are supposed to make them think you are. (*Robert enters*)

ROBERT: Dolores.

DOLORES: What?

ROBERT: The children are on the phone.

DOLORES: What do they want?

ROBERT: They want to talk to you.

DOLORES: Ask them what they want. Tell them I can't talk now.

(*Sarah Nancy is looking at the yearbook*)

SARAH NANCY: How did you make the beauty page at two colleges?

DOLORES: Personality. I always knew how to keep a conversation going.

ROBERT: Dolores.

DOLORES: Yes.

ROBERT: They say they won't tell me what they want. They'll only tell you.

DOLORES: All right. (*She goes*)

SARAH NANCY: Did you go to college with Aunt Dolores?

ROBERT: We met the year she graduated.

SARAH NANCY: She was beautiful.

ROBERT: I guess she was. (*Dolores comes in*)

DOLORES: They forgot their teddy bears. I said you would bring them over.

ROBERT: They're nine and ten years old. What do they want with teddy bears?

DOLORES: They still sleep with them. You know that.

ROBERT: Well, I'm not driving anywhere with two teddy bears for two half-grown children.

DOLORES: Why are you being so difficult?

ROBERT: I am not difficult. I am hungry and tired. I worked hard all day.

DOLORES: Well, I didn't exactly have a ball today myself, mister. If I find you something to eat, will you take those teddy bears over to the children?

ROBERT: All right. I'll be the laughing stock of the town, but I'll do it. (*She goes*)

SARAH NANCY: How do you get on a beauty page?

ROBERT: Well, you have to be pretty to start with, I guess. I think a committee of some kind looks the girls on campus over and makes recommendations and I guess they have judges. But I really don't know. You'll have to ask your aunt that.

SARAH NANCY: How did you meet Aunt Dolores?

ROBERT: At a dance. I think. Yes, I think it was at a dance the first time I met her. And I asked her for a date and six weeks later I popped the question.

SARAH NANCY: What does that mean?

ROBERT: What?

SARAH NANCY: Popping the question.

ROBERT: You know. I asked her to marry me. (*Sarah Nancy makes a face*) What are you making a face about?

SARAH NANCY: I don't know. I sure hope nobody pops a question to me.

ROBERT: Well, they will some day.

SARAH NANCY: Who?

ROBERT: Some boy or other.

SARAH NANCY: I don't know any boys.

ROBERT: Of course you know some boys.

SARAH NANCY: Not any I'd want to pop the question to me. (*Dolores comes in*)

DOLORES: I opened a can of chile and a can of tamales and sliced some tomatoes. Will that do you?

ROBERT: Thanks. (*He goes*)

SARAH NANCY: Any of the dumb boys I know try popping a question to me, I'll kick them in the stomach.

DOLORES: What in the world are you talking about, honey? (*The door bell rings*) There he is. Now, quickly, let me see how you look. (*She forces Sarah Nancy to stand up*) Oh, pretty. (*Sarah Nancy sticks out her tongue*) Oh, Sarah Nancy. (*Dolores goes to the door and opens it*) Come in, Felix. (*Felix comes in*) How handsome you look. I believe you two have met?

FELIX: Yes.

SARAH NANCY: What church do you attend?

FELIX: What?

SARAH NANCY: What church do you attend?

FELIX: Methodist.

DOLORES: (*Jumping in nervously*) Sarah Nancy is an Episcopalian. She is very devout. Felix is very devout, too, you know.

SARAH NANCY: Who is going to win the football game on Friday?

FELIX: We are.

SARAH NANCY: Why?

FELIX: Because we are the best team.

SARAH NANCY: Who says so?

FELIX: Everybody know that. Do you like football?

SARAH NANCY: No.

FELIX: No?

SARAH NANCY: No.

FELIX: Do you like...

SARAH NANCY: I hate sports. I like to read. Do you like to read?

FELIX: No.

DOLORES: Well, you know what they say...opposites attract. (*She laughs merrily. Felix laughs. Sarah Nancy scowls*) Well, I'll stay and visit just a few minutes longer and then I'll leave you two young people alone. How is your sweet mother, Felix?

FELIX: O.K.

DOLORES: Your mother and Sarah Nancy's mother and I were all girls together. Did your mother tell you that? My, the good times we used to have together.

FELIX: Do you have a radio?

DOLORES: Yes, over there. (*He goes to the radio and turns it on*)

FELIX: Do you want to dance?

SARAH NANCY: No, I hate dancing. What church do you belong to?

DOLORES: You asked him that before, Sarah Nancy, honey, remember? He said he was a Methodist and I said you were an Episcopalian.

SARAH NANCY: Oh. (*Dolores finds a way to get behind Felix and she begins mouthing a question for Sarah Nancy to ask*) What do you do?

FELIX: What do you mean?

SARAH NANCY: For a living.

FELIX: Right now I'm in insurance. But I'm leaving that. Not enough money in it. I'm going to be a mortician.

SARAH NANCY: What's that?

DOLORES: An undertaker, honey.

SARAH NANCY: How do you get to do that?

FELIX: You go to school.

SARAH NANCY: What kind of school?

FELIX: A mortician school.

SARAH NANCY: Oh, who teaches you?

FELIX: Other morticians. (*Dolores begins to subtly mouth another question; Sarah Nancy continues to ignore her, so Dolores finally gives up*)

DOLORES: I'm going now and leave you two young people alone to enjoy yourselves. (*She goes. He goes to the radio and moves the dial from one program to another*)

FELIX: There is nothing on I want to hear. (*He turns the radio off. He sits down and looks at Sarah Nancy, smiling.*) Having a good time on your visit here?

SARAH NANCY: It's okay.

FELIX: Let's play some games. What games do you like to play?

SARAH NANCY: I never played any.

FELIX: Never played any games?

SARAH NANCY: No.

FELIX: All right, I'll teach you one. How about ghosts?

SARAH NANCY: Ghosts.

FELIX: It's the name of the game. You start a word to be spelled and the one that spells a word is a third of a ghost. Get it?

SARAH NANCY: No.

FELIX: Well, maybe it isn't too much fun with just two playing. I know, let's see who can name the most books of the Bible. I'll go first. (*He doesn't wait for her to comment and he begins to rattle off the names of the Bible*) Genesis, Exodus, Leviticus...(*He closes his eyes as he thinks of them and he takes it all very seriously. Sarah Nancy stares at him as if he is insane. When he gets to Daniel she slips quietly out of the room and is gone by the time he begins the New Testament. He is not aware she is gone. Robert comes in. Felix is so concentrated he doesn't see him. Robert looks at him like he is crazy, shakes his head in disbelief and leaves the room. Felix is unaware of any of it. He says the names very fast as if speed were part of the game, so fast in fact that the names should not always be distinct. When he finishes, he opens his eyes*) How did I do? I think I got every one. (*He looks at his watch*) I did it in pretty fair amount of time, too. Now let's see what you can do. (*He suddenly becomes aware she is not in the room. Calling*) Sarah Nancy. (*He is puzzled by her disappearance and is about to go to the door leading into the rest of the house to call her when Robert comes in with two teddy bears*)

ROBERT: Hello, Felix. (*They shake hands*) What's new?

FELIX: Not a whole lot.

ROBERT: You're looking well.

FELIX: Thank you, sir. (*Robert starts out the front door*) Excuse me. Do you know where Sarah Nancy is?

ROBERT: No, I don't, son.

FELIX: She was here a minute ago. We were having a contest to see who could name the most books of the Bible.

ROBERT: Who won?

FELIX: I don't know. She was here when I started, but when I finished and opened my eyes, she was gone.

ROBERT: Just sit down and relax. She'll be back.

FELIX: Yes, sir. (*Robert goes out. Felix sits down. Dolores comes in looking stricken*)

DOLORES: Felix, Sarah Nancy has sent me out to apologize to you and beg your forgiveness. She has been stricken, suddenly, with a very bad sick headache. She's suffered from them, she says, since childhood, and the worst of it is the poor darling never, never knows when they will strike. She says she was sitting here listening to you rattle off all the books of the Bible and having one of the liveliest times of her life, when her attack began. She is just heartbroken, the poor little thing. She slipped out not wanting to disturb you, to take an aspirin, hoping to find relief for her headache, so she could resume the lovely time she was having with you, but she got no relief from the aspirin, and she says now the only relief are cold packs on her head and total, total silence. She is quite stricken, poor sweet thing. Too stricken to even come and say good night. Whatever will Felix think of me, she said. "Why precious darling," I reassured her, "he will most certainly understand." I know you do. Don't you?

FELIX: Oh, yes, ma'am.

DOLORES: How is your sweet mother?

FELIX: Just fine, thank you, ma'am.

DOLORES: And your daddy's well?

FELIX: Oh, yes ma'am.

DOLORES: Tell your mother and daddy hello for me.

FELIX: I will. (*A pause*) They said when I came over here to say hello for them.

DOLORES: Thank you. (*A pause*)

FELIX: Well, I guess I'll be going on home.

DOLORES: All right, Felix.

FELIX: Tell Nancy Sarah...

DOLORES: Sarah Nancy.

FELIX: Oh, yes. Sarah Nancy. Tell her I hope she feels better.

DOLORES: I will.

FELIX: Tell her I said all the books in the Bible under ten minutes, and if she thinks she can beat that to call me up and I'll come over and time her.

DOLORES: I'll tell her that.

FELIX: Well, good night again.

DOLORES: Good night to you, Felix, dear. (*He goes. Dolores sighs. She begins to turn the lights off when Sarah Nancy comes out*) What are you doing out here, Sarah Nancy?

SARAH NANCY: I want to listen to the radio.

DOLORES: You cannot listen to the radio. You can be seen from the street if you sit in this room listening to the radio. I told that boy that you were mortally ill with a sick headache and you cannot appear five minutes later perfectly well and sit in the living room and listen to the radio.

SARAH NANCY: I want to hear Rudy Vallee.

DOLORES: You will not hear Rudy Vallee and run the risk of someone seeing you and telling Felix about it. What possesses you? I ask two lovely young men over last week and you refuse to speak to either of them all evening. I ask this sweet, charming boy over tonight and you walk out of the room while he is saying the books of the Bible. Well, I tell you one thing, I will not ask another single boy over here again until you decide to be gracious. And I know you can be gracious, as gracious as any girl here. Anyone with the lovely mother you have can certainly be gracious. (*Robert enters*) Oh, you gave me such a start. I thought you were Felix. How were the children?

ROBERT: All right.

DOLORES: Did you tell them to behave themselves and to mind Hannah and to get to bed when she told them to?

ROBERT: No.

DOLORES: Why not?

ROBERT: Because it would have done no good. They were all running around like a bunch of wild Indians. They weren't any more interested in those teddy bears than I am. Did Felix pop the question to you, Sarah Nancy?

SARAH NANCY: No. And if he had, I'd have knocked his head off.

DOLORES: What's all this about popping questions?

ROBERT: I was telling Sarah Nancy how we met and after six weeks I asked you to marry me.

DOLORES: Six weeks? It was three months.

ROBERT: Six weeks.

DOLORES: I only went out twice with you in the first six weeks. We didn't start going steady until our third date. You took me to a tea dance at your frat house and you asked me to wear your fraternity pin and I said I had to think about it, as I wasn't in the habit of just casually accepting fraternity pins like some girls I knew. (*The door opens and Felix enters*)

FELIX: Excuse me. I left my hat.

DOLORES: Oh, Felix. Isn't this remarkable. I was just about to go to the phone and call you and tell you that Sarah Nancy had completely recovered from her headache. You hadn't gone five minutes when she came out and said the aspirin worked after all and where is Felix and she was so distressed that you had gone that she insisted I go to the phone and see if you wouldn't come back, which I was about to do. Isn't that so, Sarah Nancy? (*Sarah Nancy doesn't answer*)

FELIX: Did Mrs. Henry tell you I said all the names of the Bible in under ten minutes?

DOLORES: Yes, I did. Didn't I, Sarah Nancy? (*Sarah Nancy doesn't answer*) And she was so impressed. Weren't you, Sarah Nancy? (*Again no answer from Sarah Nancy*)

FELIX: Want to hear me do it again? You can time me this time.

SARAH NANCY: No.

FELIX: Want to play another game then? How about movie stars?

DOLORES: That sounds like fun. Doesn't it, Robert? How do you play that?

FELIX: Well, you think of initials like R.V., and you all try to guess who I'm thinking of.

SARAH NANCY: Rudy Vallee.

FELIX: No, you give up?

DOLORES: I do. I never can think of anything. Can you think of who it is, Robert?

ROBERT: No.

FELIX: Do you give up, Sarah Nancy?

SARAH NANCY: No. (*A pause. There is silence*)

FELIX: Now do you give up?

SARAH NANCY: I'll die before I give up. (*Again silence*)

DOLORES: Honey, you can't take all night. It won't be any fun then. I think there should be a time limit, Felix, and if we don't guess it...

FELIX: (*Interrupting*) Give up?

SARAH NANCY: No.

DOLORES: Let's have a five minute time limit. (*She looks at her watch*) Five minutes is almost up.

FELIX: Give up?

SARAH NANCY: No.

DOLORES: Time is up. Who is it?

FELIX: Rudolph Valentino.

DOLORES: Rudolph Valentino. Imagine. Now why couldn't I have thought of that? Isn't that a fun game, Sarah Nancy, honey? Why don't you pick some initials.

SARAH NANCY: O.B.

DOLORES: O.B. My. O.B. Can you think of an O.B., Felix?

FELIX: Not yet.

DOLORES: Can you, Robert?

ROBERT: No.

DOLORES: My, you picked a hard one, Sarah, honey. O.B. Can she give us a clue?

FELIX: Yes. You can ask things like, is it a man or a woman.

DOLORES: Is it a man or a woman?

SARAH NANCY: A woman.

DOLORES: A woman. My goodness.

SARAH NANCY: Give up?

DOLORES: I do. Do you, Felix?

FELIX: Yes. Who is it?

SARAH NANCY: Olive Blue.

FELIX: Olive Blue. Who is she?

SARAH NANCY: A girl back home.

FELIX: She's not a movie star.

SARAH NANCY: Who said she was?

FELIX: Well, goose. They're supposed to be movie stars.

SARAH NANCY: You're a goose, yourself.

DOLORES: Sarah Nancy.

SARAH NANCY: It's a dumb game anyway.

FELIX: Well, let's play popular songs.

DOLORES: That sounds like fun. How do you do that?

FELIX: Well, you hum or whistle part of a song and the others have to guess what it is.

DOLORES: Oh, grand. Doesn't that sound like fun, Sarah Nancy? (*Again no answer from Sarah Nancy*) Why don't you whistle something, Sarah Nancy?

SARAH NANCY: I can't whistle.

DOLORES: Well, then hum something.

SARAH NANCY: I can't hum either.

FELIX: I'll hum and you all guess. (*He hums flatly*) Can you guess?

DOLORES: I can't. Can you, Robert?

ROBERT: No.

DOLORES: Can you, Sarah Nancy?

SARAH NANCY: No, but I never will be able to guess what he hums, because he can't carry a tune.

DOLORES: Well, I don't agree at all. I think Felix has a very sweet voice.

ROBERT: Then how come you can't tell what he's humming?

DOLORES: Because I didn't know the song, I suppose.

ROBERT: What was the song, Felix?

FELIX: "Missouri Waltz."

ROBERT: Don't you know the "Missouri Waltz" when you hear it?

DOLORES: Yes, I know the "Missouri Waltz" when I hear it. Hum something else, Felix. (*He hums another tune. Again very flat*) Now what's the name of that, honey?

FELIX: "Home Sweet Home."

ROBERT: "Home Sweet Home." My God! (*Dolores glares at Robert*)

DOLORES: Oh, of course. It was on the tip of your tongue. All right, Sarah Nancy, honey, it's your turn.

FELIX: No, it's still my turn. I keep on until you guess what I'm singing.

SARAH NANCY: How are we going to guess what you're singing when you can't sing?

FELIX: I certainly can sing. I'm in the choir at the Methodist Church. I'm in a quartet that sings twice a year at the Lion's Club.

SARAH NANCY: If you can sing, a screech owl can sing.

DOLORES: Sarah Nancy, honey.

SARAH NANCY: I'd rather listen to a jackass bray than you sing. You look like a warthog and you bray like a jackass.

FELIX: Who looks like a warthog?

SARAH NANCY: You do.

FELIX: I'm rubber and you're glue, everything you say bounces off of me and sticks on you.

SARAH NANCY: Warthog. You are a stinking warthog and I wish you would go on home so I could listen to Rudy Vallee in peace.

FELIX: Don't worry. I'm going home. I didn't want to come over here in the first place but my mama bribed me to come over here. Well, a million dollars couldn't make me stay here now and two million couldn't ever get me here again if you were here. (*He leaves*)

DOLORES: Oh, my God. I have never seen such carrying on in my life. Sarah Nancy, what am I going to tell Sister? She will take to her bed when I report this. Absolutely have a breakdown.

SARAH NANCY: I'm sorry. I'm not going to lie and tell some old fool jackass they can sing when they can't.

ROBERT: I agree with Sarah Nancy. He can't carry a tune at all.

DOLORES: Nobody asked your opinion.

ROBERT: Well, I'm giving it to you whether you asked for it or not.

DOLORES: And I don't want to hear it. How can you expect Sarah Nancy to learn to be gracious if we don't set an example?

ROBERT: I didn't tell her not to be gracious. I just told her that I agreed with what she said about his singing. I'm being honest. If that's ungracious, all right. I'd rather be honest than gracious.

DOLORES: That's all right for you. You're a man. But let me tell you right now, I didn't get on two beauty pages by being honest, but by being gracious to people. But I'm whipped now and worn out. I've done all I can do. I can do no more. (*She leaves*)

ROBERT: I guess your aunt's a little upset.

SARAH NANCY: I guess so. Do you mind if I listen to Rudy Vallee on the radio?

ROBERT: No. (*She turns on the radio. She turns the dial*)

SARAH NANCY: What time is it?

ROBERT: Almost ten.

SARAH NANCY: Shoot. I missed Rudy Vallee.

ROBERT: Well, you can hear him next week.

SARAH NANCY: I'll be home next week.

ROBERT: I'm going to go see to your aunt. Will you be all right?

SARAH NANCY: Sure. (*He goes. She gets the yearbooks. She looks at one and then the other. Felix comes in*)

FELIX: Where's Mrs. Henry?

SARAH NANCY: I don't know.

FELIX: I told my mama what happened and she said I owed Mrs. Henry an apology for speaking like I did. I told her what you said to me and she said it didn't matter how other people acted, I had to remember that I was a gentleman and that I was always to act in a gentlemanly fashion. So tell Mrs. Henry I'm here and I want to apologize. (*She goes. He sees the yearbooks. He looks at them. Sarah Nancy comes in*) Did you tell her?

SARAH NANCY: No. I couldn't. She's gone to bed. She has a sick headache.

FELIX: (*He points to the book*) She was pretty, wasn't she?

SARAH NANCY: Yes, she was.

FELIX: You don't sing any better than I do.

SARAH NANCY: I didn't say I did.

FELIX: And you're never going to be on any beauty pages, I bet.

SARAH NANCY: I didn't say I would.

FELIX: Don't you care?

SARAH NANCY: No. (*There is silence. An uncomfortable silence. He closes the yearbook*)

FELIX: I can't think of a whole lot to talk about. Can you?

SARAH NANCY: No.

FELIX: You aunt is quite a conversationalist. It's easy to talk when she's around.

SARAH NANCY: I guess. (*A pause. Silence*)

FELIX: Do you mind if I stay on here for a while?

SARAH NANCY: No.

FELIX: I told my mother I'd stay at least another hour. If you get sleepy, you just go on to bed. I'll just sit here and look at these yearbooks.

SARAH NANCY: I'm not sleepy.

FELIX: You want one of the yearbooks?

SARAH NANCY: Thank you. (*He hands her one. She opens it. He takes one and opens it. After a beat they are both completely absorbed in looking at the yearbooks. They continue looking at them as the light fades*)

The End

Timothy Mason

BEARCLAW

Timothy Mason

Now living in New York City, Timothy Mason is a native of Minneapolis, Minnesota, where he spent most of his life working in theater, first as an actor, then as a playwright. Among his writing accomplishments in Minnesota were seventeen plays which he composed for young audiences, produced by the Minneapolis Children's Theatre Company.

Bearclaw was originally commissioned by The Actors Theatre of Louisville. The first version of the script received its premiere in 1984 at the White Barn Theatre in Westport, Connecticut, in a production co-produced by Lucille Lortell and the Circle Repertory Company of New York City. The play was subsequently produced in the present version by the Seattle Repertory Company in Seattle, Washington in 1985. Mr. Mason reports that the subject matter—the situation of an elderly father in a nursing home—reflects the concerns of his own father: "My father spent many years as a national advocate for the elderly, doing his best to expose what he called 'warehouses for the living dead,' and to create decent, humane homes for the aged." Reflecting on the ideas in the play, Mr. Mason writes: "*Bearclaw* is about a very personal brand of fascism, one that can be practiced in the comfort of one's own home. Perhaps the initial impulse behind any fascistic act is benevolent. The danger arises when one confuses a desire to do good for others with a conviction that one know what is best for them."

Mr. Mason's other plays include *In a Northern Landscape*, first produced by the The Actors Theatre of Louisville in 1983; *Levitation*, which premiered in Manhattan at the Circle Repertory Company in 1984, and *Before I Got My Eye Put Out*, commissioned in 1984 by the South Coast Repertory in Costa Mesa, California. Mr. Mason dedicates *Bearclaw* "To Victor."

Characters:

>PAUL, *twenty-two*
>CONSTANCE, *mid-thirties*
>PETER, *sixty-eight*
>PETER JR, *mid-thirties*

Scene One:

>*A nursing home in St. Paul, Minnesota.*
>*As the house goes to black, a voice on the public address system:* "Testing, two three. Good morning. The title of Reverend Wee's sermon this Sunday will be 'Life at the Crossroads.' Special music will be provided by the St. Paul Cathedral School Boys Choir. Remember now, that's Sunday, 10 a.m. in the chapel. 'Life at the Crossroads.'"
>*Morning light. A clean, well-appointed room in a modern nursing home. Paul is making up the bed, while Constance goes through closets and drawers, collecting leftover odds and ends. Paul is dressed as an orderly; Constance is dressed as a nurse.*
>*They work in silence for some time.*

PAUL: How can you tell if you've got a hernia?

CONSTANCE: Believe me, you'd know. (*Finding a pair*) Shoe-trees. You need any?

PAUL: For sneakers? (*Constance looks at Paul's feet, then drops the shoe-trees into a bag and turns back to the closet*) Mrs. Swenson. God. Blimping right out on me. She calls, I come, I lift, I put her down on the toilet. I wait. She thinks. She hums. She says she's not in the mood. Lift, carry, back to the bed, plunk. Ten minutes later, she calls again.

CONSTANCE: Feel your groin.

PAUL: That's a habit I'm trying to break.

CONSTANCE: Go on. Is there a lump on either side? Is it tender?

PAUL: (*Feeling*) A little tender. No lumps.

CONSTANCE: You'll be fine.

PAUL: Easy for you to say.

CONSTANCE: (*Finding a small object at the bottom of a drawer*) Weird ring.

PAUL: Lemme see.

CONSTANCE: (Giving it to Paul) It's huge.

PAUL: It's an ashtray.

CONSTANCE: An ashtray?

PAUL: I love it.

CONSTANCE: It's yours.

PAUL: I mean it, I love it.

CONSTANCE: Catch you smoking on the floor again, your ass is grass.

PAUL: I know, I know.

(*They work in silence for a time*)

CONSTANCE: Your father was out here again this morning.

PAUL: Right.

CONSTANCE: You found him?

PAUL: I found him.

CONSTANCE: Sprawled out in the lobby when I came on.

PAUL: I took care of it, okay?

CONSTANCE: I gave him some coffee.

PAUL: Thanks.

CONSTANCE: He looked terrible.

PAUL: I know how he looked.

CONSTANCE: What do you do, give him money?

PAUL: Sometimes.

CONSTANCE: Does he have somewhere to stay? I mean it's snowing out.

PAUL: *I* don't know.

CONSTANCE: Where does he go when it gets really cold?

PAUL: Acapulco. (*They work in silence*) I'm done here.

CONSTANCE: (*Finding a small packet at the bottom of a drawer*) You won't believe this.

PAUL: What is it? (*She holds up the packet for him to see*) I don't believe it. *Rubbers*? Let me see.

CONSTANCE: (*Giving him the packet*) Can you believe it?

PAUL: I mean this guy couldn't cut his own food.

CONSTANCE: Hope springs eternal. You want 'em?

PAUL: You're a riot. Hey, I gotta go.

CONSTANCE: Where? North wing?

PAUL: South. Mrs. Swenson's in the mood for a bath.

CONSTANCE: Mmmm. Go get her, Bearclaw. (*Paul stops in his tracks, glares at Constance*) Okay, okay, Paul.

PAUL: See you at lunch.

CONSTANCE: Thanksgiving lunch.

PAUL: Yeah. Turkey loaf.

(*Paul exits. Constance finds one sock and a pair of suspenders in the last drawer. She puts them into the bag. She makes a final survey of the room, clipboard in hand. When she is finished, she tears off the top sheet on the clipboard, crumples it into a wad and tosses it into the wastebasket. The lights drop to the level of a winter afternoon.*

A voice on the public address system: "Sheryl, call for you on line 13. You got a call. Sheryl, please pick up 13.")

Scene Two:

Peter, dressed in an overcoat, opens the door. Constance reads from the next sheet on her clipboard.

CONSTANCE: Asgard, Peter T.

PETER: Ahs-gard.

CONSTANCE: Ahs-gard. Well, it really is one of the nicest. Of course, it's small...

PETER: Oh, no, this is going to be all right.

CONSTANCE: Those glass doors go out to your own little terrace.

PETER: (*Starting down toward the doors*) Terrific.

CONSTANCE: They're locked. Regulations.

PETER: (*Stopping*) Of course.

CONSTANCE: In the summertime we unlock them. It's really pretty out there. Trees...

PETER: I can imagine.

CONSTANCE: (*Indicating*) Lots of closet space.

PETER: Great.

CONSTANCE: Bath, easy chair, writing desk, straight-backed chair, motorized bed...

PETER: My Lord, I wouldn't ever have to leave this room. (*She looks at him*) Ah-hah. I guess that's the point.

CONSTANCE: You look too young to be here.

PETER: I suppose I am relatively.

CONSTANCE: Well, there's all kinds of activities...(*A beat*) I have this feeling you're not really big on bingo.

PETER: No, no, no...it's all fine. I chose this place myself.

CONSTANCE: Oh.

PETER: I chose the room for the light.

CONSTANCE: Well, there certainly is a lot of it during the day.

PETER: I'm a Sunday painter.

CONSTANCE: Really?

PETER: Drawing, mainly. Charcoal sketches, pastels. I just started last year.

CONSTANCE: Take off your coat, why don't you.

PETER: I'm working my way up to primitive.

CONSTANCE: (*Helping him off with his coat*) Well, you'll have to draw me some day. (*She puts his coat on a hanger and hangs it in the closet. While she's in the closet, Paul enters carrying a poinsettia*)

PAUL: (*To Peter*) Hi.

PETER: Hello.

PAUL: Mr. Asgard?

PETER: Ahs-gard.

PAUL: For you.

PETER: You shouldn't have.

(*Constance emerges from the closet*)

CONSTANCE: This is Paul, one of our orderlies.

PETER: How do you do.

PAUL: Where do you want it?

PETER: I'd rather you kept it.

PAUL: Reception says it's from your son.

PETER: I know, I know. It's the sort of thing that would make this place look like a hospital room. You keep it, Paul. Really.

CONSTANCE: Don't be silly. It's for you.

PETER: I don't care for poinsettias. They've never had an appeal for me. Bah, humbug, I say to this poinsettia.

PAUL: I think it's nice.

PETER: (*A flash of anger*) Then keep it! (*Beat*) Ah, just put it anywhere. (*Paul puts the plant on the writing desk and starts to leave*) Thank you.

PAUL: (*Turning back*) Sure. (*Paul exits*)

CONSTANCE: Well, unless there's anything I can do for you...

PETER: No, not a thing.

CONSTANCE: I want to welcome you, Mr. Asgard. You're going to like it here, I know.

PETER: I've ordered newspaper delivery, several of them. When will that start?

CONSTANCE: (*Consulting her clipboard*) Let me see. Well, well. Quite a list of them. You speak all those languages?

PETER: Temporarily.

CONSTANCE: No kidding. Well, I suppose you could have the

local papers beginning tomorrow, but some of these others may take a few weeks to get going.

PETER: Fine.

CONSTANCE: All set, now?

PETER: All set.

CONSTANCE: Okay, then. Five-thirty in the cafeteria for supper.

PETER: (*Dismayed*) Five-thirty!

CONSTANCE: I'll check in on you later.

(*She exits. Peter looks about him for a moment. He picks up the poinsettia, looks for another place to put it, and then wearily puts it down on the writing desk again. He picks up the card from the plant, puts on reading glasses, and sits at the desk. He reads the card. He puts it back in the plant and takes off the glasses. He sits in the twilight that comes in through the glass doors.*

A voice on the public address system: "Hello, hello! It's Monday night, and that means bingo. Seven-thirty in the north wing lounge—bingo lovers, unite!")

Scene Three:

The light fades rapidly. The door opens and Paul, carrying a dinner tray in one hand, switches on the overhead light with the other.

PETER: (*With a start*) What? Who's there? What is it? Turn off that light!

(*Paul sets the tray down on the bed, switches off the overhead light, and goes to Peter. He puts his hands on Peter's shoulders*)

PAUL: Hey, it's okay.

PETER: Don't touch me!

PAUL: It's okay. You're gonna be okay.

PETER: Don't touch!

(*Paul takes his hands off Peter's shoulders*)

PAUL: All right.

PETER: Who are you?

PAUL: I'm Paul. Remember? (*Paul switches on the desk lamp, and Peter looks up into his face*)

PETER: No. No, I don't. Where am I?

PAUL: You're in the home, Mr. Asgard. (*A beat*)

PETER: Oh. (*Pause*) Oh, yes. The Home.

PAUL: You missed supper. I brought a tray for you.

PETER: And you're an orderly here.

PAUL: More or less. Do you want something to eat?

PETER: I remember now. I remember you.

PAUL: Shoot. I'm unforgettable. How about something to eat?

PETER: No. No, thank you.

PAUL: You gotta eat.

PETER: How's the food?

PAUL: Tonight? Awful.

PETER: In that case, no thanks.

PAUL: I'm afraid I can't take no for an answer. (*Paul goes and brings the tray from the bed to the desk*)

PETER: I see. I see. You're a fascist.

PAUL: Sure. But I'm a cute fascist. (*Paul sets the tray down and uncovers it*) God, are you in luck. Fish patties.

PETER: I didn't remember you at all. For a moment there, I had no memory of this place, or coming here or any of it.

PAUL: Creamed corn, french fries, prune juice, you'll love it.

PETER: And now I remember it all.

PAUL: (*Picking up a fork and offering it*) Come on, Mr. Asgard. Eat up.

PETER: Look! I do not yet need to be fed!

PAUL: Okay. Feed yourself. (*Pause*)

PETER: I just don't want everybody being suddenly solicitous all over me.

PAUL: Don't worry. I won't be. What is that? Solicitous?

PETER: Ah...concerned. Overly concerned.

PAUL: No problem.

PETER: The doctors say I have to expect these lapses of memory. Get used to them, they say. Get used to them!

PAUL: What's wrong with you?

PETER: Nothing's wrong with me! (*A beat*) I had an accident.

PAUL: Yeah?

PETER: That's actually what they call it. Cerebral vascular accident. Like I stepped on a banana peel.

PAUL: You had a stroke.

PETER: Not bad, moderate. Year and a half ago. The only lingering effect was a little trouble with the right side of my body. (*Talking out of the side of his mouth*) Talked like this for a while, you know? Like Jimmy Cagney. (*Normal voice*) So, I got into physical therapy, started drawing, worked my way back to near-normal. *But.* The medications the doctors pump into me are scrambling my brains.

PAUL: What are they giving you?

PETER: Coumadin and Centrax.

PAUL: Oh, God. What's the Centrax for?

PETER: To "reduce behavioral problems."

PAUL: Behavioral problems?

PETER: Ten milligrams, two to three times daily.

PAUL: Oh, boy. A regular troublemaker.

PETER: I can't live without the junk, and I can't live decently with it. At home, I'd find myself in the kitchen without a clue where the bathroom was. The connections in my brain simply disconnect.

PAUL: What a total fuck.

PETER: (*With a laugh*) Yeah. Well put. You don't notice it at first. At first you just say to yourself, now where did I put those damn keys, or...or you're talking to someone and the right word is there on the tip of your tongue and that's exactly where it stays.

PAUL: (*Genuine*) Oh, my God. That sounds just like me. (*Peter laughs*)

PETER: I hope you'll call me Peter.

PAUL: I mean it, that sort of stuff happens to me all the time.

PETER: Listen, I don't think you've got anything to worry about.

PAUL: Easy for you to say. (*Indicating the tray*) You're not going to eat any of that crap, are you?

PETER: Nope.

PAUL: It's not always this bad.

PETER: I hope not.

PAUL: If I cover for you tonight, you gotta promise to eat every damn thing they give you tomorrow. Promise?

PETER: Fascist! From the Latin word, *fasces.* A symbol of power in ancient Rome. A symbol of authority. It was a bundle of sticks with a single axe projecting out of them. You see? Fascism: a lot of little sticks supporting one big stick.

PAUL: Oh, that helps a lot. You talk like a teacher.

PETER: History.

PAUL: College?

PETER: High school.

PAUL: I knew there was somthing about you I didn't like. Which high school?

PETER: Southwest.

PAUL: Rich kids' school.

PETER: You?

PAUL: South.

PETER: Poor kids' school.

PAUL: That's me. Do you mind if I smoke? I'm not allowed to smoke on the floor, but...

PETER: It's a destructive habit. And expensive. And pointless. Go ahead. (*Paul produces his ashtray, fits it on his finger, pops it open and lights a cigarette*) Remarkable.

PAUL: Nice, huh?

PETER: Mankind has come a long way. High school. Did you graduate?

PAUL: (*Bristling just a little*) Yes, I graduated.

PETER: What have you been doing since then?

PAUL: What does it look like? Clawing my way to the top.

PETER: Do you plan on going to college?

PAUL: No.

PETER: Why not?

PAUL: I just don't.

PETER: You're not planning to spend your life doing this?

PAUL: I don't know. After a while you get sort of attached to bedpans.

PETER: That's no attitude.

PAUL: It's one attitude. Come on, what is this?

PETER: You came here straight from high school?

PAUL: No. Look they'll be paging me in a minute.

PETER: What else did you do?

PAUL: Worked.

PETER: Doing what?

PAUL: God, get you going, you don't stop!

PETER: What did you do?

PAUL: Sold men's clothes.

PETER: Where?

PAUL: Fitzroy's.

PETER: Exclusive store.

PAUL: I suppose.

PETER: So? You had a job selling men's wear in a fashionable shop. What happened?

PAUL: What do you mean, what happened? Nothing happened.

PETER: You quit.

PAUL: Sure.

PETER: They fired you?

PAUL: Jesus!

PETER: What happened?

PAUL: I fell in love with the merchandise, okay?

PETER: I see. You stole.

PAUL: God, I'm loving this. It's like high school all over again.

PETER: You didn't like high school?

PAUL: Stop! Enough! No more questions!

PETER: Just trying to get to know you.

PAUL: *(Rising to leave)* Yeah, right. I'll see you around.

PETER: Look, I'm curious, that's all.

PAUL: Curious! You're like a dentist with a drill!

PETER: So were you arrested, or what?

PAUL: Oh, your students must have loved you, man.

PETER: *(Defensively)* My students did love me.

PAUL: Yeah? So where are they? Where's the wife, the kids, the students who loved you so much? People don't usually check into this place alone, you know.

PETER: *(Angry)* I wanted to do this on my own! It was my idea, wise guy.

PAUL: *(After a beat)* Sorry.

PETER: I insisted!

PAUL: I'm sorry.

PETER: *(After a pause)* My wife passed away. I have a son. *(Pause. Peter beginning to drift)* My students...Students are transient.

PAUL: What's that? Transient? *(A beat)* Peter? What's your son's name? *(A beat)*

PETER: What?

PAUL: Are you feeling okay?

PETER: There's a boy...Very small. He has my name...

PAUL: Who's this, your grandson?

PETER: A sailor suit. Blue. And a white cap and he's standing in a boat...

PAUL: This is your grandson, right? *(A beat)* Peter?

PETER: Never stand up in a boat, dammit!

PAUL: I'll go get the nurse, Mr. Asgard.

PETER: Never!

PAUL: *(Shaking Peter)* Peter?

PETER: *(Looking up at Paul)* Do I know you?

PAUL: Sure you do.

PETER: You're sure?

PAUL: You know me. I'm Paul, your orderly.

PETER: Orderly?

PAUL: Your friend. South High School.

PETER: Oh. Oh, yes.

PAUL: Paul, remember?

PETER: Poor kids' school.

PAUL: Now you got me. (*Pause*) You gonna be all right?

PETER: When I forget, it's like a window opens at night, a round window, the porthole of a ship, maybe, and outside there's just a circle of deep dark blue.

PAUL: (*After a pause*) No stars?

PETER: It's very quiet out there.

PAUL: You feeling better now?

PETER: Oh, sure. It just opens and closes.

PAUL: Well, I gotta go.

PETER: It's blurry out there. Murky. Like some painting by Turner. Do you know Turner?

PAUL: I know Tina Turner.

PETER: Joseph Mallord William Turner was a great English painter. Most of his works hang in a London gallery called the Tate. Seascapes. Interiors. Murky.

PAUL: Right. Sure. Well. Do you want the nurse?

PETER: Whatever for?

PAUL: Good question. Okay, then.

PETER: You'll come back?

PAUL: Don't worry.

PETER: I'll tell you all about fascism.

PAUL: Oh, great. History lessons. (*Paul picks up the tray*)

PETER: Good night.

(*Paul exits, carrying the tray. Peter stands, takes off his jacket and tie, and drapes them over the back of his chair. He sits again. After a moment he switches off the desk lamp.*
A voice on the public address system: "Paging Dr. Lindholm, please. Dr. Lindholm, please pick up a house phone.")

Scene Four:

Three weeks later, the room is filled with midmorning light. Peter stares at his watch, bewildered and frightened. Constance knocks at the door and enters, followed by Peter Jr.

CONSTANCE: *Here* we are.

PETER JR: That's him, all right.

PETER: Peter. Good morning.

CONSTANCE: Another Peter!

PETER JR: Junior.

CONSTANCE: Right, right. You haven't been here before.

PETER JR: He didn't permit me.

CONSTANCE: (*Picking up Peter's jacket and tie*) No kidding.

PETER JR: I guess he was a little touchy at first. About being here.

CONSTANCE: But he's adjusting so *well.*

PETER: And he's here, present in the room, and can be addressed directly. (*Pause*)

CONSTANCE: Right. (*A beat*) Well, I'll see you Peters later.

PETER JR: Goodbye. (*She goes*) Have you been waiting long?

PETER: Waiting? Oh, yes, you've thrown off my schedule for the entire day.

PETER JR: Sorry.

PETER: I may have even missed the bingo. (*A beat*) What time *is* it?

PETER JR: A little after eleven. (*Peter looks at his own watch*) Your watch stop?

PETER: (*Listening to his watch*) No, no, it's not that.

PETER JR: How are you doing?

PETER: Pretty well. No complaints.

PETER JR: That would be a first. You like it here?

PETER: It takes some getting used to.

PETER JR: They treating you all right?

PETER: Oh, yes. Nice people.

PETER JR: And the other residents?

PETER: Old. Very old.

PETER JR: What did you expect?

PETER: I don't know that I expected anything. (*He looks at his watch again*) A little after eleven you say?

PETER JR: Why the mystery, Dad?

PETER: Mystery?

PETER JR: All of this—on your own. You didn't have to give up the house, you know. You just...didn't have to do it.

PETER: How else could I pay for this place?

PETER JR: I would have helped you, you know that. Anyway, you don't belong here.

PETER: I do now.

PETER JR: You're too young to be here.

PETER: For how long am I too young? A matter of months? A year?

PETER JR: Well, then, come and live with us. Fran would welcome it, I would welcome it, we'd both feel so much better about it all.

PETER: A man has to face the realities of his situation, and adjust to them. That's something I always tried to teach you.

PETER JR: And I'm telling you we're ready to make the necessary adjustments, we would do any amount of adjusting.

PETER: And I would have twenty-four-hour-a-day witnesses to my decline.

PETER JR: Witnesses? I'm your son, for God's sake!

PETER: It's easier this way, easier all around.

PETER JR: Never give an inch.

PETER: I'm doing it his way for your sake as well as mine.

PETER JR: Never let anyone else give an inch.

(*Paul appears at the door, carrying a tray of medications*)

PETER: (*Noticing Paul*) Here they're neutral. I'm just part of the job.

PETER JR: (*Not wanting to go on with this in front of anyone*) Dad...

PETER: Ah, Paul? This is Peter, my son, the lawyer. Peter, meet Paul, my friend, who is at present working as an orderly. Until he discovers what it is he's *supposed* to be doing.

PAUL: Hi.

PETER JR: How are you.

PAUL: (*To Peter*) Your medications.

PETER: Oh, good. For the falling-apart.

PETER JR: What are they giving you these days?

PETER: Glue. (*Paul laughs alone, then falls silent*)

PETER JR: You know it's going to be no problem to and from this place to ours, getting here and back, I checked it out on the map and you just take Highway 12 right on into the city, through the loop till you link up with 194 and then it's a straight shot across the river all the way to the Summit Avenue exit.

PETER: (*Swallowing a pill with water from a white paper cup*) You took Summit?

PETER JR: Wait a minute. Was it Summit? No.

PETER: Como.

PETER JR: Como, of course! Right.

PETER: What about Lake Street?

PETER JR: Lake Street?

PETER: You avoid the freeways with Lake Street.

PETER JR: Well, yes, sure.

PETER: Get on Excelsior Boulevard right there in St. Louis Park, it turns into Lake Street...

PETER JR: Straight shot down Lake into the city . . .

PETER: Across the Lake Street bridge and keep on going when Lake turns into Marshall all the way to Summit.

PETER JR: To Summit, sure.

PETER: Of course, if you were in a hurry, you wouldn't *want* to avoid the freeways.

PETER JR: No, no, right.

PETER: But you could still take Lake to 31st and pick up 135, take 135 to 194, across the river to St. Paul and all the way to Como. (*Peter takes another pill*)

PETER JR: I'll try that. I'll definitely give that a try.

PETER: You wouldn't have to mess with Highway 12 at all.

PETER JR: I hadn't thought of that.

PETER: But if I were doing it, I'd take Excelsior to Lake to Marshall to Summit to Como.

PAUL: Where would you park?

PETER: In the lot. (*Realizes Paul is having him on*) Wise guy.

PETER JR: You will spend Christmas with us, won't you?

PETER: Oh, yes. Of course. Yes. Thank you. And thanks for the plant.

PETER JR: You liked it?

PETER: I liked it.

PETER JR: Great, I'll just keep them coming then. So. Pick you up Thursday afternoon?

PETER: Why?

PETER JR: Christmas Eve.

PETER: Oh. Oh, yes. We're not exchanging gifts, are we?

PETER JR: (*After a pause, controlled*) It had entered my mind.

PETER: You mean you've already gone and got something for me? Dammit, you know how I feel about that!

PETER JR: It's something people do for each other, this time of year. The holly and the ivy. You've heard of it?

PETER: It seems so pointless among adults...

PETER JR: Dad, do not get started on that.

PETER: What the hell am I supposed to give you? Or your wife, for that matter?

PETER JR: From you she doesn't expect a thing!

PAUL: I'll come back later...

PETER: (*To Paul*) You stay put!

PETER JR: (*To Paul*) Don't worry, I'm on my way out.

PETER: (*To Peter Jr*) You want me to make something for you in occupational therapy? A napkin holder, maybe?

PETER JR: We are not talking about Christmas presents here, is that obvious to everyone?

PAUL: I'll see you all later...

PETER: (*To Paul*) You're not going anywhere!

PETER JR: Dad. This is ridiculous. A drawing. One of your sketches.

PETER: They're not good enough.

PETER JR: Geez! A gesture. That's all it's about. Gestures.

PETER: Christmas gifts in a home without children make no sense.

PETER JR: At last! This is what we're talking about!

PAUL: (*To Peter*) I thought you had a grandson.

PETER: I should be so lucky.

PETER JR: Dad...

PETER: They *choose* not to have children, that's the point.

PETER JR: Dad, we do not have to go into this in front of...in front of...

PAUL: Paul.

PETER JR: Paul.

PETER: Children *redeem* a household.

PETER JR: Private! This is private! (*Silence*) I'm sorry. (*To Paul*) Really. This is nothing. Just a well-rehearsed two-step. (*A beat*) Forgive us. (*A beat*) We're sorry, right, Dad? (*A beat*) Right. (*To Peter*) No gifts this year, okay?

PETER: Well, if you've already gone to the trouble...

PETER JR: No gifts! Just us. And a wonderful meal.

PETER: I suppose I could pick up something or other here in the gift shop...

PETER JR: No gifts! (*A beat*) Please. You'll come?

PETER: Sure. Of course.

PETER JR: Spend the night with us. Spend as long as you want. All right?

PETER: Thursday, then.

PETER JR: Right. (*To Paul*) Take good care of him, okay?

PAUL: I'll try.

PETER JR: And don't let him give you any of his crap.

PAUL: Now that's asking a lot.

PETER JR: Bye, Dad.

PETER: Thursday.

(*Peter Jr. goes*)

PAUL: You guys should be on T.V. (*Offering a paper cup of pills and a paper cup of water*) Come on, Mr. A. Bottoms up. I've got other pills to push.

PETER: Don't go. Please. I'm...a little anxious.

PAUL: What's up?

PETER: Look at this. (*He extends his arm and shows his wristwatch*) My watch. Look. (*Paul looks at Peter's watch*)

PAUL: Yeah?

PETER: It doesn't mean a thing to me. I look at it and I see it and I see the face and I remember *watches* and *clocks* but it doesn't mean a damned thing to me, big hand, little hand, Paul, I can't tell time anymore, I can't tell what time it is.

PAUL: (*After a pause, putting his hands on Peter's shoulders*) What a total fuck.

(*Blackout*)

Scene Five:

From down the hall, the sound of an elderly senile resident calling out, "Mavis?" again and again. The lights rise on Peter in bed, Constance standing above him, taking his blood pressure. Evening. The poinsettia is gone. A crocus stands in its place.

PETER: That old man is going to drive me out of my mind.

CONSTANCE: He can't help it.

PETER: "Mavis, Mavis."

CONSTANCE: He's calling his wife.

PETER: Well, why the hell doesn't she answer!

CONSTANCE: She's dead.

PETER: Great. That's just great. I end up in a loony bin.

CONSTANCE: After this last stunt of yours, you are in no position to talk.

PETER: Stunt?

CONSTANCE: Those people wanted to play bingo, they did not want to hear a lecture on the Industrial Revolution.

PETER: I thought they were a very appreciative audience.

CONSTANCE: Anyway, your doctor has increased your Centrax as a result. Is that what you wanted?

PETER: My doctor is nearly senile himself.

CONSTANCE: He know what's best for you.

PETER: How long is this going to take?

CONSTANCE: As long as I say.

PETER: Viva il Duce.

CONSTANCE: Do I smell smoke?

PETER: My blood pressure is nowhere near that high. Are you about finished with me?

CONSTANCE: Yes, thank God. (*She unwraps the band from his arm*)

PETER: What's the verdict?

CONSTANCE: You'll live.

PETER: You sound disappointed.

CONSTANCE: You *don't* have cigarettes in here, do you?

PETER: An expensive habit, and filthy, and pointless.

CONSTANCE: (*Hanging the clipboard on the end of the bed*) All right. Just holler if you need anything.

PETER: I do not holler. Mavis's *husband* hollers. Can't you shut the door to his room?

CONSTANCE: If I do, I won't be able to hear him.

PETER: If you don't, I *will* be able to hear him!

CONSTANCE: Goodnight, Mr. Asgard. (*She exits*)

PETER: (*After a pause*) The coast is clear! (*The bathroom door opens, and Paul sticks his head out*)

PAUL: God. She nearly caught me. (*Paul enters the room*)

PETER: What do you expect? The air in here is blue.

PAUL: Blue? I had one cigarette.

PETER: And that's one too many.

PAUL: Didn't you ever smoke?

PETER: Certainly I did. Corn silk behind the corn crib.

PAUL: Too much, man.

PETER: Yes, it was, as a matter of fact. Got sick as a dog and never tried it again.

PAUL: Kind of a daredevil, weren't you?

PETER: Lippy. A lippy boy. Anyway, there's no need for you to smoke in class.

PAUL: In *class*!

PETER: I mean...You know what I mean.

PAUL: Look, Peter, I'm off duty, I'm hungry, I've got a friend waiting for me at home.

PETER: Now, where was I before we were interrupted?

PAUL: God. World War I.

PETER: World War I. So. Strictly speaking, fascism was born out of the social and economic chaos which followed the First World War. Believe me, the time was ripe.

PAUL: (*Lighting a cigarette*) You were there, right?

PETER: I'll ignore that. The various growing fascistic movements found recruits easily enough from the ranks of the three main classes.

PAUL: What was your wife's name?

PETER: What? Hannah. Three main classes, each of which was nurturing its own particular grievance: One, the defeated military. Two, a generation of frustrated youth.

PAUL: How did you first meet?

PETER: Who? Hannah? Church social. These were kids who had been too young to fight in the war, and who were attracted by fascism's two-pronged thrust: violent action, and the all-embracing leadership of a single charismatic figure.

PAUL: When did she die?

PETER: A long time ago. Someone to tell them what to do, and when and where and how. Someone who knew what was best for them.

PAUL: How long ago?

PETER: Pay attention, will you? Before you were born. Am I wasting my breath here?

PAUL: No.

PETER: All right. Finally, number three, the single most dangerous group of them all: the vast disenfranchised middle class. Why dangerous, you ask?

PAUL: I didn't, but...

PETER: Simple. Inflation. When there's a universal pinch in the pocket, nothing's uglier than the mood of the shopkeeper, the bureaucrat, the lawyer, the truck driver...

PAUL: The schoolteacher.

PETER: The schoolteacher. Most of them have worked for what they have with a single-mindedness which has closed them off to any of the other compensations that make living on this planet worthwhile: an appreciation of beauty, nature, travel, the arts, you name it. Inflation robs them of the only thing they possess in their stunted value systems.

PAUL: Not pretty.

PETER: They feel cheated, but they don't know who it was who cheated them, they don't know whom to blame. What does it lead to?

PAUL: I give up.

PETER: Anger. Racism. Bigotry. Persecution. When people feel the presence of an enemy, but don't know who or what it is, what do they do?

PAUL: They get scared.

PETER: Go to the head of the class. Exactly! They get scared. (*Pause*)

PAUL: I gotta go, Peter, I'm late already.

PETER: Fine, fine. So who's this friend waiting for you?

PAUL: A friend, all right? My roommate.

PETER: What's his name?

PAUL: Joe. Joe.

PETER: Joe the fellow who picks you up after work?

PAUL: You don't miss a thing, do you.

PETER: He drops you off in the mornings, too.

PAUL: He's an early riser.

PETER: What's that little car he drives?

PAUL: An Audi, and yes, he should have bought American.

PETER: Do you have relations with this fellow?

PAUL: What?

PETER: You know what I'm talking about. I was a schoolteacher for thirty years, I've seen it all, believe me.

PAUL: I'll bet you have.

PETER: So you are queer then.

PAUL: Jesus! (*A beat*) You don't approve?

PETER: Oh, it's none of *my* business.

PAUL: Hah!

PETER: How did you meet?

PAUL: (*Sullen*) Church social.

PETER: Wise guy. What does this Joe fellow do for a living?

PAUL: He writes for the paper.

PETER: Which one?

PAUL: *The Dispatch.*

PETER: Well, that's something, anyway. (*Paul lights another cigarette*) Didn't you ever try it with girls?

PAUL: God. Yes. Sure.

PETER: So what went wrong?

PAUL: Nothing went wrong!

PETER: It didn't work? You didn't like it?

PAUL: It worked! I liked it!

PETER: I guess I don't understand.

PAUL: No, I guess you don't. (*A knock at the door*) God. (*Paul quickly stubs out his cigarette and disappears into the bathroom*)

PETER: Who is it?

(*Constance opens the door. Peter Jr stands behind her, a cookie tin in his hands*)

CONSTANCE: (*Musical*) Surprise, surprise.

PETER JR: (*Entering*) Hi, Dad.

PETER: Peter.

PETER JR: So. How about some cookies?

PETER: Cookies?

PETER JR: Sure I made this huge batch after dinner. Fran was at the health club for the evening and I was all alone and feeling kind of hungry and so I said to myself, why not? And I just sort of got going and kept on going and I ended up with a few dozen more than I ever intended, so I thought why not just hop in the car and bring you a crateful. (*A beat*) Peanut butter.

PETER: None for me, thanks.

CONSTANCE: Not right now, thanks.

PETER JR: Right. So how are things?

PETER: Couldn't be better. They're turning me into a junkie.

PETER JR: More Centrax?

CONSTANCE: He gives us no choice.

PETER: (*With some pride*) You heard about my *cause célèbre*?

PETER JR: Ah, the lecture? I did hear something...

PETER: The word spreads like wildfire. The walkers were clattering up and down the halls, dentures were cracking...

CONSTANCE: You really got a kick out of it, didn't you?

PETER: It beats bingo.

CONSTANCE: Did you ever think how *they* felt? Carl Lundquist's card was nearly full when you took over the microphone, he was in tears.

PETER: Look: When Paul finally hauled me out of there, I got a round of applause!

CONSTANCE: The applause was for Paul! (*She is at the bathroom door*) Okay, Smokey the Bear, you can come out now. (*After a pause, Paul emerges, sullen and embarrassed*)

PETER JR: My God. What the hell is going on here?

PETER: We were going over a few of the elements of fascism.

CONSTANCE: Smoking again, right? Am I going to have to report you to the supervisor, Paul?

PAUL: I gotta go.

PETER: He's got a date.

PAUL: (*To Peter*) You shut up about that!

PETER JR: Now look here, Buster...

PAUL: Get out of my way.

PETER: Don't keep your date waiting. (*Paul exits, slamming the door behind him*)

CONSTANCE: Paul! (*On her way out, to Peter*) You! Are more trouble than you're worth! (*She exits*)

(*Long pause*)

PETER JR: Your blood pressure still up?

PETER: They don't tell me a thing.

PETER JR: I know the feeling. (*Gesturing toward the bathroom door*) You got any more in there? Like clowns out of a Volkswagen, one hundred and forty-six orderlies come tumbling...He's getting to be a regular, isn't he?

PETER: He's getting to be a regular pain in the neck.

PETER JR: Remember when you found out I smoked? You told me to stop, so I did, but the only way I could was to chew a lot of gum, and then you told me what sugar would do to my teeth. I switched to sugarless. He talks to you?

PETER: What? Paul? Ach. Kids. Thinks he's in love. *You* know.

PETER JR: He comes in, talks, smokes, you counsel him, sort of?

PETER: It's difficult to break the habits of a lifetime.

PETER JR: God, don't I know it. (*A beat*) I see you got the crocus.

PETER: Yes. Thanks. It's lovely.

PETER JR: Like this one habit of mine. Trying too hard. You know? After Mom died. I tried too hard, didn't I? *You* know. With you. Worked at it too much.

PETER: What are you talking about?

PETER JR: The habits of a lifetime. Like when I was in school, second year, I fell in love with this British girl, law student, black hair and white skin. Deirdre, can you believe it? And it was a total mistake from the word go. You mind if I talk here, for a minute?

PETER: Go right ahead.

PETER JR: I start taking her out. Dinner, walks along the Esplanade, in the Public Gardens. And it's all fine. She likes me well enough. She talks, she listens. A little preoccupied, maybe, but she listens. The same in bed.

PETER: Peter...

PETER JR: A little preoccupied, but she's there, anyway. Sort of. What isn't fine about it all is that her...reserve...is driving me totally out of my head. The cooler she gets the hotter I get. Crazy. Completely. I'm beginning to make a fool of myself, trying too hard, calling her, seeing her, giving her things, I can't keep my hands off her...

PETER: (*Overlapping*) Peter, please...

PETER JR: (*Overlapping*) ...Which is a mistake, of course, I know that, everybody knows that, but I can't help myself. Every time I make a vow to let her alone, I break it. And by now she's avoiding me for all she's worth, making up excuses, *hiding* from me, and I just keep bashing my head against the wall, and I wonder, what's wrong with me? (*A beat*) You won't believe what I did.

PETER: What did you do?

PETER JR: I got a can of bright green spray paint one night, and on the sidewalk right outside her dorm I wrote in huge letters, "I AM A PIG FOR YOU, DEIRDRE." (*A beat*) She never spoke to me again. (*A beat*) So what was wrong with me? That I kept on trying when I knew it was no use?

PETER: I don't know.

PETER JR: Neither do I. (*A beat*) I'll leave the cookies here. (*He sets the box on the writing desk and exits. Slow fade to black. After a moment, in the darkness, a voice on the public address system:* "Hello, hello! The semifinals of the Scrabble tournament will begin promptly at six-thirty in the north wing lounge. Coffee and cake are being served by the ladies of the Naomi Circle, and *all* pocket dictionaries will be checked at the door. This means you, Mr. Lundquist. Now, go get 'em, all you semifinalists!")

Scene Six:

In the darkness, "Goodnight Irene" on the harmonica. The lights rise on Peter and Paul. Peter is doing a charcoal sketch of Paul, who poses with a harmonica to his lips, occasionally playing it. The crocus has been replaced by a large Easter lily.

PETER: The trouble with van Gogh was, van Gogh didn't believe in himself. (*Pause. Peter sketching*) He didn't. No matter how brilliant you and I may know he was, he wasn't buying it. That was his tragedy. Every man has his own tragedy, and that was his.

PAUL: So he took a pair of scissors and cut his ear off.

PETER: Part of it.

PAUL: I wonder:—why the ear?

PETER: Don't move around like that.

PAUL: Why not the hand he painted with, or a finger, at least, if he thought he was so bad?

PETER: Come on, Poetry-in-Motion, hold still.

PAUL: Maybe he figured he'd heard enough.

PETER: All that talent, that vision, but when he looked at himself, he just couldn't see it.

PAUL: When I look at myself, I don't even think about amputation.

PETER: Well, Paul, that's why I like you. (*Long pause: Peter sketching, Paul playing "Goodnight, Irene" on his harmonica*) Paul. What's your last name, anyway? (*Pause. Paul continuing to play the harmonica*) What's your last name? (*A beat*) Paul?

PAUL: That's it. Just Paul.

PETER: Don't give me that. What's your last name.

PAUL: What's up? You want to call me on the telephone?

PETER: Oh, come on. What is it?

PAUL: Paul. Just Paul, okay?

PETER: Okay, okay. (*Pause*) Know why I have you posed like that? With your harmonica?

PAUL: I give up.

PETER: I'm afraid of your lips. Your mouth. Eyes, ears, nose and throat I can do, no problem, but a mouth—that's another doctor.

PAUL: Coward.

PETER: I suppose so. Tell you another secret.

PAUL: Yeah?

PETER: Hands are a total bitch. But the way you cup them around that harmonica, like they're one solid ball, it's a breeze.

PAUL: Are you telling me you don't believe in yourself?

PETER: What a little wiseguy you turned out to be.

PAUL: He doesn't believe in himself. Hide the scissors.

PETER: When I first met you, little did I know. (*Pause, Peter sketching*)

PAUL: Peter?

PETER: Yes?

PAUL: I've decided to take your advice.

PETER: How so?

PAUL: I'm gonna take some classes.

PETER: (*Putting down his sketch pad*) Well. That is simply the best news I've had in a long, long time. Good *going*, Paul.

PAUL: Thanks.

PETER: Thank *you*. What are you going to study?

PAUL: (*Genuinely proud*) Watercolour painting and karate.

PETER: (*After a beat*) What did you say?

PAUL: In Hawaii.

PETER: Hawaii.

PAUL: I'm sick of these winters, man. And I met this guy who's a travel agent and he says there are some great charters going to Hawaii and he's gonna get me some brochures.

PETER: (*Anger rising*) Watercolour painting and *karate*?

PAUL: (*A little defensive*) You said watercolour had to be one of the biggest challenges you could face.

PETER: And *karate*?

PAUL: I'm sick of being defenseless, man.

PETER: Of all the utterly *stupid*...I urge you to get a grip on your life, and you decide to...I don't believe it. This is not my advice you are taking. This is some drugs you are taking, it has to be!

PAUL: (*Hurt*) I thought you'd be proud.

PETER: Proud? Proud? You are a hairbrain. A fluff-head!

PAUL: Cut it, okay?

PETER: Dizzy!

PAUL: Just cut it! It was only an idea, anyways...

(*Constance enters, carrying a newspaper*)

CONSTANCE: (*Musical*) Hello, hello!

PETER: (*Grim*) Hello, Sunshine.

PAUL: (*To Peter, sullen*) It was just a thought, for God's sake.

PETER: (*To Paul*) Take my advice: don't think.

CONSTANCE: Sounds like we're having a *swell* time. That German newspaper you ordered?

PETER: (*Taking it*) *Die Zeit*? I don't believe it.

CONSTANCE: (*Looking over Peter's shoulder*) Say—that is really pretty good.

PETER: Thank you.

CONSTANCE: No—I mean it.

PETER: It never occurred to me you didn't mean it.

CONSTANCE: A little condescending this morning, aren't we. Paul, you had a visitor.

PAUL: Oh, God.

CONSTANCE: It's okay. I gave him some coffee.

PAUL: He's gone?

CONSTANCE: Yup. Oh, and Joe's been on the phone for you, and beds in the south wing haven't been made up yet.

PAUL: Right. Thank you.

PETER: And thanks for the paper. It's only three months old, you know.

CONSTANCE: You can always look at the pictures, Asgard.(*She exits*)

PETER: Whoops.

PAUL: You treat her like she's stupid or something. She's not.

PETER: I know that. She's a mental giant. So who's this visitor of yours? (*He tosses the newspaper aside*)

PAUL: My accountant. How long is this gonna take?

PETER: The trouble with you is, you're not willing to put a little effort into the things you do.

PAUL: Yeah, that's my tragedy. (*Pause. Peter sketching*)

PETER: Roger Hecht. Class of '68. When I first got hold of that boy he was completely nowhere. A total disaster. Didn't know who he was and didn't care.

PAUL: I got this feeling you set old Roger straight.

PETER: Damn right I set him straight! I opened his eyes to himself. Showed him that the road he was on was nothing but an absolute dead end, no question. I let him know that there were worlds out there he never dreamt of: art, history, philosophy, music, uplifting books...

PAUL: How did old Rog feel about all this?

PETER: I'll tell you exactly how he felt. He felt grateful. To me. For the two years that I had him, I didn't let up on that boy for one minute.

PAUL: Dear God.

PETER: Hey, sit still.

PAUL: What's this guy up to now? Wait. Don't tell me. He's an astronaut.

PETER: Roger Hecht is now a very well-respected member of his community. Hold your pose, for God's sake.

PAUL: What does he do?

PETER: I got a Christmas card from him. Four, maybe five years ago. Photo of the family. Nice looking wife, three beautiful little girls. Maybe it was six years ago...

PAUL: For a living, what does the guy do? To support all those women?

PETER: (*Sketching, after a pause*) He sells lawn furniture.

PAUL: Oh, that's great!

PETER: Will you put that harmonica back in your big mouth!

PAUL: You give old Rog the world on a platter, and he ends up peddling lawn furniture. And all he's good for is one lousy card in all these years? That's really good.

PETER: (*After a pause*) And the son of a bitch was only trying to sell me a patio suite. (*After a beat, the two of them laugh together*) Terrible skin! In thirty years of teaching history to acne victims, old Rog was the worst! (*They laugh again, fall silent, and Peter continues to sketch while Paul plays the harmonica*) But that doesn't alter the point I've been trying to hammer home with you. Not by a jot.

PAUL: Paul, you gotta go to college. Paul, you gotta take life seriously. Paul, you gotta make something of yourself.

PETER: Yes, yes, and yes.

PAUL: Paul, trust me: I know what's best for you.

PETER: You *want* to be stuck in this place for the rest of your life?

PAUL: Well, *you* are, goddammit! Maybe I don't have any more choice than you! (*A beat*)

PETER: You can't hurt me that easily, if that's what you're after.

PAUL: Shit. I'm sorry.

PETER: It'll take a lot more than a little lip from you to get me going.

PAUL: Jesus, though, you're always riding me, you never let up.

PETER: It's for your own good.

PAUL: Exactly! You know everything! You have an education, you've travelled overseas, you speak all those languages, so of course, you know all about me!

PETER: What I know about is the infinite potential of every single one of God's creatures.

PAUL: Oh, great. Now he's a missionary.

PETER: "Little lamb, who made thee? Dost thou know who made thee?"

PAUL: Dear God.

PETER: The man who wrote those words was an artist, and you can see his drawings hanging in one wing of...

PAUL: (*Overlapping*) Of the Tate Gallery in London, England.

PETER: (*Overlapping*)...The Tate Gallery in London, England. William Blake. He had a vision, and he followed it. That's all I'm trying to say to you. Find your vision. Follow it.

PAUL: Yeah. Right. Session's over.

PETER: Paul?

PAUL: God, I'm stiff.

PETER: Please.

PAUL: This little lamb is a little short on cash. Makes it hard to move, much less follow a vision.

PETER: That's bullshit.

PAUL: Bullshit? I don't have the money to go to college! I don't have the brains! And besides, I don't fucking want to!

PETER: Pure bullshit. Brains, you don't have to worry about, you've got more than enough. And you don't want to only because you're afraid to. As for money, that's just a question of discipline. How do you spend the money you make here?

PAUL: Jewelry, mostly. Now and then a fur coat.

PETER: Sure, be a wiseguy.

PAUL: What do you think I make for hauling old folks' shit all day? For lifting Mrs. Swenson and carrying her to the toilet? For coming home at night with piss all over my whites? I should be making a fortune. Guess what: I don't.

PETER: What about this Joe fellow? Would he help you?

PAUL: He owns too much of me already. Besides, he's barely getting by as it is.

PETER: Are your parents in a position to help at all?

PAUL: My father is in the position of being dead. My mother's got three little kids to take care of, okay?

PETER: I'm sorry.

PAUL: (*Still angry*) Don't be.

PETER: Your father must have been very young. When did he

pass away?

PAUL: Many moons ago.

PETER: Come on, Paul. How did he die?

PAUL: Forget it.

PETER: How?

PAUL: Forget it, I said.

PETER: I want to know!

PAUL: God. (*A beat*) He was a fireman. There was a fire.

PETER: I'm very sorry.

PAUL: Yeah.

PETER: Wait a minute. Wouldn't your mother be receiving benefits? Pension? Insurance?

PAUL: It's not enough.

PETER: How old were you when it happened?

PAUL: I don't know. Twelve.

PETER: Twelve. (*A beat*) Well. There you have it. Something to strive for. Something to live up to. The memory of your father.

PAUL: (*Very angry*) Dear God, will you give me a break! Just shut up, will you!

PETER: Don't talk to me like that.

PAUL: You? You can't talk to your own son without getting constipated!

PETER: (*Also very angry*) Now you hold it right there!

PAUL: You can't talk to him, he can't talk to you, put the two of you in a room together, you get instant constipation, both of you!

PETER: How dare you!

PAUL: Mister Fucking Know-it-All!

PETER: You're shackled, you're in chains!

PAUL: To me, you're just part of the job!

PETER: I'm telling you, you're too scared to live!

PAUL: And I'm telling you, you are a total fuck!

PETER: Get out!

PAUL: I'm going!

PETER: Don't come back!

PAUL: Don't worry! (*Paul goes out, slamming the door. Peter picks up the Easter lily, opens the door, and flings it out into the hall. He slams the door and goes to the bed. He droops, sits slowly on the bed, and puts his head into his hands*)

Scene Seven:

The lights shift to a nighttime blue, coming in through the glass doors. Peter Jr. enters, followed by Constance, who carries a vase of bleeding hearts.

PETER: Hannah? Hannah, is that you? Hannah?

PETER JR: How long has he been like this?

CONSTANCE: Off and on for about a week.

PETER: Where is he, Hannah?

PETER JR: He's talking to Mom.

PETER: Hannah?

CONSTANCE: It's me, Mr. Asgard. Connie. Constance. You know that.

PETER: Hannah, where's that boy who used to visit?

CONSTANCE: Who?

PETER: What's become of him?

CONSTANCE: You mean Paul? He's still around. He's got the night shift now. You're probably asleep when he's on duty.

(A beat)

PETER: Let's go camping this summer, like we used to.

CONSTANCE: Oh, God.

PETER: Bay Lake, Pelican, Whitefish, Trout Lake. We wouldn't have to go tenting, I know that was a burden for you, we could rent a cabin.

CONSTANCE: Peter.

PETER: We could be tourists for a change, instead of trailblazers, what do you say?

CONSTANCE: *(After a beat)* I think that sounds just fine, Peter.

PETER: Was I hard on you, Hannah? A little overbearing, maybe?

PETER JR: *(Grasping Peter's shoulders)* Dad.

PETER: A little bossy?

PETER JR: Dad?

PETER: What. Peter? What.

PETER JR: How are you doing?

PETER: When did you get here?

PETER JR: Just now. How are you feeling?

PETER: Ach. Little woozy. Stuff they give me before bed. Packs a punch.

PETER JR: *(To Constance)* Can't they ease up on those damned pills a little?

CONSTANCE: When we do, he starts wandering off, all over the building.

PETER: "Wandering off." Used to be when I went somewhere I was "going places." It's late, isn't it?

CONSTANCE: A little after eleven.

PETER JR: I stayed late at the office getting that stuff about Paul you asked for.

PETER: What? Oh. Oh, yes. Thank you.

CONSTANCE: What stuff about Paul?

PETER JR: Oh, you know, his background, family records, that sort of thing.

PETER: Look, she does not have to hear about...

PETER JR: My office has a department that investigates insurance claimants, so Dad asked me to check out this Paul.

CONSTANCE: If you wanted to know about him, why didn't you just ask him?

PETER JR: Ask *him.*

PETER: (*Taking the portfolio from Peter Jr.*) If you will excuse me, I would like to retire now.

CONSTANCE: Be my guest, I got off at eleven anyway.

PETER: In that case, goodbye.

CONSTANCE: Oh, come on, Asgard. I'll help you. (*She begins to unbutton his shirt*)

PETER: Please. Let me. (*Peter begins unbuttoning his shirt, slowly and with difficulty*)

CONSTANCE: I'll get the cuffs, they're always a problem.

PETER: (*Flailing at her*) Will you please just...!

CONSTANCE: Okay, okay. (*Long pause. At first Peter Jr. and Constance watch as Peter struggles laboriously and unsuccessfully with his buttons. When it becomes embarrassing, they both turn and look out the glass doors.*)

PETER JR: Won't be long now, you can get out onto the terrace.

CONSTANCE: Oh, it's wild, everything just blooming away.

PETER JR: You know I actually had to mow the lawn this week?

CONSTANCE: No kidding. Already?

PETER JR: It was that long.

CONSTANCE: Wow. Already.

PETER JR: Take your sketch pad out there, your charcoals. Did you know he's half-Indian?

CONSTANCE: Paul?

PETER: Indian?

CONSTANCE: Well, sure. His name is Bearclaw, for God's sake. Did you think he was French?

PETER: Bearclaw.

CONSTANCE: On the floor we call him The Gay Brave. (*A beat*)

PETER JR: *Also* he is *gay*?

CONSTANCE: All orderlies are gay.

PETER JR: God.

CONSTANCE: You wouldn't be prejudiced, would you?

PETER JR: What, me? Oh no, oh no.

CONSTANCE: Most of them are very gentle with the residents, and they spend so much time working out, they're certainly strong enough to do the job. (*A beat*)

PETER JR: You should have an easel for out there on the terrace. How about I pick you up an easel? Have your coffee out there, your morning papers, the crossword, and then get down to work. What a setup. About three years ago he was arrested, shoplifting from the store he worked for. Shoes, mainly. A few silk ties, some shirts, mainly shoes.

CONSTANCE: Hey, that's all in the past.

PETER JR: What isn't? His father's been in and out of jails for years.

PETER: His father.

PETER JR: Drunk and disorderly, for the most part. Some petty theft. He doesn't look it, particularly. Paul. Indian.

CONSTANCE: So have you investigated me, too?

PETER JR: (*With a smile*) Not yet.

CONSTANCE: That's a relief.

PETER JR: You taking all this in, Dad? Or is this nothing new. Dad? (*Long pause*)

PETER: (*Finally, still fumbling with his buttons*) My fingers... get confused.

CONSTANCE: Well, if you'd just let me help you ...

PETER JR: I'll take care of it.

CONSTANCE: You'll get him to bed?

PETER JR: Sure.

CONSTANCE: That all right with you, Peter?

PETER: Good night.

CONSTANCE: I'll check in on you later. (*She exits. Peter Jr. begins to unbutton his father's shirt*)

PETER JR: Losers. Creeps. All of them. Oh, I'm sure he's a

perfectly nice kid. A nice kid, perfectly. So it's not him, is it, Dad. It's why do I spend my life crazy jealous of this long line of losers you pick up? Huh? In your classes, on the street, God knows, the supermarket.

PETER: I stood by you, didn't I? When it looked like you were the loser?

PETER JR: Let's get that belt buckle.

PETER: I didn't turn my back on you, not for a minute.

PETER JR: Nope.

PETER: Through all the drugs and the crazy screwed-up philosophies, the hair and the clothes and the anger...your terrible anger towards me...I always let you know that you could come back. Just that. Come back.

PETER JR: No questions asked.

PETER: No questions asked.

PETER JR: And I came back.

PETER: And you came back.

PETER JR: And no questions were asked.

PETER: Nope.

PETER JR: Not one. (*Peter Jr. eases Peter's shirt off his shoulders*)

PETER: Peter?

PETER JR: Oh, yeah, I was some kind of hippie, wasn't I, Dad. For twelve months, exactly. I did the whole thing by the book, went to San Francisco...put some flowers in my hair...It was like a junior year abroad. (*He drapes the robe over Peter's shoulders*) Okay, off with the pants. (*Peter Jr. slides Peter's trousers off*) I did hold your interest for a while though, didn't I?

PETER: I was never uninterested in you.

PETER JR: You cared for the creeps, so I had a fling at being one. Didn't work. Doesn't matter.

PETER: I cared for you always. I still do. It's just that...I'm a teacher. It's my calling. And some of those kids were in such need.

PETER JR: Where's your pyjamas?

PETER: Look! The physician doesn't tend the healthy.

PETER JR: (*Erupting*) It wasn't my fault! It wasn't my fault I was healthy!

PETER: Peter...I never said...

PETER JR: You said! You said! You didn't say a goddam thing! The two of us locked in that big house together, without her, just two men looking at each other all those years. But you never stopped talking to her. I was there, and she wasn't, but she was the one you talked to. God, I tried. I tried, but all I ever heard from you was nothing! (*A beat*) I was a pig for you, Dad. (*Long pause*)

PETER: Is it because of me? You don't want children because of me?

PETER JR: (*Weary*) Oh, fuck.

PETER: I screwed up with you, so you don't want to screw up with yours. (*A beat*) It's because of me.

PETER JR: Look. It's still an open question. (*Pause*)

PETER: I took you away, remember? After? We went away together, Bay Lake, Pelican Lake, Trout, Whitefish, all the old places. From one lake to another, all that summer after she died, don't you remember? The two of us.

PETER JR: I remember.

PETER: All that summer. (*Pause*)

PETER JR: She just shouldn't have left us, should she?

PETER: No.

PETER JR: We needed her.

PETER: Yes. (*Pause*)

PETER JR: How many languages do you suppose we have, Dad? Between the two of us. Six? Seven? Seven with my Latin.

PETER: I have Latin too, you know.

PETER JR: Of course. (*A beat*) We just never spoke the same one at the same time. (*Long pause. Then Constance knocks at the door, and enters*)

CONSTANCE: Everything all right in here? (*Pause*) Let's get you into bed.

PETER JR: Yes. You should be going to bed.

PETER: Yes. I need to sleep.

CONSTANCE: I'll take over from here.

PETER JR: Okay.

PETER: Peter?

PETER JR: Dad?

PETER: Goodnight.

PETER JR: Goodnight.

CONSTANCE: I'm going to pull the curtains now.

PETER JR: Sure.

(*She draws the curtains around the bed, and disappears with Peter behind them. Peter Jr. goes to the glass doors and looks out into the night, standing in the same place that Paul has occupied earlier while he smoked. Peter Jr. takes a stick of sugar-*

less gum from his pocket, unwraps it, and chews. Finally, Constance tiptoes out from behind the curtains)

CONSTANCE: Out like a light. In the morning, he'll be clear as a bell.

PETER JR: *(As they leave the room)* Thanks for all your help. I know you're off duty…

CONSTANCE: Thank you for all the flowers. You know, bleeding hearts were my favourites when I was growing up?

PETER JR: Yes?

CONSTANCE: Bleeding hearts and baby's breath. *(They exit the room, Constance turning off the light. A very long pause. Then Paul enters the room quietly. He looks at the curtained bed. He walks down to the glass doors and lights a cigarette. He looks out into the night, smoking. The dim light fades to black)*

Scene Eight:

In the darkness, a voice on the public address system: "May I have your attention, please. The representative from H & R Block will be available for tax consultations on Tuesday and Thursday of next week, because it's that time of year again, folks. All those residents who would like a little tax-talk should make an appointment with Sheryl at the nursing station. Thank you."

Bright early morning light streams in through the glass doors. Peter, dressed in pyjamas and dressing gown, is poised to sketch Constance.

CONSTANCE: So. Do you want me sitting or standing or what?

PETER: Suit yourself.

CONSTANCE: I think I'll sit.

PETER: Why don't you stand?

CONSTANCE: I'd rather sit.

PETER: If you insist. *(She sits)* All it took was a little research and a couple of phone calls.

CONSTANCE: Don't you think you should let Paul in on this?

PETER: If the Bureau of Indian Affairs is passing out scholarships, why shouldn't Paul get one? He certainly qualifies. But don't you breathe a word about this to Paul. I want to surprise him.

CONSTANCE: My lips are sealed.

PETER: He comes in here when he thinks I'm asleep. I can smell the smoke.

CONSTANCE: And you don't say anything?

PETER: We're not speaking.

CONSTANCE: Well, if you're not speaking, how are you going to surprise him? (*A beat*)

PETER: This is going to be very difficult.

CONSTANCE: What is?

PETER: Can't you put something in front of your mouth?

CONSTANCE: *What?*

PETER: You could wear one of those surgical masks.

CONSTANCE: What on earth are you talking about?

PETER: I have a little trouble drawing the human mouth, d'you mind?

CONSTANCE: (*Rising*) Well if you think I'm gonna sit here wearing a *mask* for God's sake...

PETER: It doesn't have to be a mask necessarily...

CONSTANCE: This is my *portrait* you're doing!

PETER: Sit down!

CONSTANCE: Why? I thought you wanted me standing!

PETER: I don't particularly want you at all, if it comes to that! (*Constance starts to leave*)

CONSTANCE: It's no wonder Paul asked for the night shift.

PETER: You! Stop! Right there, young lady! (*Constance stops. A Beat. She turns back to face Peter, smiling in spite of herself*)

CONSTANCE: Young lady? One minute I could choke you, the next...*Young lady*? Asgard, I'm yours.

PETER: If at first you don't succeed, quit, this is your motto, all of you.

(*Constance sits. Peter regards her. He gets the vase of bleeding hearts and puts it in her hands*)

CONSTANCE: Now we're getting somewhere. When I was a teenager, bleeding hearts were very big with me. I don't think you ever fall in love again quite so hard. Or so hopelessly. (*Peter is in position with his sketch pad, scrutinizing her*) And at that age, heartbreak is part of it all, somehow. Heartbreak. Love wouldn't be the same without it.

PETER: Hmmmmm.

CONSTANCE: My father grew a row of these in the back garden, along the driveway. Bleeding hearts and baby's breath. Eventually you trade one for the other.

PETER: A little less talk?

CONSTANCE: Yeah. Right. (*A beat*)

PETER: Mm-mm. No. (*He goes to her*) You're breathing them, get the picture? Their aroma.

CONSTANCE: But bleeding hearts don't have an...

PETER: Just...do it.

CONSTANCE: Yes, sir. (*She smells the bleeding hearts*)

PETER: More like this. (*He positions the vase of flowers so that it obscures her face, and then goes back to his sketch pad*)

CONSTANCE: (*After a pause, deliberately*) You have completely covered up my face, have you not.

PETER: Oh, I wouldn't say completely . . .

CONSTANCE: (*Rising*) Well, anyway, we tried.

PETER: Wait a minute! I'm not giving up that easily. If at first you don't succeed, quit. Take you, for instance. All this medical training in your background. Did you ever consider taking it a step further? Did you ever once consider becoming a doctor?

CONSTANCE: No.

PETER: There, you see? So easily contented. So easily defeated.

CONSTANCE: Defeated?

PETER: Pamela Branschweiger, class of '72. Classic non-achiever. Small dreams. I'm telling you, this girl's dreams were minute! *And.* She was a gum-snapper. What do you want out of life, Pamela? Snap. What do you hope for? Snap. What do want to make of yourself? Bubble, scratch, check the fingernails, snap! I mean this girl enacted the entire story of her life within her own oral cavity! (*A beat*) Stop laughing, it's no joke.

CONSTANCE: Yes, sir.

PETER: Okay. Sure. So she was overweight. (*A beat*) You're laughing again.

CONSTANCE: I can't help it.

PETER: That's what Pamela said. I can't help it. I'm fat now, I always have been fat, and I always will be fat. Snap.

CONSTANCE: And?

PETER: *And*, I got that girl on the most austere diet in the history of diets. I got the gum out of her mouth, and some decent food into it, and not too much of it. Okay. It was a start. I spent every lunch hour for six months in the student cafeteria. I practically had to sit on her, but I did it.

CONSTANCE: Congratulations.

PETER: Thank you.

CONSTANCE: But I never wanted to be a doctor. I always wanted to be a nurse. It's that simple. I'm doing exactly what I always wanted to do. And I'm loving it. I wouldn't call that a defeat.

PETER: You're married?

CONSTANCE: Was.

PETER: Divorced?

CONSTANCE: Yup.

PETER: If at first you don't succeed...

CONSTANCE: We're talking about things that are none of our business now, aren't we?

PETER: Any kids?

CONSTANCE: A girl.

PETER: Fatherless.

CONSTANCE: Okay, Jack, let's put the lid on it, shall we? I don't know what planet you come from, but here on mine some things work out and some don't, and nobody really has a lot of control over either. And if you haven't learned that by now, when will you? (*A beat*) I was married before I graduated from high school, for God's sake. I was a child. (*A beat*) You're in such a hurry to give people The Word. Like you're in such a hurry to get Paul out of here. Okay. He's an orderly. Not glamorous, not lucrative. But he works hard. He's good with the people. He's good *for* the people. So where do you get off making him feel miserable for *that*? Huh? (*Peter is silent*) You know, in this place, I shouldn't say it, but it's true, people come and people go, and some you notice and some you don't, and that's just the way it is. You—you, notice. You're the resident sore thumb, as a matter of fact, and with that poor kid of yours limping around here all the time with his flowers and his cookies and his *face*, Jesus! Scrubbed and shining and giving you chances right and left and you miss the boat every damned chance you get!

PETER: (*Pained*) I am not unaware...

CONSTANCE: Well, Jack, when you're a *nurse*, you have many duties, and one of the things you get to do as a *nurse* is, you get to count the comings and the goings and you get to count the chances that people get and I'm telling you *already* you've had more than your share. What does a nurse do? She tells you time's up. (*A beat*) I've go to go now. (*She goes to look at the blank page of the sketch pad*) Well, there's one thing anyway. At this point you could go almost anywhere with it. (*She exits. Peter does not move*)

(*A voice on the public address system:* "Sheryl, we need you in

203 immediately. Sheryl, please report to the south wing immediately.")

Scene Nine:

The lights fade to nighttime levels, and then rise slightly with the first glimmer of dawn. After a pause Paul enters quietly. He does not notice Peter sitting in the bed, partly obscured by the bedside curtain. Paul stands looking out the glass doors. He produces his ashtray and lights a cigarette. Long pause.

PETER: You really shouldn't smoke.
PAUL: God. (*A beat*) I didn't mean to wake you.
PETER: You didn't wake me.
PAUL: Oh. Good.
PETER: What time is it, anyway?
PAUL: I don't know. Dawn. Well. I guess I'll shove off.
PETER: Well. If you have to.
PAUL: I just came in to check on things.
PETER: You come in here to smoke, night after night. (*A beat*)
PAUL: That's not why I come in here.
PETER: No?
PAUL: Tell the truth, I missed talking to you.
PETER: You should take those cigarettes and throw them out the window.
PAUL: That's what I missed. Advice.
PETER: Oh, God, just can't stop, can I? Well, I'm swearing off it. No more advice. For anyone, ever.
PAUL: That's a long time, Peter. (*A beat*)
PETER: It's been a while.
PAUL: Over a month.
PETER: So how have you been?
PAUL: Oh, you know.
PETER: No, I don't know, that's why I asked—oh, God, there I go again.
PAUL: Hey, it's okay.
PETER: Grilling you. I know what's going to heppen. I'll die. That's a given. And with any luck I'll make my way up to St. Peter and he'll say, "How you doin', old fella?" And I'll say to him, "Look at yourself. Wasted potential. One of the most famous saints in history, and you end up a doorman."

PAUL: Talk about wasted potential. You should have been on T.V. (*A beat*) So how *are* you doing?

PETER: Pretty well. Given there's a little time bomb somewhere in my brain, ticking away, I'm doing pretty well. How was your night?

PAUL: Mrs. Swenson died.

PETER: Oh.

PAUL: I was with her.

PETER: Oh.

PAUL: Yeah. Old Tons of Fun. I'm gonna miss her.

PETER: You know what time is, Paul? You want me to tell you? Time is a total fuck. (*A beat*) Now you listen to this because it's the very last piece of advice I'm ever going to give anybody.

PAUL: I knew you wouldn't last.

PETER: I'm serious. You've got to stop denying your name, you've got to stop denying your father, you've got to find him, the two of you have to find each other, and you've got to do it while there's still time. (*Pause. Paul is stunned*) You have a beautiful last name. (*A beat*) Bearclaw. Beautiful. (*A beat*) It's a little unusual, isn't it, a white woman marrying an Indian?

PAUL: Chippewa. Mom has a mind of her own. Did he show up here?

PETER: No.

PAUL: Then how did you...? I won't ask. Anyway you probably figured by now he wasn't a fireman, he didn't die, he's out there somewhere, drunk as an Indian.

PETER: He's your father.

PAUL: Tell me about it.

PETER: You've got to talk to each other.

PAUL: You try talking to him.

PETER: Before it's too late.

PAUL: It was always too late.

PETER: Maybe...maybe you're just not talking the same language.

PAUL: Yeah? Well, I don't know where you go to school to learn that one. (*A beat*) Beautiful? You think my name is *beautiful*?

PETER: Yes. Yes, it is. And it's yours.

PAUL: (*Bitter*) Well, it was pretty popular back on the reservation.

PETER: The reservation?

PAUL: You know, the bearclaw is a very big thing with us.

Because the bear is a very big thing with us. So it stands for all kinds of stuff. But my father told me once, we were sitting in front of the T.V., I forget what we were watching, and he was still sober enough to talk. I don't know, I think I was twelve or something and already he had a pretty good idea I was queer. Indians got a real nose for that kind of thing. Anyway, he said the father bear looks at his cubs and if they're okay he pulls in his claws and gives them a pat and if they're not, he puts his claws out and rips them open. (*A beat*) I think it was "Bowling for Dollars." (*Pause*)

PETER: Oh, dear God. (*A beat*) There are scholarships available to Indians, Paul. You could get one, you're eligible.

PAUL: Forget it, Peter.

PETER: College scholarships.

PAUL: Look. I already tried it. The Bureau of Indian Affairs, they're a bunch of total fucks. You know why they won't give me a scholarship? Because my father never had a birth certificate, can you believe it? They weren't so good at making certificates back on the reservation. And so, Mr. Bearclaw isn't an Indian. He's not Chippewa because according to the BIA he ain't even been born. (*A beat*)

PETER: There must be other avenues.

PAUL: Hey—I don't know what I'm gonna do. I'll figure it out for myself.

PETER: You grew up on a reservation?

PAUL: No, here in town. But my father did, so we'd go back sometimes. Visit the old family plantation.

PETER: Yes?

PAUL: We'd go ricing. In that part of the country, the Indian is allowed one industry, just one. Wild rice. It was hard work, but I loved it. You go along in a canoe, right through the stalks, and you beat them with sticks, and the wild rice falls into the canoe. It's good money, too, man. I remember once, I was about six years old. I bought a pair of brand-new leather shoes with the money I made ricing. It was my birthday, and that was my birthday present to myself. (*A beat*) I put those shoes right next to my bed. I kissed the soles before I went to sleep. I was only six, right?

PETER: When's your birthday?

PAUL: (*Evasive*) What?

PETER: Your birthday. When is it?

PAUL: Many moons. When the rice is in the canoe.

PETER: Wiseguy. I'll find out, just watch me.

PAUL: I don't need leather shoes anymore, Mr. A. Nothing but sneakers from here on in.

PETER: Peter Junior's birthday is coming up.

PAUL: Yeah?

PETER: Oh, I've got something planned for him, don't you worry about that.

PAUL: I thought you didn't like giving gifts.

PETER: Some things you just get out of practice.

PAUL: He's a lot like you.

PETER: Peter? You're out of your mind.

(*Paul reaches for a cigarette, and winces painfully with a stitch in his side*)

PAUL: Ooo.

PETER: What's the matter? You hurt yourself?

PAUL: Yeah, I hurt myself.

PETER: How?

PAUL: It's no big deal, Peter, I just got some tape on my ribs that's driving me crazy.

PETER: You've got your ribs taped up and it's no big deal? What happened?

PAUL: I forgot to learn karate.

PETER: Tell me.

PAUL: A couple of cops tried to flirt with me outside a gay bar. They were a little clumsy. Eat that for breakfast, Mr. Onward-and-Upward.

PETER: But that's appalling. They struck you? Well, we've got to do something. Register a complaint...

PAUL: Yeah, right. They'd be delighted to hear from us.

PETER: What were you doing outside a gay bar?

PAUL: I was coming out of it.

PETER: What were you doing *in* the bar?

PAUL: Research.

PETER: Sure, be a wiseguy. How does that Joe guy feel about you going to places like that?

PAUL: I wouldn't know. I don't live with him anymore.

PETER: What?

PAUL: I split.

PETER: You left him? Oh, that's great, just great.

PAUL: (*Dangerous*) I don't want to talk about this, Peter.

PETER: The one stable thing in your life and you throw it away.

PAUL: I mean it.

PETER: Sure it was weird, but at least it was stable.

PAUL: I thought you weren't going to grill me anymore!

PETER: Why did you do it? So you could go running around to bars?

PAUL: No! No! I don't know why! Because he always had to be on top, how's that? (*A beat*) He tried to help me. And help me, and help me, and help me. Somebody trying to help you all the time, it gets so you think you need help. (*A beat*) Like you. This condition you've got? The stroke, the medication, all of it? That's not your tragedy. Your tragedy is you've always gotta be on top! (*A beat*)

PETER: I hurt everyone I touch.

PAUL: Goddamn right you do!

PETER: My students. My wife. You. I've got a son who's afraid to conceive a child because of what I did to him. (*A beat*)

PAUL: Peter? Now, don't. Just don't, please. What are you crying for?

PETER: I'm not.

PAUL: Come on. Don't. You did help me, you know.

PETER: Bullshit.

PAUL: You did. You just sometimes forget to pull in those claws, that's all.

PETER: I don't know a goddamned thing about helping anybody. I can't even help myself, for God's sake.

PAUL: Now that's bullshit.

PETER: You don't know what happened tonight.

PAUL: So what happened.

PETER: I don't want to talk about it.

PAUL: So don't.

PETER: I wet my bed, that's what!

PAUL: Too much.

PETER: How dare you laugh!

PAUL: Look at it one way, it's kind of funny.

PETER: I wet the bed, goddamnit!

PAUL: You mean you've been sitting here all this time . . . Why didn't you tell me, for God's sake? Peter. What's a little pee among friends?

PETER: Go away.

PAUL: I can't do that.

PETER: If it comes down to this, what's the point of starting? Of doing any of it?

PAUL: Is this advice? Is this my career counsellor talking? (*A beat*) We'll take care of it, it's no big deal. (*A beat*) Okay. Today, I'm not peeing my pants. But someday I'm gonna. Are you telling me I just shouldn't bother with any of it? Because of *that*? (*Long pause*)

PETER: Don't leave me again, will you? I know I'm impossible...

PAUL: Don't worry. I'm sick of the night shift anyway.

PETER: You'll switch back?

PAUL: Sure. Come on.

PETER: I don't think I can move. My legs feel funny.

PAUL: No problem. We'll just give you a lift into the john, that's simple.

PETER: I don't want anyone else to see me like this.

PAUL: Who's gonna see you?

PETER: Don't let anyone else in the room.

PAUL: Over my dead body anybody gets in here. (*Paul lifts Peter out of the bed*) Ahh! Goddamn tape!

PETER: How are *you* going to keep anyone out, sissy?

PAUL: (*Carrying Peter into the bathroom*) I'll hit 'em with my purse, Peter. I'll hit 'em with my purse.

(*The dim lights fade to black. In the darkness, a harmonica playing "Goodnight Irene"*)

Scene Ten:

Peter's bed has been stripped bare. The bleeding hearts have been replaced by lilacs. Constance and Paul are making the bed from scratch: mattress pad, sheets, covers, pillowcases. They work in silence. Eventually Peter Jr. enters, dressed in a dark suit and carrying a large coffee table book.

CONSTANCE: How did it go?

PETER JR: Just fine. It was hot out there.

CONSTANCE: I'll bet.

PETER JR: A few of his old students showed up.

CONSTANCE: Great.

PETER JR: At least, I assume that's who they were.

CONSTANCE: Pamela Braunschweiger? (*Peter Jr. regards her blankly*) Never mind.

PETER JR: I'm sorry you weren't able to join us.

CONSTANCE: So am I.

PETER JR: You said there was a package for me?

CONSTANCE: It was stuck in the back of the closet. (*She goes to get it*)

PETER JR: Ah, Paul? (*He offers the book*) This was Dad's. (*Paul stares at him*) He left a note, you should have it. Turner.

CONSTANCE: Can I see? (*She takes the book, leafs through it*)

PETER: JR: He talked like some big-time traveller, but he never was. Couldn't afford it. But about ten years ago he went on a little package trip for high school teachers, toured all over England and Wales. That's when he got this book on Turner, in the gift shop of the Tate.

CONSTANCE: That's this guy? Turner? It's beautiful. (*She gives it to Paul, who takes it and turns to look out the glass doors*)

PETER JR: Well. The relatives are waiting back at the house. Paul? Fran and I would like you to come. (*A beat*) I would like you to come.

PAUL: I'm on duty.

CONSTANCE: It's nearly three, you can take off early.

PAUL: I can't make it.

CONSTANCE: I'll cover for you.

PAUL: I can't.

PETER JR: I know how you feel, Paul, but I hope you'll come.

PAUL: Please don't tell me you know how I feel. You don't, okay?

PETER JR: I can try, can't I?

PAUL: He was about the best thing ever happened to me. (*A beat*)

PETER JR: Yeah. I guess you're right. I don't know how you feel. (*A beat*)

CONSTANCE: (*Offering the envelope to Peter Jr.*) Open it.

PETER JR: What?

CONSTANCE: It says on the envelope: "Birthday, Peter Junior."

PETER JR: Ah, my birthday isn't for a week.

CONSTANCE: I think it'll be okay. (*Peter Jr. opens the envelope, pulls out several pastel drawings, and leafs through them*) Look at that. About two, three weeks before the stroke he started doing pastels. Really pretty good.

PETER JR: I remember that suit. That's me.

CONSTANCE: That little boy standing in the boat?

PETER JR: I remember that day. I wasn't far out from shore, but I started goofing off and ended up in the water. Dad jumped in and swam out to me, grabbed on and towed me back to the beach. It was a hot day, Pelican Lake. We sat on the sand, drying off in the sun.

PAUL: He drew your mouth.

PETER JR: He had a little trouble with it, didn't he? (*Peter Jr. contorts his lips into a comical grimace for a moment*)

PAUL: He never drew anyone's mouth.

PETER JR: (*Looking at the drawing*) I wasn't goofing off. I just stepped off that boat to see what he would do. He was always best if he thought you were sinking. (*Immediately, to Paul*) You coming?

PAUL: Look how I'm dressed.

PETER JR: You're very good at what you do. I think you're dressed just right.

PAUL: I don't fit in.

PETER JR: Oh, for God's sake, who does?

CONSTANCE: (*To Peter Jr., picking up the vase of lilacs*) You want these?

PETER JR: You keep them.

CONSTANCE: Well. Peter.

PETER JR: Thanks for everything, Connie.

CONSTANCE: (*On her way out*) I'll see you tomorrow, Paul. (*She exits*)

PETER JR: You want to ride with me?

PAUL: I've got a car here.

PETER JR: (*Giving Paul a calling card*) Okay, here's the address. Now you get on 135 at the Como entrance, take it to 194, take 194 to . . .

PAUL: Hey. I'll find my way.

(*Peter Jr. looks at Paul, and then exits, carrying the packet of drawings. Paul holds the book tightly to him and looks out the glass doors. After a moment he reads the calling card. The lights fade*)

The End

Laurence Holder

WHEN THE CHICKENS CAME HOME TO ROOST

Laurence Holder

Laurence Holder is one among a half-dozen black playwrights in the country to have received professional New York productions, critical acclaim, and awards for his work. Yet outside a small theatrical community, his work is relatively unknown. Hopefully, publication here will bring more attention and productions to this talented writer who has written many works based on the history and experiences of black culture in America. Though *When the Chickens Came Home to Roost* was first presented in 1981 at the New Federal Theater in Manhattan, produced by Woodie King, Jr. and Steve Tennen, it appears in print here for the first time.

At the play's New York premiere, Frank Rich, reviewer for the *New York Times*, observed that the playwright "has taken a pair of intimidating, legendary men—Elijah Muhammad and Malcolm X—and brought them to utterly convincing life." He further described the play as "a fascinating tug of war between men who once had everything in common—who indeed made history together—and who now find themselves antagonistic strangers... The two characters form a highly theatrical study in contrasts—of youth and age, of idealism and cynicism, of energy and exhaustion." The production went on to receive four awards from Audelco (the Audience Development Committee, and organization of black theatergoers): for director, Allie Woods; for leading actor Denzel Washington; for scenic designer, Robert Edmonds; and for writer, Laurence Holder.

Another Audelco nomination went to Mr. Holder as musical creator of the story of *Juba*, a dance musical based on the life of William Henry Lane, presented at New York City's La Mama Theatre and recreated later under the title *Five Points* at the AMAS Repertory Theatre.

Other plays by Mr. Holder include *Zora*, a character study of Harlem Renaissance's most controversial woman artist, Zora Neale Hurston, a famed novelist and anthropologist (originally on a double bill with *When the Chickens Came Home to Roost*). Critical acclaim was also given to Mr. Holder's jazz musical *They Were All Gardenias*, the love story of jazz musicians Billie Holliday and Lester Young. Additional plays written by Mr. Holder are: *Zora and Langston*, a play about their love affair; *Laurel Wreath*, a play on life after the bomb; *Ruby and Pearl*, a musical comedic drama of two aging burlesque queens who don't want to "take it all off"; *Hot Fingers*, a musical biography of Jelly Roll Morton; *Hot Lips*, an account of Valaida Snow, performer extraordinaire; *Man*, the story of a man born and raised in penal institutions in America; *The Fighter*, a boxing tale; *Jon and Arnie*, the story of a black man and a white man trapped in a small town jail; *Babblers*, a play about a black middle class family torn between security and conformity; *Gosperetta*, a gospel musical based on confession; and *The Blue Blocks*, a story of American schizophrenia as seen through the occult eye.

During his active career as writer and actor, Mr. Holder has worked with theater notables Rosetta LeNoire, Ellen Stewart, Woodie King, Jr., Michael Hadge, Ornette Coleman, Regge Life, Mary Alice, Phyllicia Ayers Allen, Denzel Washington, Jacquie Berger, Yvonne Southerland, Arthur Burghardt, Cynthia McPherson, Yvonne Taylor Cheyne, John Vaccaro, and the late Hazel Bryant.

Mr. Holder has also written scripts for radio and television. He created a television series that aired originally in 1977, *Watch Your Mouth*, a youth-oriented show, which focused on the need for youngsters to know a standard form of English as well as their own colorful street language. Additionally, he created and produced his own radio show, entitled *New Ark Show*.

Mr. Holder has also created and directed writing and acting workshops for numerous groups including the New Federal Theatre, the Cell Block Theatre, and American Writer Enterprises, among others. He is a member of the Dramatists Guild and now resides in Arizona where he teaches at South Mountain Community College.

Characters:

ELIJAH MUHAMMAD
MALCOLM SHABAZZ

Scene One:

In the prophet's office which is furnished with two easy chairs and a large desk, Elijah Muhammad paces uneasily. He takes a drink of water from one of two water pitchers and sits down just as the door is knocked on. He groans aloud.

ELIJAH: Who is it now?

MALCOLM: It's Malcolm.

(Elijah jumps up smiling and walks unevenly to the door)

ELIJAH: Boy, why din't ya say it was you in the first place? I been waiting for you. *(He opens the door and steps back to let in a large man, lean and bespectacled)*

MALCOLM: Salaam alaikum.

ELIJAH: As-alaikum salaam. You look like gloomy Sunday on a Monday, boy. What's the matter? *(Elijah turns and starts towards the water pitcher)*

MALCOLM: Well, you know how those news people are.

ELIJAH: I sure do. I sure do. Want some water or tea?

MALCOLM: No, thank you.

(Elijah turns away from the water pitcher, having filled his glass again, and looks at Malcolm with a huge grin. He shakes his head from side to side)

ELIJAH: Yep, you look like they run you out of town. Have a seat, Malcolm. Have a seat. *(Elijah walks over and sits in the biggest chair. Malcolm holds his briefcase in his lap)*

MALCOLM: I came because I wanted to see you, sir.

ELIJAH: Yeah, well either I want to see you or you want to see me. What's the problem?

MALCOLM: It's about the sc—...

ELIJAH: Aw, man, I don't want to hear nothing about that. I been pestered my own self with them paper people. What's happening at number seven, your mosque.

MALCOLM: The mosque? Well, everything is going just fine until this thing hit the papers. We've been be—...

ELIJAH: Yeah, yeah, that's the only problem when you start foolin' around with the devils, they always want to get deep into your business. It's a shame, too. I mean, Malcolm, (*He takes a deep swig from the glass and wets his lips with his tongue*) this thing with them paper people ought to stop. Just because I'm a successful business man, doesn't mean they can just pick my life apart. I got a wife and family too.

MALCOLM: I know. I spoke to Wallace about all this.

ELIJAH: You spoke to Wallace? (*Elijah looks at the briefcase Malcolm holds in his hands*)

MALCOLM: Yes sir, I did. I wanted to know what he thought about it all.

ELIJAH: He's just a minister. (*Elijah makes a pass for the case, but Malcolm pulls it away*)

MALCOLM: He's your son, too.

ELIJAH: You spoke to Wallace. Hmm.

MALCOLM: He thinks we can settle out of court.

ELIJAH: Of course we can settle out of court. All those girls want is some miserable money. That's all they want. They fell out of favor in the movement and now they are blackmailing me.(*Malcolm taps the brief case and fixes his glasses nervously*) And what's that supposed to mean?

MALCOLM: What, sir?

ELIJAH: The tapping of the briefcase, that's what.

MALCOLM: It...er...means that I've got their sworn testimony as to when the...er...

ELIJAH: I ain't never known you to be so slow with the words, Malcolm. What is it?

MALCOLM: When the acts took place.

ELIJAH: What acts?

MALCOLM: The acts of adultery.

ELIJAH: You got it all there in that case of yours?

(*Malcolm nods his head and adjusts his glasses again*)

MALCOLM: This isn't an easy thing to do, sir. I mean I have only the greatest respect and admiration for you. I—I love you like the father that was taken away from me.

(*Elijah gets up and walks more unsteadily towards the water pitcher*)

ELIJAH: Yep, yep, yep, I know you have those feelings, Malcolm. I feel very strongly about you. I mean you are my main man. And I've treated you better than I've treated my sons, which, by the way, they are quick to remind me. You see, Malcolm, things aren't easy anywhere.

MALCOLM: I know they aren't.

ELIJAH: And sometimes you have to step on someone's toes in order to make the right decisions. And sometimes I step on my own family's in order to do the right thing by you.

MALCOLM: Well, it isn't Wallace.

ELIJAH: No, it isn't Wallace, that's for sure. You and him are like brothers in more ways than one. I suppose that's why you went to him rather than any of the others.

MALCOLM: Well, sir, Wallace has an open mind and he can see the future more clearly than some of these self-seekers.

(*Elijah stops drinking and looks at Malcolm coldly*)

ELIJAH: That's a hard accusation, Malcolm. Very hard. You got the proof in that case, too?

(*Malcolm shakes his head. Elijah then continues his drink and returns to the seat*)

ELIJAH: The hard truth of the matter is that I never did a thing to those girls, Malcolm, and you should never have gone to Wallace with any kind of a story about me. It's one of those backbitin', reptilian, devilish things. It's like the woman who goes and tells another woman that her man has been fooling around with another woman. Now that first woman thinks she's being a friend, but you and I know better, don't we?

MALCOLM: I don't understand you. I'm trying to work out a way for all of us on this. I didn't tell the papers anything because I didn't believe the story in the first place.

ELIJAH: Come on, Malcolm. You believed the darn story. Inside you got to be pleased as pink. (*He laughs*) Now ain't that a what do you call them? A metaphor.

MALCOLM: I ain't pleased as pink. This whole thing reduces our creditability. How many young girls are going to come into the movement because of this? Not many more.

ELIJAH: You're taking this whole thing too far. You stepped out of line when you went to Wallace and more importantly when you went to those girls. (*He stops and watches the effect of his words on Malcolm, who looks at him as though he is containing his anger*) Er…just what did the girls say, Malcolm?

MALCOLM: That it happened. That you made them secretaries so they could be close to you and when the times were right, it happened.

ELIJAH: That's all they said?

MALCOLM: That's all, you see they got these babies to take care of and they've been thrown out of the movement, so there really isn't any place for them to turn to. Having babies is a family affair.

ELIJAH: It sure is. How's your family doing? I ain't seen any of them kids for a long time now. They must be growing like trees.

MALCOLM: They got a good mother. Their father they don't see much of. He's always running around trying to make something of himself.

(*Elijah starts looking at the case and smiles*)

ELIJAH: And you're doing it. You are. You're one of the most famous and dangerous men in America, Malcolm. Don't you forget that. There are some people in this country who would like to see you gone, that's for sure.

MALCOLM: If you say so.

ELIJAH: I say so, you know so. You see them leathernecks with their drunken faces staring out at you sometimes when you make those speeches of yours. You know what they're thinking, Malcolm. And if you don't, you should.

MALCOLM: They got more reason to hate me now.

ELIJAH: Why's that?

MALCOLM: Because now I'm a charlatan. I been making up stories about how decent and kind and thoughtful you are and then along comes all this news about illegal babies.

ELIJAH: Them babies is not illegal. God never said anything about illegal babies, Malcolm. Just the mans in this world. Those are the illegals. The ones who would put babies into coal mines before they're six. You ever read about the history of England? You ever read Dickens?

MALCOLM: No, sir, I haven't read Dickens, although I know about what you're saying.

ELIJAH: Save your anger and rage for them. Don't come in here and start thinking I've got to be saved and you and Wallace are the only ones who can do it. I been saving myself before you were born. And then some. Remember I started this movement.

MALCOLM: I thought Fard.

ELIJAH: Fard...the person was really The Prophet incarnated.

MALCOLM: Dear Holy Prophet...

(*Elijah stops and looks at Malcolm. There is a curious mixture of hate and love suddenly thrust into the room. Elijah gets up and walks over to the water pitcher. He pours a glass*)

ELIJAH: Fard, bless his heart, was a great man, like you, Malcolm. But Fard went in 1934 and I was there and I built this movement. I made it what it is. I had help. And recently you have been the one to help me, but it's my movement. Thanks to the constant beneficence of Allah. And Allah is the one who is going to save me, Malcolm, not you or Wallace or any other man. God is going to save me. (*Elijah looks at Malcolm, who is holding his own peace*) Malcolm, you don't believe that anymore, do you?

MALCOLM: About me and Allah?

ELIJAH: No, about me and Allah.

MALCOLM: It's a private covenant.

ELIJAH: Well, if you believe that, then why in the blazes did you have to go and get yourself mixed up in this?

MALCOLM: Because I couldn't help myself, sir. You see, some years back, when I was in prison, there was a man who came to see me, in the flesh. He told me that there was a man who could get me out of the prison and see and make a better life for myself. I believed that man. I got out of prison. I did make a life, a good one. I was doing what I wanted to do. Organize my people so they could make the kind of life they wanted. But one day, when I worked over in Detroit—God, I don't even remember where anymore— I've tried to burn it out of my mind, that man came back to me. But he wasn't the same man anymore. He looked haunted and he was saying the strangest things about you. And we were all upset. So he was kicked out of the movement. And of course he went from bad to worse. And this time he asked me for help and I couldn't give it to him. I couldn't even help him get a haircut or anything like that. And all because he was kicked out of the movement. Do you understand, sir, that I couldn't help my own flesh and blood? And he was asking, and he had given me so much direction. He was the one who had pointed the way to you. He was my John the Baptist. He was my own brother, Reg—...

ELIJAH: Don't mention his name. I know who you're speaking about. But he violated the codes we have here.

MALCOLM: But he was telling the truth! (*Malcolm jumps to his feet, no longer to contain himself*) He was trying to tell me the truth all the time, as he saw it. What good are codes if they don't help you to be true to yourself? Mr. Muhammad, I gave up on my brother for a code that didn't apply. There was something higher working here and because of my dedication to words, I missed the people.

ELIJAH: Is that why you don't relate the religious message to the people anymore?

MALCOLM: All my preaching relates to Allah.

ELIJAH: Maybe it does to you, in your mind, but it don't to me. You ain't the only one with a briefcase, you know.

MALCOLM: What? (*He sits back down*)

ELIJAH: I get transcripts of everything you say, Malcolm. You aren't delivering the message of The Prophet the way you used to. I know. I know. You are becoming more like them civil rights fools every day.

MALCOLM: We got to have rights like the rest of the Americans in this land we fought and died for.

ELIJAH: You don't have to preach to me, I know all the words. I've used them myself. But you are almost sounding like that King boy they pulled out of some old Christian church, did you know that? Huh?

MALCOLM: No.

ELIJAH: You and him are walking down the same road. Liable to meet soon also, and then what will you be saying to old Elijah then, huh? What will you say then? Uh, Uncle Elijah, we got to keep the black folks in line now, yeah, we got to do that so the white mens won't come and shoot them down. But we're past that already, Malcolm. We got the Nation of Islam. We got the Fruit of Islam. Those fine upstanding members of the American community. We look good. We stand straight. We have already got our pride because we worked for it. We ain't got to be begging for it. We don't need no special concessions from the white man. Don't you understand that?

MALCOLM: I do. There isn't a man alive who doesn't understand the significance of the Fruit of Islam. But you won't turn them loose. You won't let them make a stand with the rest of the black Americans in the country. Just imagine how a troop of the Fruit would look on one of them marches King sets up? Just imagine all the youngbloods who could be impressed by their uniforms and how that would increase our numbers. We would be a power then.

ELIJAH: And the FBI would be down our backs worse than they are now. We'd have more infiltrators than we would have people on our side. That's the whole problem with doing it your way. You would wash out the truth of the movement for numbers. And then they would kill you and where would your movement be then? I'll tell you. It'd be with you in your coffin. In your coffin, Malcolm.

Do you see what I mean?

MALCOLM: Yes, I do.

ELIJAH: It's hard to be a black man in this country because you got to be paranoid also, because no one wants a black man; they all want a black boy. Someone they can whistle for and not have to say thank you to. Do you understand?

MALCOLM: I do.

ELIJAH: That's good. You were always an understanding man, Malcolm. Wise beyond your years. It's one of the things that first impressed me, the other being that fantastic energy you have. Fantastic. You're going to be one of the superheroes in America, if I can keep you alive. Your zeal for the job is just what any movement needs, but you can't outsmart your commander and overreach your supplies. You got to approach this whole thing like it's a military campaign. And this campaign is going to take quite a few years, more than you got left on the planet in the first place. You know, Malcolm. (*Malcolm raises his head*) You make the other commanders very jealous of your success.

MALCOLM: All they have to do is what I'm doing.

ELIJAH: But that's the whole point. I'm keeping them in line. And besides you are the best. The others are still growing, and they need a model, and that's why I'm letting you go as far as you do go, so they can see what a man does. But I can't let anyone think for me; otherwise we would have been gone a long time ago. I know you are upset about your brother, that's only human.

MALCOLM: But he was right.

ELIJAH: He was wrong. He should have come to me with his information, like you did. But he wasn't a man, like you are, and that's why you don't even know where he is. Because he's not a man, and he never did believe; otherwise he would never have doubted me in the first place. I been around too long to be taken for a fool, Malcolm. Too long. There has been mens who wanted to take over this movement from right under my nose. We've had fights and arguments in this room that would have frightened even a strong man like yourself. But I'm the one who's still here, Malcolm. I was the strongest one. And I still am. Now, are you going to let me see what's in that briefcase of yours?

MALCOLM: (*Stands and shakes his head*) No, I'm not.

ELIJAH: You ain't, huh? Suppose I ordered you to.

MALCOLM: Well, then, I guess I would have to.

ELIJAH: But you don't want to. Why?

MALCOLM: It's my briefcase.

(*Elijah laughs loudly and returns to the water pitcher*)

ELIJAH: I knew when I first took you on, that the day when you didn't want to take a request would come. And here it is.

MALCOLM: I never thought it would come. I can remember the first night I saw you. I used to hallucinate when I was on the drugs, but that first night I saw you I was flabbergasted. There you were sitting on the edge of my prison cot just staring at me. I knew I was sitting with God. We didn't say a word to each other. We just sat looking at each other. Me out of my mind in jail and you just there, almost like you were saying take it easy, Malcolm Little. This too shall pass or something like that. I made up my mind, all right. The Nation of Islam had given me something to live and die for. And you were the Messenger. And when I got out, I made up my mind that I wouldn't listen to any of the gossip. I'd just do my job and hope that it was the best. And I did. Even when my brother came around, even after I began to hear stories from other people, I said, let them tell the stories, Elijah is giving them something to fill their lives with. But then I saw the women and Wallace.

ELIJAH: And now your whole mind is changed?

MALCOLM: I'm looking at things differently. I realize that a man is a man after all is said and done. And some things a man can't escape.

ELIJAH: Hmm. Some things a man can't escape.

MALCOLM: And we've got to say something to the people in the Nation.

ELIJAH: What do we have to say to them, Malcolm?

MALCOLM: (*Lowers his head*) We got to lie.

ELIJAH: Why do we have to lie?

MALCOLM: Because we can't tell them the truth.

ELIJAH: And what is the truth?

MALCOLM: That you are the father of these babies.

ELIJAH: Hmm. We don't have to say anything. We'll give them some money and that will satisfy them.

MALCOLM: But it isn't going to satisfy me. And I've got to be satisfied. I've got to be so I can keep going out and making out like I've been making out. I got to convince people that the future rests with the Nation of Islam. That people can make something out of themselves if they come on in and believe in you. Look, sir, we can tell them that it's in the Koran. It's prophecy. It's all been ordained. People need things like that. The religious and the spiritual are things they fear, but they want to know anyway. We got to say some—...(*Malcolm suddenly looks at Elijah, who has slumped in the chair*) Is there something wrong, Messenger? Shall I send for the Doctor?

ELIJAH: You young people got so much energy that has just got to be burned.

MALCOLM: You older people ain't so bad yourself.

ELIJAH: That's true. Are you sure the girls didn't say anything else about me?

MALCOLM: They all want to come back into the movement.

ELIJAH: They can't come back. That would be admitting something to them, like guilt. Guilt! It marks all of man's actions. He's always feeling something that ain't right, something that undermines him even as he's trying to do his best. And when you're at the top, other men are always looking for your weaknesses. And so you can't talk to anyone. No one wants to hear you when you're feeling weak and tired. They take it as permanent weakness and that you can be toppled. Some nights I would be here, Malcolm, and I would want to talk to you so badly, but you'd be off in California or Texas or Baltimore, and I wouldn't be able to get to you. Besides you never know who's listening to the telephone these days. But I wanted to talk, so I would invite one of them in to talk. And they would be so mothering, you know, wanting to try and please the Messenger, their leader, and before you know it, you done something bad. Something that you know you're ashamed of, but then there's no one to talk about it, so you do it again because all the time it's helping you to feel a little better. But then the guilt keeps coming and packing it on you, and then you make a change, but all the time the reason in the first place for doing the thing comes back then there's no one to talk to. And then it's done again. And the guilt.

MALCOLM: I know how you feel.

ELIJAH: Do you?

MALCOLM: Yeah, that's why me and Betty have these astronomical phone bills.

ELIJAH: Yeah, well, you in a different situation from me. You got a smart woman there who can give you advice. My wife, bless her heart, couldn't stand the strain of the things I got on my mind. She sure couldn't. But are you going to let me see the briefcase, Malcolm? That's really the question here. You've saved my legal team a lot of work. If only they could all have been like you, that's the damned problem. And they're so jealous.

(*Malcolm hands the case to Elijah*)

MALCOLM: I hope it helps, sir, because you're all I got, and if you go, I don't know what I'll do.

ELIJAH: Thanks, Malcolm. Thank you very much. Don't worry so much about the old man. He can still handle anything they throw at him. Remember that. The only thing I can't control is Allah. And he must be teaching me a lesson right now.

MALCOLM: He's teaching all of us a lesson in humility.

ELIJAH: Well, you be more humble then and leave Wallace alone, too. He ain't got too much savvy yet. Oh, he's smart and all. But he hasn't been in the world the way you have. He needs some experience.

MALCOLM: So you're going to take care of it yourself?

ELIJAH: That I am. I'll take care of it. (*He rises to his feet and takes Malcolm's hand*) I'll take care of it. You can just keep saying no comment. No comment. That'll be a change for some of those reporters, not hearing you say something to them. It'll give you credibility when you want to finally say something about something else.

MALCOLM: I can't do that. (*Malcolm rises and starts for the door*)

ELIJAH: Wait a minute! What do you mean you can't do that?

MALCOLM: Messenger, I can't leave this room and not say anything to anyone. I would look like a fool, a dummy worse than any slave you ever saw.

ELIJAH: I don't follow your thinking.

MALCOLM: I mean that the people all over the world are waiting for me to say something about what's happened here at this meeting.

ELIJAH: (*Gets up and goes in front of Malcolm*) Boy, you sure are funny. Just a minute ago you said that you were going to get a little humble and the very next minute you start acting like you're the one in charge around here. Don't you know who I am?

MALCOLM: (*Nods his head and returns to his seat*) It just doesn't make any sense since we've got to say something. People are expecting me to be doing the talking.

ELIJAH: People ain't got no right to expect anything from you except what I dictate to you. This ain't no democracy, Malcolm, this is the Nation of Islam. (*Malcolm lowers his head and Elijah walks close to him*) Malcolm, you got to understand all of this because you are sure resisting my word.

MALCOLM: I'm just trying to be rational. I have no intentions of disrespecting you or your words.

ELIJAH: Then why is it so difficult for you to be silent on this issue?

MALCOLM: Because it's a moral problem, Messenger. I told you that the young women all over the world are watching and waiting to see how the thing gets resolved.

ELIJAH: What upsets me about all of this is that you don't think I can handle the adversity.

MALCOLM: I know you can handle it. I know it, it's just that I'm in a position that demands things from me, and you're putting a muzzle on me. It isn't fair, Messenger. It's not right. I'm in your corner.

ELIJAH: We're not talking about what's right and fair. We're talking about who gives the orders around here. Be an awful place if I had to take orders from Wallace or you. And I'm the one who's in the difficult position. Let's stop for a minute and relax. How about a little dinner?

MALCOLM: Food?

ELIJAH: Yes, food. Don't you eat anymore? You look like Wily Coyote or them lean wolves you find out there on the prairie.

MALCOLM: What with traveling, I don't even remember. There are so many things to do, so many people to talk to. I should be in Los Angeles right now giving a lecture.

ELIJAH: Well, you haven't answered my question.

MALCOLM: (*Raising his head*) It would be an honor to eat with you, sir.

ELIJAH: Sure it would. (*Going to the door, opening it and wheeling in a tray*) You sure know how to say the right things at the right time. (*He takes the lids off the trays*) We got soup, oh my! Roast lamb, Malcolm. I know that's one of your favorites. Plenty of vegetables, tea. I took your advice and started using some of those Chinese herbals. They're tasty, once you get a taste for it. (*Elijah puts his plates on the desk and wheels over the tray to Malcolm*) You're still looking sad.

MALCOLM: (*Looks at the food but doesn't eat right away*) I guess I'm still nervous and anxious, sir. We've got a seri—...

ELIJAH: Forget about it now, Malcolm. Just forget it. Let's eat and remember some of the good times. How's that fighter friend of yours doing?

MALCOLM: (*Surprised*) You mean, Cassius?

ELIJAH: (*Spooning the food with great relish*) That's the one.

MALCOLM: How'd you know about that?

ELIJAH: I admit it ain't common knowledge, but the man is interested in what we got to say, isn't he?

MALCOLM: Yes, he is and he's doing fine. He's going to be a champ.

ELIJAH: He already is a champ, Malcolm. He's interested in us. See, that's what I mean. You keep letting those people's values get in the way of your own. You can't keep spending time with leopards and not start running like them. You're not eating your food. No appetite?

MALCOLM: Funny thing is I'm starving.

ELIJAH: You don't think the food is poisoned, do you? (*Elijah stops eating and looks at the food, to Malcolm, and back to the food*) Well, say something. (*But Malcolm just stares at Elijah*) Why are you staring at me?

MALCOLM: You don't think someone wants to poison you, do you?

ELIJAH: Naw! My wife would've died by now. She tastes everything. (*Elijah bursts out laughing*) By George, you've lost your sense of humor fooling with them folks.

(*Malcolm takes a deep breath and then starts picking at the food*)

MALCOLM: You had me worried.

ELIJAH: Why should you worry, Malcolm, you're next in line. I would have to leave this little empire to you.

MALCOLM: I just wasn't thinking like that, sir.

ELIJAH: (*Interrupting his eating, angrily*) Well, just how was you thinking? You been sitting here all this time and laying out all this lame talk and not once have you really spoken up about what's going on. Instead you sneak behind my back to members of my family and then you dig up dirt on me. Dirt on me, Malcolm! Now I want to know what you're thinking?

(*Malcolm puts the utensils down and gets up and goes over to Elijah*)

MALCOLM: I don't like what I've been hearing, Messenger. And I've been hearing the craziest, most preposterous things about me. And people say you've been the one to instigate these things. You think I'm talking behind your back, and you claim that you've got a dossier on my blasphemes. But it hasn't been me who's been doing the dirty, behind-the-back talk. It's you, and I can hear it in your voice. I can see the way you're patronizing me, downgrading me. You still think we're in 1934 and no one is really listening to you except for a few FBI men, but that's not the way it is anymore. There's a whole world out there. There's all those millions in Africa who are watching and waiting for us to do something. Something important. And it ain't about making babies with some stupid girls and then blaming them and kicking them out of the movement. And it ain't about running behind my back and spreading rumors that I'm trying to embarrass or humiliate you. My god! You are the last person in the world that I would ever have thought I would be talking to like this. Messenger, I got more faith in you than you have in yourself. I love you. I worship you. But I can't let you go on thinking like this about me because it isn't true. (*Returns to his chair*) It isn't true. Allah knows it isn't true.

(*Elijah sits there with a forkful of food suspended in mid-air. He finally puts it down and stands up.*)

ELIJAH: Well, I want to know who's been spreading all this negative propaganda around. That's what I want to know. Who is it? I'll summarily discharge them from the movement. No one knows more than I do how valuable you've been to me and the movement. No one. I'll bet it was those girls, huh? Them? Well, I won't give them a dime for starting those lies. Lies! Lies! They're all liars. The whole world is one boondock of lies. And you, my trusted partner in all of this movement of the black man to a place of security and well-being, you believe the lies. What am I to make of that? How can I trust you anymore? You let the liars breach the walls of faith and then you accuse me. Me! The Honorable Elijah Muhammad. The Messenger of the faith.

MALCOLM: It's in your attitude, sir. The way you talk to me. Condescending and almost nasty. You bait me. You want me to say things about what you think the others are saying about you. And I don't, so you bait me some more. But if this thing with the young women hadn't come up, I'd still be indicted by you because you think I want to take the movement over by hook or by crook. Well, this old field hand isn't biting the hand that feeds him. We'll work it out. We will. (*Goes back to picking at his food*)

ELIJAH: Back to that, huh? Back to handling the old man's problems like he's a horse with a broken leg or something.

MALCOLM: Everything is filled with scandals and people wind up forgetting about them sooner or later. That's what I mean.

ELIJAH: Oh, no, Malcolm. I know you too well to believe that.

What are you going to do?

MALCOLM: I'm not going to do anything, Messenger. I'm just going to keep my mouth shut and act like Elmer Fudd. (*Mimics Fudd*)

ELIJAH: And now you want to get sarcastic with me. Just what is getting into your head?

MALCOLM: I must need a rest from all this. We don't ever talk with each other anymore, you're right about that. You don't believe me when I say I'm sorry. You don't believe me when I say I don't think the blasphemes you think I think. I mean there isn't a man on this planet who could ever have told you that I want your job. And what's making me angrier is that I have to act like some little lovesick girl trying to convince her boyfriend that it's all right to do whatever you want to do to me because I will always love you, baby. I don't want to stand here and have my guts and blood and brains spilling all over to prove to you that I do love you. I don't want to. I'm a man and I do have pride.

ELIJAH: Well, remember pride goeth before a fall. (*Malcolm stands and looks at Elijah*) Well, don't just stand there again staring at me. It's in the Bible. A lot of colored folks know the expression.

MALCOLM: What fall are you talking about?

ELIJAH: The fall from grace, Malcolm. That's what I'm talking about.

MALCOLM: (*Sits back down*) I'll do whatever you say, sir. Whatever it is, I'm your boy. That is the expression, isn't it? And it is found in the Constitution, isn't it?

ELIJAH: More sarcasm, huh? Why don't you just let the wind out of you and enjoy the meal? That's what you should be doing. But you've gotten so much out of hand that you can't even do that.

MALCOLM: I'm angry, sir. I can't prove to you . . .

ELIJAH: Stop it, Malcolm. I've listened to the love talk long enough. I feel like the boyfriend who's been watching his girl cheat on him long enough and now I'm tired of it. I want some honest warm talk from a man I consider my friend. Someone whom I know would lay his life down for mine, it if was required.

(*Malcolm jumps to his feet*)

MALCOLM: But that's what I've been saying to you—in so many words, that is.

ELIJAH: Good, then sit down and eat. (*Malcolm sits down and a sudden smile breaks over his face*)

MALCOLM: You always were smarter than I was, Messenger.
(*Elijah smiles*)

ELIJAH: Yeah, and soon you'll take everything I know and make this empire even larger and more prestigious.

MALCOLM: Why do you say that, sir?

ELIJAH: I'm getting tired, too, boy. Real tired. Here I am, almost an old man, and I'm facing paternity suits when I should be holding my grandchildren on my lap and sitting out there in Phoenix, where the air is good for my lungs. I got a bunch of ambitious Ministers who all think they're ready to take over my job. (*Malcolm starts to object*) Everyone except you, Malcolm. But what is true is that there is a lot of disagreement about what we should do, especially with the country starting to flounder over this civil rights mess. I can't really understand how anybody in their right mind could think that guaranteeing civil rights is going to change anything for the black person in this country. You got to be a money-making machine for anyone to take notice of you in this place. And just where are the overwhelming majority of us going to get money? The Nation of Islam is the most efficient organization and look at the huge problems we have getting by.

(*Malcolm casts a furtive eye over the lush office but says nothing*)

ELIJAH: Yeah, but this soup is nice even if it is a little chilled.

MALCOLM: It certainly is, sir. And so is the lamb.

ELIJAH: Hmm hmm. So when are you going back to New York?

MALCOLM: As soon as the western coast gets swung through.

ELIJAH: Why don't you send someone in your place?

MALCOLM: I'd love to, but they all say, "Malcolm, you're the only one who can get the people in the hall." So I go and get the hall filled and we make a little more money to save some little boy or girl. It's simple logic. If I don't go, someone will get lost. Lost in the maze of this world.

ELIJAH: You believe that?

MALCOLM: Not entirely, but the others do, and that makes the difference in the minds of the publicizers. So I almost don't have a choice.

ELIJAH: You've got to spend more time with that family of yours.

MALCOLM: Oh, Betty and I have talked and she says do it now while they're still young. When they get older and want to really know about the world that's when I'd better be there.

ELIJAH: She's a wise and understanding woman.

MALCOLM: Betty is the next-to-greatest thing that ever happened to me personally. But what bothers me is I'd like to be with them. I never really had much of a family life what with my father being killed by those crackers and my mother going insane, and the rest of the kids being spread out all over the union.

ELIJAH: Yeah, you'd do good by yourself to take a little vacation.

MALCOLM: (*Looking up at the Messenger*) Is that an order, sir?

ELIJAH: No, no, just a suggestion and wistful thinking on my part. You ever have dreams, Malcolm, dreams about what you might have been or done?

MALCOLM: I had my last dream the night you came to me in prison. Since then I'm not letting any thoughts like that come through. I just want to get the job done, my job.

ELIJAH: Total dedication, Malcolm, that's what makes you different from the others.

MALCOLM: Every man does what he can do, sir. No more. No less?

(*They both laugh*)

ELIJAH: I have this strange dream and I don't know what to make out of it. And I can't talk to anyone else about it.

MALCOLM: What is it?

ELIJAH: I don't want to ever hear a word about it, Malcolm.

MALCOLM: You have my solemn promise, sir.

ELIJAH: Every night I've been dreaming about being on a farm. Just me, the wife, and the grandkids. We raise chickens, vegetables, and things like that, and the whole world is peaceful. I don't have to know anything about black and white. I don't have to hear your speeches on the radio, I don't have to make any, and I don't have to hear Wallace every third day telling me how to run the Nation of Islam. We lead a simple life and everyone is happy. And every night we watch the stars overhead and we thank Allah for all the bounty. The dream ends with me hearing a rooster cry announcing the morning sun. Ah, Malcolm, that's a dream I would love to be reality.

MALCOLM: It's a great dream.

ELIJAH: Yes, it is, Malcolm. And I want it to come true. Am I making myself clear? (*He pushes the dishes away*)

MALCOLM: I think so.

ELIJAH: (*Comes over to him*) Forget about Wallace for the next few months. Let him think his own way, my way, for a change. And about this thing with the women, what kind of a statement did you want to make?

MALCOLM: Well, sir, I thought if we could tell the brethren that a man is judged by his contributions and not his faults. There's David, Solomon, Moses just to name a few. No one remembers that they were adulterers and murderers, just the founding fathers of the church. That should explain it to them.

ELIJAH: And the press?

MALCOLM: Just denials, and then we settle out of court. You're right, they do want money. It is a form of blackmail, but the Nation doesn't need the scandal that accompanies a trial.

ELIJAH: All right, Malcolm. See to it. See to it, my boy, and take care of yourself.

MALCOLM: You're serious, sir.

(Elijah comes forward and shakes Malcolm's hand)

ELIJAH: We don't need a scandal. By the way, Malcolm, did the women, any of them say anything else about me to you?

MALCOLM: *(Smiles, winks)* They think you're some man, sir.

ELIJAH: At my age, huh?

(Malcolm nods his head and opens the door)

MALCOLM: Well, salaam-alaikum.

ELIJAH: *(Puffing his chest)* As-sa-laikum salaam. *(The door closes. His face becoming hard)* I used to be the most dangerous man in America.

(End of Scene One)

Scene Two:

(Elijah's office is in darkness. But there is a radio report about the Kennedy assassination)

RADIO VOICE: The Nation is in deep mourning over the death of President John F. Kennedy who was struck down by assassin's bullets earlier today. The President died and—and—no one knows what to say. Peole all over the world are sending their condolences. Heads of state, military leaders, all of them.

(The radio is switched off and we hear Elijah's voice)

ELIJAH: I want you to send a directive to all the Ministers. What? Yes, all of them. I do not want them to say a word about his situation with those people. It's their affair. It's business as usual for us, as I'm sure it will be for them before the night is out. They're going to swear in Lyndon Johnson as President. What? No, I don't want all of that in the directive. Just tell them to stay mum. No, not mum's the word, just be quiet about it. Who are you? Someone new? Oh, Wallace hired you. He hired you as my secretary? He did? Send the directive, Miss. Thank you. This is getting to be worse than a nursing home. Why can't anyone follow instructions? Everyone wants to be a boss. What does that white man say? I don't get no respect? Well, he's not the only one. Say, Miss, send another directive. Huh? No, this one is pursuant to the one I just gave you? What does pursuant mean? Never mind that. The second directive goes as follows: No one can say, no, that isn't right. Huh? No, I just said that isn't right. What happened to my other secretary? She quit? Really. Say: Under no circumstances are you to say anything regarding the death of the President. Period. Send both of them and this way they'll know I'm serious. Some of those boys have gotten wind of the money they can make by talking a lot. We've got Malcolm to thank for that, too. Thank you.

(*The radio clicks back on, as do finally the stage lights, which catch Malcolm as though he is in an airport. He holds his ever present briefcase in his hands and has a big smile on his face*)

RADIO INTERVIEWER: Malcolm, as the leading spokesman for the Nation of Islam, do you have any comments on the death of the President?

MALCOLM: No, I don't. I think it's unfortunate when any man is struck down in the line of duty.

ELIJAH: What are you doing, Malcolm? Can't you just say no comment?

RADIO INTERVIEWER: Well, Malcolm, I think the many listeners would like to know what your private thoughts are.

MALCOLM: Well, if I did that, then they wouldn't be private anymore.

ELIJAH: That's better. Just walk away from him now.

RADIO INTERVIEWER: Well, you don't want to say anything about it. How do you think the Nation of Islam is responding to the death of the President?

MALCOLM: Well, I guess it's still business as usual for us.

ELIJAH: Did that woman put that in the directive?

MALCOLM: You have to understand that the death of one white man doesn't really change the nature of our difficulty with the

American way of doing things. Just because he's dead, and as I've said, I'm sorry about that, but just because he's dead doesn't mean that the drugs have suddenly stopped flooding our neighborhood or that the police aren't still brutalizing our communities.

ELIJAH: You don't have to say any of that. You can just keep your mouth shut for once, can't you?

RADIO INTERVIEWER: One more time, Malcolm, do you have any thoughts or opinions about the assassination?

MALCOLM: Well, I would have to say that it seems like a case of when the chickens came home to roost. That the violence being done to my people has come full circle and struck one of them down. It's a shame but you can't live in a violent country without being touched by that violence.

(*Lights on. Malcolm and Elijah look at each other*)

MALCOLM: Salaam alaikum.

ELIJAH: Yes, how are you?

MALCOLM: I came as soon as I could.

ELIJAH: I heard you on the radio. What, did Betty teach you how to do and say all that?

MALCOLM: Could you repeat that, sir?

ELIJAH: Stop all the "sir" junk now. I'm onto you. Did you get my directives?

MALCOLM: Both of them.

ELIJAH: Well, what happened?

MALCOLM: May I sit down?

ELIJAH: Of course. Sit down. If you got the directives, what happened?

MALCOLM: Well, nothing really happened. He asked me a couple of questions . . .

ELIJAH: And you blabbed like a chicken. Against my orders you just quacked away. I suppose the next time they ask you to jump off a bridge, you would, just so you could have something else to talk about.

MALCOLM: That's not true at all.

ELIJAH: They have you dancing on a string, Malcolm, and you don't see it. You can't hear it. You're dumb. Worse than an alley cat, that's what you are.

MALCOLM: I hardly said anything. The interview lasted no more than two or three minutes.

ELIJAH: The most expensive two or three minutes in your life.

MALCOLM: What do you mean?

ELIJAH: Did you notice anything peculiar about the directive?

MALCOLM: (*Inspects the sheets of paper from his pocket*) No, it appears as though everybody got them, that's all.

ELIJAH: Have you heard Louis or any of the others on the radio?

MALCOLM: I haven't had a chance. I haven't even seen Betty.

ELIJAH: Betty, Betty, Betty. Whenever I talk to you now, it's always about Betty.

MALCOLM: She's my heart, sir. I like to talk with my heart.

ELIJAH: You should talk to me more.

MALCOLM: I do. There haven't been any repercussions about the paternity suits, have there?

ELIJAH: You'd just love to embarrass me, wouldn't you, Malcolm?

MALCOLM: Not at all.

ELIJAH: Then why did you open your mouth up about the assassination? Why did you have to be so gabby with: it looks like the chickens have come home to roost? What is that? A joke? Humor? Black humor? And the Nation of Islam is associated with it through you. Do you have any idea of the possible recriminations?

MALCOLM: There won't be any recriminations. What I said was morally straight and sympathetic, to them and to us. Violence simply is the way of this country and look at the toll.

ELIJAH: No recriminations? None? What about the farm in the south? What about the dead cattle? The poisoned water? No recriminations? People are always looking for an excuse. The more you talk, the more people have an excuse to do what they do in this country. Ah, Malcolm. Why did you think I sent the directive, for my health? No talk. Say nothing.

MALCOLM: (*Standing now*) I have a right to talk.

ELIJAH: Sure you do. You've just finished helping the old man. You're his favorite. What can happen to you? Nothing. This will wash by in a minute, too. What's the problem?

MALCOLM: That's all true...

ELIJAH: I'll tell you what the problem is, Malcolm. You're getting too big for your shoes. Your hat size is a twelve. Your ears are like an elephant's.

MALCOLM: I'm sorry. I didn't realize that expressing an opinion was violating the directive. I should have thought so. But I didn't.

ELIJAH: Sorry. Now the repentant son. Malcolm, how can I control the lesser ministers if I let you go on so? What kind of leadership can I inspire if my main man is always going off at the lip? Who the blazes do you think you are?

MALCOLM: I'm a man with thoughts and ideas of his own and I need and do express them when I want to. That's a part of the whole thing being in this world, Messenger.

ELIJAH: Well, then, you're saying that you don't have any allegiances here, is that right?

MALCOLM: I'm not saying anything of the sort. I'm saying, however, that I owe it to myself to express my thoughts and feelings because they do make a difference to the people who hear them. If I don't talk, a lot of things don't get said. I'm not down there in Washington like all the other black leaders with tears in their eyes, what the Spanish call: lágrimas de cocodrilos.

ELIJAH: "Lagarithms cocoa cola"? What are you talking about now?

MALCOLM: (*Laughs*) I feel free, Messenger. It's like a great big weight has been taken off my back. I'm free. I can say what I want to for as long as I want to until someone shuts me down. I'm going to die anyway, so I don't really have that much time. Do you understand?

ELIJAH: I understand you've been disobedient, and the first code in Islam is obedience.

MALCOLM: I understand that also. I have taught the code of the Nation since I was indoctrinated.

ELIJAH: But you forgot! You forgot!

MALCOLM: No, I didn't forget, I just said what was coming into my mind and I have a greater respect for that than any words to be found in any directive. It's my mind.

ELIJAH: Do you understand what you've just said?

MALCOLM: I understand that you may punish me for having expressed myself. I understand that's what you're leading up to. I understand that because you've been leading up to it for a long time now. The pregnant girls told me how you back-stabbed out of jealousy. They told me and I had to believe them. The same way I had to believe my own eyes and ears when I heard the rumors that were floating around the mosques. It's quite a thing when you walk into a mosque that you had a hand in building and suddenly people turn around and look at you like you're a leper. Voices drop and there's a tenseness. You can feel the people looking at you behind your back, but suddenly no one has the strength to look you in the eyes. I've seen and felt it a long time in coming. You're jealous of me, Elijah Muhammad. You wish you were like me, younger, energetic, then you could be doing some of the things I do and lots that you won't or can't do.

ELIJAH: Well, you're not leaving me any choice.

MALCOLM: It's your paranoia that's not leaving you any choice. You keep thinking that I want your job. Who's come up to you and said that? What clandestine meetings have I had with what Ministers? (*Elijah turns away and walks to the water pitcher*) You can't say, because there aren't any. No one. I'm so pure it's driving you nuts. I wish I could have taken out some of my frustrations on a woman like you have, but I believe in what I'm doing, Elijah Muhammad. I believe in it and so does my family. So I've got a hundred and fifty percent behind me. If I only put out fifty percent, I'd still be ahead. But I don't. I put out the other hundred and fifty and we keep moving.

ELIJAH: You want to withdraw from the movement?

MALCOLM: Of course not. This movement means everything to me. I've built it up from one mosque, maybe two, till there are a dozen all over the country. People that never even heard of the Nation now look through the papers for what they can find.

ELIJAH: I can't have a crazy man running around like you.

MALCOLM: I'm not crazy. I've never been saner. You know you once talked to me about how impossible it was to talk to anyone except me. Well, I told you about Betty. You won't let me talk with Wallace anymore because you think I have an undue influence on him, but you underestimate Wallace. He's the best thing in this movement. He's bright, articulate, knows languages, and knows how to express himself so that others can follow.

ELIJAH: And you think I don't?

MALCOLM: No one is following you anymore, Elijah. You're almost through. There isn't a creative idea in your head anymore and you refuse to respond to the new times. It takes a new head, a computer brain to deal with everything that is going on in the world. And you don't have it. You can't even get past the guilt of Fard.

ELIJAH: What does Fard have to do with this? Tell me?

MALCOLM: It isn't Fard, it's your guilt over him. Look, it doesn't make any difference if Fard died because you killed him or not. How does that rate with the little kid who just seconds ago was bitten by a rat because his father didn't have the money to get the family into a nicer apartment? It doesn't. Your guilt and paranoia don't go very far when you measure it up against that kid who won't be able to walk right for the rest of his life.

ELIJAH: Why are you saying all of this?

MALCOLM: Because I want you to know that when you retire or die, you should leave the Nation to Wallace. He's the natural successor.

ELIJAH: You're saying that because you want me to retract what I haven't done yet.

MALCOLM: I don't care what you do anymore, Elijah Muhammad. It doesn't matter to me anymore, and as I say, I shake in my boots. But what does matter is that you make amends with your family. Thanks to you, I've got mine and they're going to love me because I'm going to be a father and not a monster.

ELIJAH: This is beginning to sound like one of them soap operas.

MALCOLM: And that's why people watch them—because they're so much like life—a continuing saga of struggle and upliftment. But you can't uplift anymore and that's why you've leaned on me. I've done the job you were supposed to do.

ELIJAH: Lies! Lies! You're all liars!

MALCOLM: I'm scared, Mr. Muhammad. I'm really scared. When I quit drugs, I had you and the movement to lean on, and now I feel like I don't have anything. I'm not going back to drugs and I'm not leaning on my family.

ELIJAH: And you still want to be in the movement?

MALCOLM: Yes, I do.

ELIJAH: You understand that I have to punish you.

MALCOLM: I'm scared but I'm not frightened. You've done such a great job with me. I can rely on myself, which is pretty much the way it's been.

ELIJAH: I understand what you're saying, Malcolm, but I have to silence you for thirty—no, ninety days.

MALCOLM: I accept the punishment as just, Mr. Muhammad.

ELIJAH: And that means you can't speak at the mosque. I'll get someone else to speak until the sentence is served. And remember that means no talking. You are silenced.

(*Malcolm is aghast*)

MALCOLM: Mosque number seven? I can't talk there? I can't say anything there?

ELIJAH: Silenced!

MALCOLM: Like Reginald!

ELIJAH: I said silenced!

MALCOLM: I bring the truth to you. It isn't pleasant, I know that. You are a great man. I owe so much to you, but to silence me in my own mosque? I won't make any speeches. I won't whisper, but let me talk in my own mosque.

(*Elijah shakes his head and walks behind his desk*)

ELIJAH: Do you submit?

MALCOLM: I built that mosque, it feels like with my own hands, every stone, every chair. I sweated, bled, almost died doing it.

ELIJAH: Do you submit?

MALCOLM: My friends, my family. They'll all want to know and I'll look at them and not say a word?

ELIJAH: Do you submit?

MALCOLM: The media will be coming after me wanting to know what's going on and I will say nothing to them. Betty will want to know and I will look at her for ninety days in silence. I will go to the mosque like a dead dog and not bark even though my entire being will want to shriek out and say it is unjust. The directives were unjust. The whole sense of dictatorship is unjust. Absolute power vested in one person is unjust. Man has to speak up and fight back. Fight back! (*Malcolm rushes the desk and pounds his fists on it*) You can't do this to me just because I commented on the death of man you detest. You detest all of them. And I made a very honest statement about what I felt. I felt it, not you, not the Nation. It was my thought.

ELIJAH: Do you submit?

(*Malcolm looks at Elijah and then lowers his head nodding perceptibly*)

ELIJAH: I do not hear you.

MALCOLM: I submit.

ELIJAH: Good.

(*Malcolm picks up his briefcase and the light goes out on Elijah leaving Malcolm in a state of shock alone*)

MALCOLM: It is as if my happily married wife has handed me divorce papers instead of the biscuits. I hear the cluck, cluck of the chicken ministers, but I can't feel the sun or see the stars. Something is shut up inside me and will never come out again.

I know I'm being set up by Mr. Muhammad. He is behind it as he is behind everything that happens in the Nation.

But it is not death that I fear. It is the humiliation of betrayal and the wasteful sacrifice of one man to cover up the inadequacies of another.

(*Lights dim further*)

MALCOLM'S VOICE OVER: (*Both Malcolm and Elijah turn towards each other*) I can remember the first night I saw you. There you were sitting on the edge of the prison cot, just staring at me almost as if to say: Take it easy, Malcolm Little. This too shall pass.

(*Lights out*)

The End

Jack Heifner

BARGAINS

Jack Heifner

A native of Corsicana, Texas, Jack Heifner was educated at Southern Methodist University, and upon graduating from the theater department, went to New York City to begin a career as an actor. After several brief appearances, he and Garland Wright formed an Off-Off Broadway group, the Lion Theatre Company, with Heifner as actor and Wright as director.

During this time, he wrote his first play, *Casserole*, a black comedy, staged in 1975 at Playwrights Horizons. The enthusiastic response of the audience became a turning point for Mr. Heifner's career: "I couldn't believe that what I thought was funny made other people laugh, too." The response of audiences and critics prompted Heifner to "pack away his leotards and make-up box" and purchase an electric typewriter. His next script was *Vanities*, which he wrote, amazingly, in two days. *Vanities*, revealing the lives of three Texas cheerleaders, was staged originally in 1975 at the Lion at a production cost of only $200. "In the Los Angeles production, which starred Sandy Dennis, Lucie Arnaz, and Stockard Channing, the clothes alone cost $10,000," the author observed. "By the time we got to Chicago, with Elizabeth Ashley, the set cost $30,000." Returning to New York at the Chelsea Westside Theatre in 1976, the production went on to run for five years, becoming the longest-running play in Off Broadway history. Subsequent productions of *Vanities* have played worldwide.

In 1978 the author returned to the Lion Theatre Company for the production of a play based on Colette's *Music-Hall Sidelights*. This was followed in 1980 by *Star Treatment*. Two short plays, *Twister* and *Tropical Depression* were produced in 1985 at the West Bank Cafe in New York under the collective title *Natural Disasters*. Also in 1985 Mr. Heifner provided material for the Broadway musical, *Leader of the Pack*.

Among the honors received for his work are a Playwriting Grant from the Creative Artists Public Service Program (CAPS), a Creative Writing Grant from The National Endowment for the Arts, and an award from The American Society of Composers and Publishers (ASCAP) for his lyrics in *Music-Hall Sidelights*.

Mr. Heifner has written several screenplays and two pilots for television series for ABC and CBS, as well as scripts for the soap operas *Guiding Light* and *Another World*. He is presently working on another original musical and a screenplay thriller.

Mr. Heifner's last appearnace in *Best Short Plays* was in the 1980 edition with the pair *Patio* and *Porch*, two character sketches set in a small Texas town. *Bargains*, published here for the first time, was commissioned by Southern Methodist University in Dallas, Texas, and produced there in February, 1987.

MR. MEAD
SALLY
TISH
MILDRED

Setting:

A downtown department store in a central Texas town of about
20,000 people.
   The store is obviously larger than what we can see onstage;
but what we can see are several counters and tables, three cash
registers in different locations, and a large amount of merchandise. Imagine a front door stage right with large glass windows
on each side. There are mannequins and merchandise displayed
in these show windows. There are shelves, racks and mirrors on
the walls inside the store. Upstage center is a door leading to a
stock room and directly to the left of that is the door to a rest
room, which has a sign saying so.
   Sally's area is more down right—cosmetics and shoes. Tish's
area is center—candy, wigs and sportswear. Mildred's area is
left—better dresses and piece goods. There is also an area between Sally's and Tish's for jewelry and lingerie. (This is Arlene's area, but Arlene is out sick this day.) There is very little
action written into the play, but throughout the play saleswom-
en are packing, marking, arranging and moving merchandise.
They do this while they are talking about other things. Other
props include a telephone and a stool next to the center
counter.

Time:

One summer morning in 1986, shortly before 9:00 a.m.

At Curtain:

Mr. Mead, a handsome man in his late twenties, sits on a stool,
and on the counter in front of him are some computer print-out
sheets. He is going over these while he sips coffee and takes

bites out of a doughnut. Mead is dressed in a long-sleeved dress shirt, slacks and a tie. He is very "preppie." The clock on the wall behind him says twenty minutes before nine.

There is a knock on the front door of the store. Mead looks, sees Sally, looks at his watch and mutters to himself.

MEAD: Oh, brother.

(He then gets up and goes to unlock the front door since the store is not officially open at this hour.

Sally enters. She's an attractive woman in her mid-thirties. She wears a very pretty, conservative, navy blue dress with small white polka dots on it and she has on low-heeled, navy blue pumps with matching hose. She has a handbag to match and also carries a tote bag with "SALLY" monogrammed on it. It is navy blue, too. Sally is very well-groomed, but the first thing she does after she gets in is spend time touching up her make-up. After all, she does sell cosmetics.

The action begins when Mead opens the door and Sally enters)

MEAD: Morning, Sally. I see you're early, as usual.

SALLY: Now didn't you say, "Come in early. We're having a summer sale and we need to mark down a few things before we open?"

MEAD: Yes, I did. But we open at ten and I said, "Come in an hour beforehand."

SALLY: Then I could wait outside until nine if you like.

MEAD: Don't be silly. *(Locking the door and going back to his coffee)*

SALLY: It seems like no matter how I judge my time, I always get here before everybody else...sometimes before you. Usually I just kill some time walking around, window shopping and such, but it's too hot today. The temperature must be well over ninety. Don't you think?

MEAD: I'm sure that's true.

SALLY: And I can't trust that old bus...it never runs on schedule. I'm always afraid I'm going to miss it. And sure enough, every day, I get here way before the store opens. Mama gets up so early and once I get up, get her breakfast, get her settled for the day... it's still not even seven o'clock. I've got hours to kill before it's even time to come to work. But, anyway, it gives me time to get my register set up and check the tape. I hate to run out of tape in the middle of the day. I get a spare one ready to just pop in. You know, customers hate to wait. Not that we're having too many customers lately. I think it's the heat. You got my change bag?

MEAD: Let me get it.

SALLY: Yes sir, I can certainly see why you're having a summer sale. My areas haven't been too busy at all. Nobody's buying shoes and hose...but so many people forget hose when it's hot.

Now I wouldn't go out of the house without my hose, but then ... I'm not your run-of-the-mill type of person. I know some of the girls don't wear hose to work anymore, but I feel sort of undressed without them. Habit. When I started working here, Mr. Wilks always made us wear black or dark blue dresses, high heels and hose. Of course, times change and I don't mind what people wear as long as it's clean and not too outlandish, but I took the bus out to that discount store on the highway on my day off last week...you know, that store that's certainly giving us a run for our money... or you might say, ruining all our business...and, I'll swear, some of the salesgirls had on jeans, and one even had on a pair of loud Bermuda shorts. It's just not right. Is it?

MEAD: (*Giving her the change bag and going back to have his coffee, and he continues trying to read the print-outs*) Here you go.

SALLY: Thank you. Now what do we do about this sale?

MEAD: We'll mark down a few things when the rest of the girls get here. There's no rush.

SALLY: No rush . . . just enjoy your coffee and doughnut. It sure looks yummy! (*She dumps her change out on the counter*) I'll just sort this so I'll be ready to go when the first customer comes in. I've had better luck with cosmetics than shoes this week. Monday, it was nail polish. Tuesday, everybody wanted mascara. Today, I'll bet it's lipstick. But then, my customers may surprise me! They may all want nail files, and then where will I be?

(*She laughs, Mead laughs with her and then he slips in the following information*)

MEAD: Arlene just called in sick.

SALLY: (*Changing moods*) Already? So what's wrong this time?

MEAD: Backache.

SALLY: If I've told her once, I've told her a million times... you can't stand on your feet all day in cheap, spike heels and not end up with a sore back. See these I'm wearing?

MEAD: Do we sell those?

SALLY: On, no...I mail order these. Like them?

MEAD: Very pretty.

SALLY: Very comfortable but very expensive on my budget, but I can't work in cheap shoes. I've never had a sore back once since I got them. I think I'm going to need another roll of quarters and a few more singles, when you have the time...just enjoy your coffee.

MEAD: I'm trying.

(*Sally starts to deal with her cosmetic counter*)

SALLY: How's Mrs. Mead and the kids?

MEAD: The family's fine.

SALLY: Well, it's a fine family. I always love talking to Mrs. Mead when she comes in. With me working like I do, I never have the time to watch daytime TV...but your wife always fills me in on all the shows. That way I can go home and discuss the story lines with Mama. She sees them all.

MEAD: About all my wife does is watch TV.

SALLY: Oh, now...I'm sure you're exaggerating. Even though I've never been inside your house, I'm sure Mrs. Mead keeps a lovely home.

MEAD: The maid does that.

SALLY: Well, I always notice your house, every day, when I pass by on the bus and it looks just like a showplace...and sometimes Little Krystle and Little Blake are out front playing in the yard...and I tell you, you certainly chose the right names for those kids because they really do look like a couple of movie star children.

MEAD: They're spoiled rotten.

SALLY: Oh, they'll grow out of that. Every time they come in here they practically tear the store apart, but then that's fine with me...they can do whatever they like because their Daddy's the manager. Right?

MEAD: Right...I guess.

SALLY: And I know your wife doesn't watch TV all the time because I saw her picture in last night's paper. I didn't know she was a model. Did she ever do that professionally? I mean, back when you were living in Dallas?

(*Mead takes her the extra singles and the change she requested*)

MEAD: No...she wasn't a professional model. It was just something she used to do before we were married. When she was in college, she was on the modeling squad.

SALLY: The modeling squad? I've never heard of such a thing. I heard of "The Mod Squad" and the Bomb Squad and Ghostbusters

...is it anything like that?

(*Note: Sally is a lot smarter than she plays at times. She is trying to get information*)

MEAD: No...it was just some of the sorority girls who were chosen to model for college events. So when the Muscular Dystrophy people here asked her to help out with their fashion show/fund raiser...she got involved in modeling again. It's a one-time thing. (*He goes back to his coffee*)

SALLY: And it's a very good thing, I'm sure. Even though I wonder if she should be modeling clothes from a rival store of ours. Is that good for our business?

MEAD: I don't think the people who buy from "The Exceptional Woman" are the same kind of people who shop here.

SALLY: True. Heavens, I walked into "The Exceptional Woman" the day I was looking for a new funeral dress and practically died.

MEAD: A new funeral dress?

SALLY: Yes, I always try to have one really smart dress I put aside just for funerals. Some people will wear just about anything these days...even white or pastels or what practically looks like a cocktail dress...but I always wear black. Anyway, I went into "The Exceptional Woman" and what they were charging for dresses is about what an exceptional funeral would cost! Who ever heard of two and three hundred dollars for anything other than a wedding gown?

MEAD: Unfortunately, I have. My wife spends an awful lot on clothes. That dress she was wearing in the picture came in at just under five. She got so many compliments on it at the fashion show that, naturally, she bought it.

SALLY: Five hundred dollars! My goodness, I couldn't sleep at night if I spent that much on a dress. And that thing she was wearing in the picture didn't even look like an all-purpose outfit. It couldn't have had more than a yard of material in it. In fact, when I first looked at it, I thought she was modeling a child's sundress.

MEAD: It was by a big name designer.

SALLY: Well, everything is designed by somebody and all of them have names...but I can't see paying more for that. I certainly hope some of the proceeds from selling her that big name dress went to charity.

MEAD: Maybe I could deduct it. I'll see.

SALLY: You should. Frankly, I've never liked Muscular Dystrophy much, but that has more to do with Jerry Lewis and his telethon than the disease itself. I just can't stand him. Just can't understand anybody getting paid good money to act so silly. What do you think?

MEAD: About what?

SALLY: About Jerry Lewis.

MEAD: I can either take him or leave him.

SALLY: Well, "leave him" is the way I feel. But I have nothing against the disease. In fact, I always drop whatever change I have left in those containers for the March of Dimes they have sitting sometimes beside cash registers. Isn't it odd we don't have any of those in here?

MEAD: It's against company policy to have any solicitation in the store. They set the rules.

SALLY: They sure do. I don't know how you keep up with all of them. Seems to me you are always reading memo after memo from the big bosses, and the funny thing is not a one of them has ever seen this store. Ever drove down from New York, New York, to even take a peek at what we're doing. They don't have a clue what this place looks like or have ever even bothered to come in and introduce themselves to their salespeople.

MEAD: It's a big company and having a few department stores is only a small part of their business. They're primarily into real estate...building offices and condos and shopping centers.

SALLY: Build, build, build! But you can't stop progress, can you?

MEAD: Well, who wants to?

SALLY: Well, sometimes I do. And speaking of time...could I get started with the sale items? I'd love to have my departments all ready when you fling open those doors!

MEAD: I guess with Arlene out today, you're going to have to cover costume jewelry and lingerie.

SALLY: (*Not pleased*) What?

MEAD: Just work her area along with yours.

SALLY: What if I get too busy in cosmetics?

MEAD: Then call Mildred over to help you.

SALLY: Mildred doesn't know anything about shoes *or* cosmetics. Besides, I'll have my make-up counter all arranged and she'll mess it all up.

MEAD: I need you to cover for each other.

SALLY: It's just that I know this whole store. At one time or another, I've worked in every department; but Mildred's never done anything except notions, piece goods and better dresses. Her knowledge is limited.

MEAD: Sally, I know how protective you feel about your departments, but this really isn't a ladies' department store anymore.

SALLY: It most certainly is not.

MEAD: We sell a little bit of everything, so you're going to have to do a little bit of everything.

SALLY: But in the old days, we weren't allowed to work outside our own areas, and I rather liked that rule.

MEAD: You've got new rules now; and as hard as it may be for you to change your ways, just try not to be so inflexible.

SALLY: Inflexible? Me?

MEAD: Just do as I say for once and spare me from hearing about the way you used to do things. Okay?

SALLY: Whatever you say, Mr. Mead. I don't suppose it matters what I think.

MEAD: No, not really.

SALLY: I might as well just keep my mouth shut.

(*There's a knock on the front door. Mead goes to let Tish in. She's a pretty girl, about nineteen, not very well-dressed and about seven months pregnant*)

MEAD: Good morning, Tish.

TISH: Morning, Mr. Mead. Hi, Sally.

MEAD: I'm going to the stockroom and start pulling things for the sale. One thing I know I'm getting rid of are those chocolate covered cherries, so you might as well mark those half-price, Tish.

TISH: Sure will. (*Mead exits to the stock room. Sally continues to work at her counter. Tish goes to hers and starts dealing with boxes of candy*) Sally, you haven't even said "hello." What's wrong?

SALLY: I'm just keeping my mouth shut since Mead snapped at me because Arlene's sick as usual, and he had the nerve to ask me to cover for her again. Look at this counter! It's a disaster! I like mine neat and tidy.

TISH: So what's wrong with Arlene?

SALLY AND TISH: Bad back? (*They both laugh*)

SALLY: What else? Her back's no worse off than the rest of ours. She feels well enough to go out on dates all the time, but not to work. I think Mildred ought to cover jewelry...she never sells any notions or dresses. I'm up to my neck in cosmetic sales!

TISH: Mildred's not in yet?

SALLY: Are you kidding? We're the only two around here who have any sense of responsibility. I'm sure Mildred's still asleep. She'll probably wander in here about eleven, like she did yesterday ...and just you watch! Mead won't say a word. He lets her get away with murder. That's because she flirts with him.

TISH: She thinks he's sort of cute.

SALLY: She thinks any man's cute.

TISH: He's not bad-looking.

SALLY: Well, it all depends on what you're looking for. Want me to help you open your register?

TISH: If you like.

SALLY: Oh, I like doing it. Honey, have you checked your tape lately?

TISH: Not lately.

SALLY: Look! You're going to run out soon! I'll get you one and put it right here beside the register for you to just pop in. Customers hate to wait.

TISH: Look at this mess. Mead over-ordered candy and half of it's either stale or all melted together.

SALLY: I tell you, I couldn't work candy. You've got your hands full with both that and wigs and sportswear.

TISH: Have a bonbon.

SALLY: I had a big breakfast, honey. Save me one for later.

TISH: I keep munching. I don't even like candy, but I'll bet I've put on ten pounds in the last month from this junk.

SALLY: Well, it's normal in your condition to gain weight. Isn't it?

TISH: Yes, but all this sugar can't be too good for the baby.

SALLY: I'll bet it's going to be a sweet thing, all right. What do you wish for? A boy or a girl?

TISH: Oh, I don't want to think about it.

SALLY: Well, we'll just have to give you all yellow gifts at your shower. That way you'll be safe either way.

TISH: Being pregnant sure does make me tired.

SALLY: Maybe you should stop work soon.

TISH: I've only been here two months and, believe me, this is a whole lot easier than frying McNuggets all day.

SALLY: I'm sure that's true.

TISH: Besides, we can't make ends meet if I don't keep working. No matter how hard he tries, Donny can't seem to find a job.

SALLY: Day before yesterday, when he was in here...I thought he said he was applying for some chef's job. I didn't know he was a chef.

TISH: He's not. Sure he applied, but you can't be head chef at the Sky Room at the Holiday Inn if you can't cook.

SALLY: I don't know why they call it the Sky Room. Isn't it on the first floor?

TISH: Donny's so depressed all the time, he just spends most of the day sitting around in his underwear watching TV.

SALLY: He ought to get together with Mrs. Mead.

TISH: What do you mean?

SALLY: All Mrs. Mead does is watch TV all day and that's a quote. You know, I certainly hope you end up naming your child something decent. Can you believe that woman named her kids "Krystle" and "Blake?" But then, I'll bet the whole country's full of uppity women who go around calling their kids "Little Alexis" or "Little Dex" or "Little Fallon." What a name! Fallon!

TISH: I haven't thought about what to call him or her.

SALLY: Just stick with something sane and to the point. Like John or Jim or Mary...or Sally.

TISH: Would you look at what I'm doing? Just stuffing my face with this mess. Mr. Mead is going to have to put me someplace else because I've just got no will power.

SALLY: According to him, we can work the whole store. We don't really have departments anymore...so you can have "shoes." I'll gladly part with it.

TISH: Thanks, but no thanks.

SALLY: I already know what I'm going to have to do today. Put all these summer sandals out. All these tacky sandals nobody will touch until you mark them half-price and then they just go like wildfire.

TISH: I guess getting rid of them is the idea.

SALLY: And good riddance! Did you know I have to send all the boxes back to the warehouse? This new management won't even let me throw away an empty shoe box. I've heard of cheap people, but...(*Tish swoons, knocking over a few wigs. Sally runs to her*) Are you all right, honey?

TISH: Just tired, I guess. I haven't been sleeping too well.

SALLY: Well, they always say the first one is the hardest; even though I'm sure numbers two and three are no picnic. Why don't you sit down a minute?

TISH: Oh, no...I'll be fine.

SALLY: Don't let anybody ever tell you what we do is not tiring. Last week, I had to mark all the pantyhose down to two for 99¢... then when Mr. Mead saw how fast they were selling, he told me to mark them all up to two for $1.99. They didn't cost two for $1.99 to begin with, and they're not worth a dime. And, no matter what, it doesn't seem right to charge more for them on sale than the original price. Does it?

TISH: No.

SALLY: No. I tell you, confidentially, sometimes I just have the feeling we're working for crooks. Everything in this store is just...well, irregular...rotten, if you ask me. And I'm not just referring to my shoe department. Mildred's piece goods are the same. They're seconds. You unroll a bolt of material and there are flaws everywhere. It's hard to play like you're giving your customer three yards of good fabric when you know she's got a flaw as big as a football field right in the middle...and then, when she tries to bring it back...you've got to point to the sign, "NO RETURN ON PIECE GOODS." It's embarrassing. The shoes fall apart and they try to return them. The fabrics...the hose...anything you buy at this store is guaranteed to fall apart. Of course, I keep my mouth shut, but I wouldn't shop here if my life depended on it.

TISH: But the prices are low.

SALLY: And so is the merchandise.

TISH: I guess you get what you pay for.

SALLY: Bargains. I tell you, when I started working here, we carried nothing but quality goods...then eight months ago Mr. Mead breezes in here with all his education and his college background and his wife and kids with their Hollywood names... but he doesn't know about people. He doesn't realize you've got to educate people. Sure, they'll buy anything...but once they've had a really good pair of shoes or something that lasts and lasts...until you finally give it away because you're tired of it...not because it's worn out...once you've felt what it's like to have something nice, not because it's expensive; but because it's well made, conservative and tasteful...you won't settle for less. A real bargain is something that lasts forever.

TISH: I never thought of it that way.

SALLY: It's my own philosophy, of course, and nobody has to believe what I believe. It's just, Tish, if you had been born in this town and could have seen what it was like...well, all I can say, is that I never thought it would turn out to be so...well...changed.

When I started working here, I was in high school.

TISH: High school?

SALLY: Afternoons, after classes...I would walk from the old high school, where the K-Mart is now, past rows and rows of the prettiest homes...stop at the drug store for a cherry phosphate.

TISH: A what?

SALLY: Oh, it was a heavenly soda fountain drink...they'd mix cherry syrup and carbonated water together in a big soda fountain glass with ice and a slice of lime...there used to be a wonderful old drugstore right across the street...right where that new Roy Rogers is now...then I'd come in to work refreshed. And it was a pleasure to work here...I used to feel honored to handle such beautiful things. Now, after I handle some of this stuff, I have to go wash my hands. And the customers! I won't even help a woman try on shoes anymore. I just hand her a footlet and let her put them on herself. We certainly cater to a different class of customer.

TISH: I guess what we sell is all some people can afford. I know I don't like having to just make do all the time, but I certainly can't afford expensive things. Especially now with me having to buy maternity clothes.

SALLY: Oh, honey...I wasn't referring to you when I was just chattering on and on...I was just talking about the state of things. Lord knows, Mama and I don't have much...but then, we have a nice home. It was a lot nicer before that trailer park opened up down the block and a lot quieter before we had that Dunkin' Donuts across the street...but most people sold out to progress. Moved to new homes out on the edge of town. Mama and I like being where we are...and since I don't drive, I have to be on the bus route.

TISH: You ought to learn to drive, Sally. In fact, why don't I get Donny to teach you.

SALLY: Me? Drive? Drive what? I'd have to get a car.

TISH: What would be wrong with that?

SALLY: I just don't have any need to drive. I get where I'm going without one.

TISH: I can't imagine not being able to just get in the car and go wherever I want to go. Not that I've ever been anywhere except from my little hometown to here. But I like the idea of freedom driving a car gives you.

SALLY: Oh, I think this idea of "freedom" is highly overrated. Sometimes even shocking. Did you see the Mrs. America Pageant on TV last night? With Richard Dawson and Miss Vicki Carr? Did you know Vicki is a Mexican? With a name like Carr? But anyway...I couldn't get over how some of the contestants in the parade of states were dressed like an ear of corn or a black-eyed Susan...and one woman even had on a clam outfit. I didn't think a clam outfit was appropriate at all. Frankly, I don't know if I like seeing married women in beauty contests. They even paraded in swimsuits! If you're going to parade you should be single... beauty queens should be single. I got the feeling none of those women on TV could make it when they were single...so they got married and had kids, then one day the old dream reappeared. What they really wanted was to be a beauty queen...so they tried again. I guess some dreams never die, but some are better off forgotten. I mean, the majority of the contestants couldn't make the grade the first time and they're not going to make it the second...and if there's one thing truly tragic it's a dream tried twice that didn't come true. And if I was a husband, I wouldn't want my wife parading on TV in a swimsuit. The only kind of man who enjoys that is the kind who would like to see *all* women in swimsuits, all the time or worse yet, naked all the time!

TISH: Sally!

SALLY: Sex maniacs! But these husbands and wives obviously have no shame. They probably run around in swimsuits all day! To the mall, to the car wash, to pick up the kids...who probably wear just swimsuits...entire families in nothing but swimsuits! Then... then to top it all off...you'd be surprised how many of the contestants said that they taught Sunday school! Probably in a swimsuit! And they had all sorts of weird hobbies...roping lizards, raising fleas, iguana farms. Really. Who are they kidding?

TISH: Not you!

SALLY: Not me! Sunday school teachers shouldn't enter beauty pageants. Sunday school teachers shouldn't rope lizards. Sunday school teachers should be good examples. If I had a child and found out any of the women on that show were trying to teach him about the baby Jesus, I'd pull my kid out of that class. If it was up to her she'd probably say Christ went to the beach on Sundays... in a swimsuit!

So where was I? Oh...the winner! Well, it got down to a race between Mrs. California, a blonde of course, and Mrs. Mississippi, a redheaded, black girl. The runner-up got a silver tray. All that work and all she got was a puny little tray. I liked the winner... the blonde. She was my favorite all along. She won a mink coat, a trip to Waikiki, and a tiny Korean car. Well, honey, it was quite a show. You should have seen it.

TISH: I saw it.

SALLY: What? Tish, if you saw it, why'd you let me go on and on about it?

TISH: I wanted to see if you got it right.

SALLY: Well, did I?

TISH: Yes! Every last minute of it!

(They are laughing. Mr. Mead enters from the stockroom with some boxes)

MEAD: I didn't realize working here was so much fun.

TISH: Oh, it isn't...I mean, we were just laughing about something on TV last night...the Mrs. America pageant.

MEAD: Oh, yeah...my wife watched it. She was telling me all about it when I got home from the Lions Club meeting.

SALLY: Now wait a minute. You were at the Lions Club meeting last night?

MEAD: Yes. My wife got so excited about that show, she's thinking of entering the contest next year.

SALLY: Oh, she'd make a wonderful Mrs. America. I'm sure she looks cute in a swimsuit.

MEAD: She does.

(Sally and Tish giggle again, even though they are busy dealing with merchandise)

SALLY: And with all that modeling experience she's had...well, walking a runway must come as easy to her as falling off a log backwards.

TISH: What are you talking about?

SALLY: Didn't you see Mrs. Mead in the paper last night? She was a charity model.

TISH: Really?

SALLY: Oh, she looked like a million dollars, but the little sundress she was wearing only cost five hundred.

TISH: Five hundred? Dollars? Who in their right mind would spend five hundred dollars on a sundress?

SALLY: *(Not looking at Mr. Mead)* Well...

MEAD: *(Jumping in)* Well, have a good time marking down these dresses. *(He puts down a large box of dresses. Sally stops laughing)*

SALLY: Isn't that Mildred's department? But, since she's late, I guess we'll have to help out.

TISH: How much?

MEAD: Mark them one-third off. They're all different prices, so you're going to have to change each tag.

SALLY: (*Going through the box of dresses*) Are these better dresses or regular? I swear, I can't tell the difference.

MEAD: Better. I'll get the sportswear and the lingerie out next. (*He exits to the back of the store*)

SALLY: Better? Can you believe it? Better than what? And can you believe Mrs. Mead spent five hundred dollars on a skimpy little spaghetti-strapped sundress? Mr. Mead must be taking home quite a salary from this place...none of us are certainly sharing in the wealth.

TISH: I'm just getting minimum wage.

SALLY: And I'm not doing much better. But with the small amount we're selling these days, our fancy New York, New York, bosses must be using this store as a tax loss...either that or they're going to tear the whole place down. Then where will I be? I can't go over to "The Exceptional Woman" and get a job. Not because I don't have the experience, I do. I just couldn't with a Christian conscience sell anybody a dress costing more than it would take to feed a family of four for a month. But I admit, I wouldn't mind selling nicer clothes. I mean, Tish...(*Sally is holding up a dress*) ...have you ever seen anything uglier than this outfit? And can you believe the original price? $59.95...what's one-third off that?

TISH: I'm no good with math. I could never even figure out how many McNuggets to put in a box.

SALLY: I guess I'll have to get the calculator. Oh, no...this is horrible! (*She pulls out another dress*) Even Mildred has the good sense not to hang this tacky thing on the rack.

TISH: She was holding that one for me, on layaway.

SALLY: (*Trying to cover*) Well, it is a younger type dress and with your coloring it would look good...

TISH: Oh, Sally, I was just kidding.

SALLY: Oh, you had me worried for a minute.

(*They both laugh...Mildred is knocking on the locked door. Tish goes to let her in. Mildred rushes in, out of breath, she has a paper bag with a container of coffee in it. She plops herself down on the stool and starts on her coffee. Mildred is about Sally's age. She is in a bright dress and wears very high heels. She also has on a lot of jewelry and make-up. She is not tacky,*

just a bit flashy. Her hair is a very strange navy blue color)
MILDRED: Am I late?

SALLY: It's early for you, Mildred. It's not even eleven.

MILDRED: Well, my alarm clock didn't go off.

SALLY: (*She stops dealing with the dresses*) We're all going to chip in and get you another clock for your birthday, Mildred. After all these years of hearing about yours not going off, I think it's time you had a new one.

(*Mildred feels a bit better after having a sip of her coffee, Sally starts dealing with the costume jewelry*)

MILDRED: Well, I was up late. My brother was doing my hair until way past one in the morning.

TISH: Why'd he start doing you hair so late?

MILDRED: He didn't...he started at 8:30, it just took him until after one to get finished.

TISH: That is a long time.

MILDRED: Especially just for a shampoo, rinse and set. I'll swear I don't know what's going to happen to Lothar. I don't think he'll ever make it as a beauty operator, but he's tried everything.

TISH: Everything?

MILDRED: Yes. First he went to nursing school but he was so squeamish he couldn't even empty a bedpan. Next he wanted to become a professional ballroom dancer...studied with Arthur Murray in Houston for six months and was doing quite well. Then he injured his back so badly when he fell off that float at the Mardi Gras Parade in New Orleans, he had to stop dancing. So now he's trying hairdressing, but he just doesn't have the knack. I think this rinse he gave me is an odd color. I can't wait for it to wear off, but Lothar and Dennis say I look divine.

TISH: Who's Dennis?

MILDRED: Lothar's new friend.

SALLY: Dennis? Not Dennis from "Buds and Blooms" down the street?

MILDRED: Yes.

SALLY: Why I think he's sweet. I stop in "Buds and Blooms" every now and then just to look at all his beautiful flowers. Sometimes he even gives me a rose or a carnation. I like Dennis.

MILDRED: I wish Lothar would stop trying to do something so hard like hair...Lordy, you have to pass tests and get a state license ...and open up some sort of business like Dennis's. Maybe a dry cleaners or a muffler shop or a taco stand. But every time I even mention it. Lothar throws a hissy fit...says I don't understand him ... so I'm just better off keeping my mouth shut. After all, I'm just his sister.

SALLY: Isn't it odd, Mildred...a brother and sister living together at your age?

MILDRED: Not any odder, Sally, than a woman and her mother living together at yours. Poor Lothar's always been a little lost about what he wanted to do, so he's staying with me until he finds himself. Seeing how we're both orphans, I feel responsible.

TISH: You mean you have no other living relatives anyplace?

MILDRED: No, it's been just Lothar and me against the world ever since that vacation trip to Northern California. I was only nine and he was just a baby when that tree fell on Mommy and Daddy.

TISH: A tree fell on your parents?

MILDRED: A giant redwood.

TISH: How horrible.

MILDRED: Oh, honey, you should have seen it. Squashed the living daylights out of them. To this day I can't look at a redwood picnic table without breaking into hysterics. It all comes flooding back. Thank God, baby Lothar was too young to remember it. He's got enough problems.

SALLY: You know, Mildred, I can see your little trailer down the block from my house. You sure do have a lot of men in and out of there. It must get awfully cramped when you entertain as much as you and Lothar do.

MILDRED: Well, I can see your house from my trailer, too ...and next time I know you're sitting there for hours, looking out the window watching my every move, I'll remember to wave at you.

SALLY: You do that...that would be quite neighborly of you.

(*Before Sally and Mildred kill each other, Tish decides to change the subject*)

TISH: Would you two stop! Mildred, these better dresses need to be marked down one-third. They're your department. I've got to get back to my candy. My peanut clusters look all moldy.

MILDRED: Yeah, yeah...just let me finish my coffee. Where's Mead?

TISH: Pulling out more junk for the sale.

MILDRED: Oh, Lordy... and her majesty, Miss Arlene?

TISH: Out.

MILDRED: Again? That's two days in a row. What is it this time?

ALL THREE WOMEN: Bad back? (*They all laugh*)

MILDRED: You'd think anybody who stayed on her back as much as Arlene does would feel better if she got out of bed.

(*All three women laugh*)

TISH: Did you hear what she said to that customer the other day? I couldn't believe it. This big woman came in here and asked for a "Cross Your Heart" bra in a size 48 double D. Arlene said they didn't make them that big and then added, "Honey, you don't need a 'Cross Your Heart Bra' to hold you up...Hands Across America couldn't hold you up!" I just about died! (*They all laugh*)

SALLY: Well, I loved the one time that woman asked you for a sympathetic wig. It took the longest time for us to figure out she meant a "synthetic wig." A sympathetic wig!

MILDRED: Or how about that customer who came in here to get some nylons last week and asked you for "a pair of pantywhores with a cotton crutch!" (*All three women laugh—then sigh*) Okay ...where's that pen? Let me mark these dresses down. How'd this one get in here? This is the one you put on layaway.

TISH: I decided I didn't want it. I'm too big for it anyway.

(*Sally is pretending she's not hearing this*)

SALLY: Arlene should be tarred and feathered for the way she keeps her jewelry!

(*Tish swoons again and knocks over a few boxes*)

MILDRED: Are you feeling okay?

TISH: Me? Oh, yes...just full...maybe it's the candy.

MILDRED: How's Donny?

TISH: Oh, like Lothar...he's a bit lost. Doesn't know what to do about work. He hasn't been able to hold down a job for more than a month in the entire year we've been married. He just sits around in his underwear.

MILDRED: Donny's a good man...and a good-looking man. He should think about becoming a movie star. He's ten times better looking than most of those guys on TV. There's not a single woman in this town who doesn't get just a little bit of a damp feeling when that husband of yours comes walking down the street.

SALLY: Mildred, you are just plain nasty!

MILDRED: I am not. I tell it like it is. Donny's a dreamboat. Maybe he should model underwear for a living?

TISH: Maybe I should open a stand outside on Main Street and charge people a dollar to look at him.

MILDRED: You'd make a fortune! Lordy, how did you ever land such a hunk?

SALLY: Tish "landed" him because Tish is a sweet, lovely girl, Mildred, and it's really none of your business.

MILDRED: Oh, you're just as interested as I am, Sally...so get down off your high horse!

TISH: Well, I didn't always look like this. I think women break faster than men.

MILDRED: Break?

TISH: You know, begin to show their age or the effect of hard living...you know, break. When we were kids, last year in high school, dating, we were just wild about each other. And coming from such a small town as we did, we were sort of the most popular ...the king and queen of it all. I guess that's easy in a place with only fifty people and especially if you're ignorant like we are.

SALLY: I don't think you're ignorant at all.

TISH: Yes, I am...so is Donny. We're not stupid, mind you; we just don't know much. I mean, when we got married...oh, I'm ashamed to say this, because it sounds so hicky...but then, I am a hick...but now I know a bit more. Anyway, when we got married ...it was Halloween, and I was so silly I thought it would be clever to have the wedding reception with Halloween decorations. I mean, my chosen colors for my wedding were orange and black.

MILDRED: Are you kidding?

TISH: No. We got married in this country church and there was my bridesmaid, Donny's sister, Marie, in an orange and black dress.

MILDRED: Donny's sister is named Marie? Are you making this up?

TISH: No. Oh, Lord...and we had the reception afterwards and there were pictures of witches and ghosts and orange and black crepe paper streamers decorating the place...and I thought it was so neat. I didn't know any better. And then we moved here and discovered neither Donny or me know anything...and now we're having a baby. And that baby may have the sexiest Daddy in the world, but he don't know how to do anything...except look sexy and he don't even have to try to do that...(*She starts crying*) ...and here I am, married only a year, seven months pregnant and...and, I swear to God, Donny's running around on me.

(*Mildred and Sally rush to Tish*)

SALLY: Mildred, see what you've done!

MILDRED: Me? Now, now, honey...for God's sake, Sally don't we have some Kleenex or a handkerchief for sale in this damn store?

(*Sally runs for a hankie*)

SALLY: Oh, here...Tish, you're just getting all upset for nothing.

TISH: It's not for nothing. He could have any woman in this town. Mildred said so herself.

MILDRED: I didn't mean it. I'm a bold-faced liar.

TISH: But he is having somebody. I know.

SALLY: It's just your delicate condition...and getting yourself all upset isn't going to help.

TISH: (*Still crying*) I couldn't tell this to anyone, but I've been keeping this to myself for days.

MILDRED: Don't keep it in...let it out.

SALLY: For once, Mildred's right...let it out.

TISH: You mustn't breathe a word, but I was at the laundromat a couple of nights ago after work and I was just taking things out of the dryer and folding them...and, Sally, you know those false eyelashes you sell...those fake ones over there?

SALLY: Oh, the Glamour-Lashes; the ones you glue on for long, luxurious lashes that won't come off not matter how much you bat them?

TISH: Yes...well, they come off...at least sometimes, because as I was folding clothes...there, stuck right on the front of one pair of Donny's undershorts was one-half of a pair of long, luxurious false eyelashes. Right in the front!

MILDRED: Well...well maybe it was in the dryer before you put your things in.

SALLY: Right, some woman stuck her head in to get her clothes out and lost one of her lashes.

TISH: Oh, I don't know what to do. Donny and I should have never come to this town...where he could meet someone prettier and sexier and...oh, I'm going to be sick. (*She runs toward the rest room*)

SALLY: Do you want me to come with you?

TISH: No, no...I'll just splash some cold water on my face and sit in the bathroom for awhile, and try to think about other things; except I don't have anything else to think about.

MILDRED: Well, just yell if you need help.

(*Tish rushes out. Mildred and Sally come close together*)

SALLY: Poor little thing. How could Donny do that to her?

MILDRED: Poor soul. I wonder who Donny is doing?

SALLY: Oh, that Donny! Those Glamour-Lashes don't come off

easily at all. Do they?

MILDRED: Well, don't look at me...I don't wear the damn things. Who do you think he's seeing?

SALLY: Well, I don't know.

MILDRED: Think! Who've you sold some of those to lately?

SALLY: This is not the only store in this town that sells eyelashes.

MILDRED: How did that eyelash get all the way from some woman's eyelid and get stuck on the front of big Donny's crotch?

SALLY: Mildred, I simply don't want to think about it.

MILDRED: Poor little Tish.

SALLY: Poor little thing.

MILDRED: I, for one, however, am not surprised. Lord, that man is something! Whatever it is Donny's got ought to be outlawed. It makes women, like me, go wild!

SALLY: Women like you go wild because women like you don't ever think about anything else but men. Well, do you?

MILDRED: Well, no...and it wouldn't hurt you to think about one now and then...or just once.

SALLY: For your information, I've dated men. It's been awhile, but frankly I haven't found anybody in this town worth going out with lately.

MILDRED: When did you ever have a date?

SALLY: It must have been before you moved here, Mildred.

MILDRED: Then it must have been more than ten years ago, Sally.

SALLY: I was quite well thought of when I was younger; but after my Daddy died and with Mama's heart being so weak...I stayed right by her side. We only had Daddy's railroad pension coming in, so I had to work. I'm proud I didn't desert my Mama or put her in a nursing home; but the years go by and suddenly everybody thinks I'm an old maid. Well, it wasn't by choice. It was out of duty...and they say, it's never too late.

MILDRED: I hope not...more for my sake than yours.

SALLY: But you've been married twice.

MILDRED: And divorced twice.

SALLY: So you're not any wonderful example of why anybody should get married, Mildred.

MILDRED: No, but I am a fabulous example of someone who likes to date.

SALLY: I know...and frankly, I'm shocked at some of the people you go out with.

MILDRED: Oh, they're not that bad. They look a lot better up close than they do from your window. And I'm not that picky. Listen, sitting across the table from just about anybody, having a few beers and conversation, beats the hell out of sitting home alone.

SALLY: But Mildred...sometimes I know you let them stay the night. I'll get up, walk past your trailer to get the bus to come to work and there are oftentimes more cars sitting around your place than there in the parking lot at the Dunkin' Donuts.

MILDRED: Oh, well...sometimes they sleep on the couch. Sometimes I give 'em my bed and I go sleep with Lothar. And, yes, sometimes I even let my date climb in bed with me. This is the real world, Sally, and each day is not perfect...and each date is not perfect...but I do know how to make do with whatever the good Lord hands me.

SALLY: How can you bring the Lord into this? I don't think He likes what you're doing at all.

MILDRED: I don't think He really cares too much. He'd just as soon I be having a good time as sitting home wishing I was. What's going on in my cramped trailer between me and Lothar and anybody else who happens to march in don't mean diddley-squat to the Lord...just to nosey busybodies like you!

MEAD: (*Entering*) I can hear you girls all the way back in the stockroom! You're going to scare off all the customers! (*He puts down some more boxes*)

MILDRED: They're not exactly crushed against the doors waiting for this summer sale you're having. Oh, you do look so nice this morning...but your tie's all crooked. Let me fix it for you. (*She goes to him and works on his tie*)

SALLY: (*Furious*) I've organized all my things and all of Arlene's jewelry. I don't know if Mildred's gotten her stock done. She just this second got here.

MILDRED: I've been here for quite some time now. I tell you, Mr. Mead, whatever that cologne is you're wearing, is sending me into hog heaven.

SALLY: That's a short trip for you, Mildred.

MILDRED: You mean you smell this way all on your own?

MEAD: I guess so...so...here's a box of sportswear...shorts and tops. Where's Tish?

MILDRED: In the little girl's room. (*She goes back to work*)

SALLY: I'll do it for her. You know how it is with expectant mothers. I'm sure Mrs. Mead felt puny when she had Little Blake and Little Krystle.

MEAD: I don't remember my wife having any trouble; in fact, she even drove herself to the hospital when she went into labor ...both times.

SALLY: Mercy me! If she enters the pageant, she must remember to tell the judges about that. I'll bet they'll give her extra points for originality or talent.

MILDRED: What pageant?

SALLY: Before you got here...late...Mr. Mead and I were discussing the Mrs. America contest that was on TV last night. And, from my point of view, Mrs. Mead has an excellent chance of winning because she is such an exceptional woman. Like the store where she shops.

MILDRED: She is awfully pretty. Is that her natural haircolor?

SALLY: Mildred, how can you ask that? That's personal.

MILDRED: I'm just interested in her color because mine's so messed up. If she gets hers out of a bottle, then I might like to buy some.

MEAD: She has it done every week at "The Best Little Hairhouse," but she's been a blonde as long as I've known her.

MILDRED: "The Best Little Hairhouse"...oh, that's such a fancy place. Lothar has dreams of getting on there when he graduates. It just makes me want to cry. Poor Lothar.

SALLY: I took Mama to "The Best Little Hairhouse" once and they practically ruined her hair. She likes it all tight and curly, and she came out of there with a real modern, pouffy do. We barely got home on the bus before her hair had gotten all straight and droopy. And you can't imagine what it cost. That's why I do both her hair and mine every Saturday night. It's cheaper, it's the way we like it, and there's no tip!

MILDRED: I could send Lothar over this Saturday to work on you and your Mama. He's good at tight and curly. And you won't have to tip. I'll even pay you to let him get some experience.

SALLY: I'm not a guinea pig, Mildred. Although I might consider letting him do Mama. I'll think about it.

MEAD: Let's get to work, ladies.

SALLY: So how much do I mark these...these, what are these? Majorette outfits? Are they one-third off?

MEAD: Make it half, but leave it for Tish.

SALLY: Maybe I'd better check on her. Tish, honey? (*She goes and knocks on the bathroom door*) Tish, baby, are you okay?

TISH: I'll be right out.

SALLY: (*Coming back from the bathroom*) I was getting worried she might have passed out, hit her head on the toilet and knocked herself unconscious. Mama slipped off the pot one time and...

MEAD: (*Interrupting*) I've got something else for you to do, Sally.

SALLY: Look at this backstock of lingerie. If Arlene came in a little more often, maybe things would move faster in her department.

MEAD: What I'm thinking about doing is putting a few tables out on the sidewalk and piling some of this lingerie out there ...maybe with all the sale shoes...then when people drive by, it will sort of get their attention. They'll stop and then maybe come in the store and buy a few things.

MILDRED: It'll be like a lure. Good thinking! You are so smart.

MEAD: So I don't see any need in marking all these separately. We'll just put a sign up...all bras $3.99...all panties $1.99...and all shoes $4.99. So you can put all those summer sandals out front, and whatever dress shoes and house slippers we've got left over. One price for all.

SALLY: I guess that would make things easier. It's certainly unusual.

MEAD: Be sure and save those boxes.

SALLY: I always do. Now...Tish has marked all her candy. We're about out of these cheap Afro wigs...and all my cosmetics are ready to go.

MEAD: Let's get rid of some of those. Anything that's not selling too well, put all of it in one place and mark it 99¢.

SALLY: This green lipstick didn't sell at all. It's supposed to change color according to people's moods. But it's always the same...just green. So either it's a hoax or everybody in this town is always in the same mood.

MEAD: Don't bother with the perfume.

SALLY: Yes, it moves fast enough. Especially "Tigress," which is nice. And "Musk," which smells like old feet to me. So what about the rest? I've got odds and ends, but some are expensive items...like these creams.

MEAD: I'll box up all the things you have that are too expensive to put on the sale table and send them back to the warehouse.

SALLY: I think this "Youth Cream" has been sitting on the shelf about thirty years. It's too old to still be "Youth Cream." Now what about this eye make-up? Mark it 99¢?

MEAD: Sure. And what about these Glamour-Lashes? How many pairs have you got left?

SALLY: Only two.

MEAD: Well, I'll just take them home to the Mrs. She's always losing hers. It's hardly worth sending two pair of false eyelashes back to the warehouse. (*Both Sally and Mildred have stopped dead*) How we doing on the dresses? Mildred?

MILDRED: What?

MEAD: The dresses...your department...wake up, Mildred.

MILDRED: Oh, well...there's an awful slew of them. Some are even winter dresses left over from last year. It's too hot for eyelashes...*wool* ...it's too hot for wool right now.

SALLY: (*Covering*) Should I make some signs? I put a magic marker right here in my own register just for that purpose.

MEAD: That'll be fine, Sally. Once you get everything marked, we'll put some of these things out on the sidewalk. Get everything sorted and we'll be ready to go. (*As he passes the bathroom*) Tish? Everything okay in there?

(*Sally and Mildred freeze with fear*)

TISH: I just need about a minute more.

MEAD: Are you morning sick?

TISH: (*Her voice coming from the rest room*) No...I'm just upset about what Donny's done.

MEAD: What's he done?

TISH: He's just...he's just not being a very good husband.

MEAD: I'll see if I can't have a talk with him. Don't forget he's young and maybe fatherhood scares him.

TISH: The idea of him becoming a father sure scares me.

MEAD: Don't worry...just try and feel better.

TISH: I'll try. Thank you.

MEAD: You're welcome. What are you two staring at? Get to work (*He exits into the stock room*)

MILDRED: (*Running to Sally*) For God's sake, Sally, what in the world is going on between Donny and Mrs. Mead? God, I thought Tish was going to say something about the eyelash to Mr. Mead and then all hell would break loose! I could just wring that Donny's neck!

SALLY: Oh, I wouldn't be too quick to blame Donny. I'm sure

Mrs. Mead enticed him into the situation.

MILDRED: I've always noticed how she flirts with the menfolk. Remember the Christmas party the store gave us at the Ramada Inn last year?

SALLY: I've got a good memory, Mildred. Better than yours, because we didn't have the Christmas party at the Ramada Inn last year. We had it at the Howard Johnson's.

MILDRED: Whatever...and Mr. Mead gave us all those cheap canned hams as presents? Remember?

SALLY: How could I forget. A five pound canned ham! Not even a bonus!

MILDRED: And when Mrs. Mead was passing out those hams, giving them to us...*presenting* them to us like they were some sort of extravagant gift . . .

SALLY: That ham was so tough, Mama made me throw it away. She took one bite of it and practically choked to death. Mama is very picky about her food and if there's one thing she knows it's bad ham.

MILDRED: Sally, I'm trying to make a point! When Mrs. Mead came up to give me my ham...Lothar was sitting there next to me ...and she winked at him! (*Mildred is all worked up ...Sally takes a pause*)

SALLY: So?

MILDRED: She was trying to make a pass at him!

SALLY: Oh, don't be silly, Mildred. What would she do with Lothar?

MILDRED: That's not the point...the point is, when she sees a man...any man...she can't resist. Poor Mr. Mead.

SALLY: Oh, no! You're not going to start feeling sorry for him! As far as I'm concerned, any man who marries someone who even has the slightest desire to parade in a swimsuit in front of God and everybody else watching TV, gets what is coming to him.

MILDRED: But do you think he suspects anything about Donny and the Mrs.?

SALLY: He doesn't seem to care much what she does.

MILDRED: Well, I don't see what Donny sees in her. Do you think if I called "The Best Little Hairhouse" they'd give me the name of her haircolor?

SALLY: Mildred, I feel I must tell you something. I've kept this to myself for quite some time now, because I am by nature a discreet person...but one day I was having, or trying to have, a converstaion with Mrs. Mead. You know how she always sort of talks over you...like you were too low to kiss the hem of her garment? Well, she came in here to get a dress. Now it's a proven fact Mrs. Mead wouldn't wear anything we sell here. So when she picked out what I considered to be just about the prettiest dress you have ever put out on your rack...and there have been so few pretty ones, but this one I might have considered wearing...

MILDRED: Where was I when this happened?

SALLY: It was early, Mildred, early in the morning and you were probably still in bed...but that's another subject. Anyway, she had this dress...and I said, "Mrs. Mead, that dress would look just lovely on you." And she said, "Don't be silly, Sally. This isn't for me to wear seriously. I'm just buying it to wear to a costume party." And I said, "What costume party?" And, "What are you going as?"

MILDRED: And what did she say?

SALLY: She said, once a year the sorority she belonged to when she was a coed back in Dallas, has a big carnival and all the alumni come back to visit. And everybody wears costumes...and she said she was going to her sorority dressed as, and I quote, "A typical example of the type of poor white trash who live in this horrible town my husband has forced me to end up in!"

MILDRED: Well, I never.

SALLY: Poor white trash, Mildred. She was going to a party in Dallas dressed as a symbol of what she thinks you and I are. And I was just floored! I mean, the dress was a simple navy blue number with just the tiniest hint of a design worked into it...a muted little bird motif...and it wasn't at all the tackiest thing in your department. In fact, it was the best of all your better dresses!

MILDRED: I remember that dress! I loved it! Well, she certainly has a lot of gall. Then what happened?

SALLY: Then I said..."Mrs Mead, you must be kidding?" And she said, "You bet I am. This whole place is a joke!" A joke, Mildred. She thinks the town where we live and the place we work in and the kind of lives we lead is some sort of joke. Now I admit, things aren't what they used to be...but I still take some sort of pride in what I do and I have never had any desire to leave this town, as awful as some of it has become. I'm sure it's not that much different from the rest of the country.

Normal people every place now shop in stores like we have and eat out in fast-food restaurants...and even though I miss a lot about this town and don't like the way things have changed so fast...I take consolation in the fact that if I went someplace else, life would be just like it is right here. For better or worse, this place is my home.

Mrs. Mead, however, is living in some sort of dream world. She watches her soap operas and her TV shows, because her maid does everything else; and she spends a fortune on herself, not charity; and she thinks it's okay to go around on her high horse hurting people's feelings and running around with other people's husbands. I mean, what sane woman would name her kids Little Blake and Little Krystle if she didn't have delusions of being something other than what she is? My Mama watches the soaps every afternoon, but when I come home at night she's not all decked out like Alexis expecting caviar for her supper. Some people know what's real and what's only make believe. We're out here, Mildred, dealing with the real world and the real people in it...and even though I can't stand most of them, I don't treat them like garbage.

MILDRED: Now you'll have to admit, most of the time when a woman asks to try on a shoe...you just hand her a footlet.

SALLY: That has to do with hygiene. I'm always very mannerly when I do that.

MILDRED: That you are.

SALLY: It's just like why I won't let ladies try on lipsticks. You never know where somebody's mouth has been.

MILDRED: This is true.

SALLY: And if I ran the lingerie department...I'd make the same rule about panties.

MILDRED: Good idea.

SALLY: Arlene, however, is always too concerned about herself to pay any attention to her job. But you, I must say, keep the piece goods quite tidy and I love the way you arrange the dresses by color. It takes time and care to do that. Even though it makes it more difficult to find the right size.

MILDRED: I have an eye for color. I've always known that. Very few things really irk me, but I just can't stand it when some people try to put things together that don't match.

SALLY: I noticed yesterday how you talked that woman out of buying that red dress she thought went so perfectly with her red handbag. You missed out on a sale.

MILDRED: There are a million shades of red, and what she had was a pinkish-purpley tint dress and an orangey-red handbag. I just couldn't stomach that. I kept telling Lothar last night, I wanted a black rinse on my hair...not blue-black, not magenta-black, just pure-dee black. That's not what I got at all.

SALLY: No, it's not.

MILDRED: I just don't think anybody as color blind as Lothar should be working on hair. Oh, we got in the worst argument over the color he painted his room in the trailer. He said he was going to do the bedroom "chalk."

SALLY: "Chalk?" Is that a color? Like blackboard chalk?

MILDRED: Yes...and when he finished, I thought it looked more like a sort of "cheesy" color. So did Dennis, and Dennis knows color. Anyway, Lothar just screamed at the both of us. The bedroom, he said, was not cheese but "chalk" and the accent color was "mushroom." Looked more like gray to me. He saw some picture in "House and Garden" he was trying to recreate in his bedroom. He got all these pots and filled them with dead brown weeds and statues from the garden shop at the K-Mart and spray painted them to look like old antiques...and he thought the bedroom was just like the one in the picture. Actually, the weeds he chose were ragweed and poor Dennis can't even sleep in there without having a sneezing fit...and I don't think a bunch of plaster ducks and deers look antique just because they're sprayed gold...but you can't tell that to Lothar. Lord, I hope he doesn't get some idea about becoming an interior decorator next or he'll be barking up another dead-end career.

SALLY: I must say, you have the patience of Job when it comes to Lothar.

MILDRED: If I don't stick by him, who will? I've dedicated my life to trying to make Lothar content...hoping someday he'll discover what he wants to do. I mean, he's my own flesh and blood; but he is also a cross for me to bear.

SALLY: I understand what you mean. Sometimes Mama and our situation gets too much for me, too. I guess I've never admitted it, but occasionally I do feel a bit cheated out of some of the things I wanted to do...just because I've always thought it was more important to try and make her last months on earth happy ones. The doctors told her because of her weak heart, she had less than a year to live. But that was fifteen years ago. And now I'm beginning to wonder if the doctors ever told her that or if she just told me that, so I wouldn't up and leave her. But I guess, any way you look at it, I won't have any regrets. At least as far as she's concerned. But I wouldn't know what to do, Mildred, if I found out my own Mama had been lying to me all along just to keep me there; while all this time I could have been doing something else with my life instead of just taking care of her.

MILDRED:Oh, honey...isn't it funny...we're both just sort of stuck in the same boat.

SALLY: Waiting on somebody else...here or at home...I've spent my whole life waiting on somebody else.

MILDRED: I know what you mean.

MEAD: (*Entering from the stock room*) About finished?

MILDRED: About. I just have a few more dresses to go.

MEAD: Good. Now, if you'll help me move some of these tables out on the sidewalk...we'll get going on this sale. Well, come on.

(*Mildred and Sally go to move a table. Tish is coming out of the rest room*)

MILDRED: Baby, how you feeling?

TISH: Oh, fine...don't make a fuss over me.

(*Mildred is. Sally is in a strange mood, ever since talking about her Mama. She seems distracted*)

MILDRED: Well, we were worried.

TISH: I'm sorry, Mr. Mead, for not doing my work...but I'm all better now. What are you doing?

MILDRED: Mr. Mead is having a sidewalk sale.

TISH: He's selling the sidewalk? (*She's serious, but Mildred saves her*)

MILDRED: No! Oh, Tish made a joke! Did you hear that, Mr. Mead? Tish thought you were selling the sidewalk? Oh, that's funny!

TISH: What's a sidewalk sale then?

MILDRED: He's decided to pile the lingerie and some shoes out there to attract customers.

TISH: Oh, that sounds good.

MEAD: So, let's see...(*Mead and Sally are coming in from putting a table of lingerie outside*)...Tish, if you and Mildred can cover all the departments in the store...Sally can stay out on the sidewalk.

(*Sally stops what she's doing*)

SALLY: I can do what?

MEAD: You can stay out there and sell those bras and panties, along with your shoes.

SALLY: I'm supposed to stand out on the sidewalk in my home town in front of God and everybody selling bras and panties?

MEAD: Sure.

SALLY: But I don't want to do that.

MEAD: What?

SALLY: I said, I don't want to do that. (*She's not angry, but he is getting there*)

MEAD: Are you saying you won't do that?

TISH: I'll do it.

SALLY: Tish, you have no business being out in that heat. Furthermore, it's going to melt those cheap bras if they sit out in that hot sun.

MILDRED: Oh, for Pete's sake, Sally...what's the big deal? I'll do it.

MEAD: I need you to keep marking dresses, Mildred. Sally's got all her departments done. So she'll go outside.

SALLY: But I can't do that.

MEAD: What is your problem? Simply go ouside, stand there and if anybody wants to buy something, take their money.

SALLY: But there are some things that I don't think are proper, Mr. Mead. Now you can pile whatever you like outside, but there's no way I can stand on that sidewalk and sell ladies' intimate apparel like I was in some sideshow at the circus.

MEAD: That's not what I'm asking you to do!

MILDRED: Oh, come on...let me do it. I've got no shame, and I can sit out there and work on my suntan.

MEAD: You stay out of this. (*He is getting angry. Tish is starting to cry*)

TISH: Sally, would you stop this? Just go outside. I can't stand arguing! I come down here to get away from the screaming!

MEAD: Tish, either go back to the bathroom and cry, or get busy with your candy. Mildred, get to marking those dresses, this minute!

(*Tish and Mildred run to their areas. Sally is calm, but stands her ground. Mead is fuming*)

SALLY: I didn't know you could be so unreasonable. Is that something they teach in manager's school these days?

MEAD: There are a lot of things you don't know, Miss Banks.

Now I don't care how many years you've worked here...

SALLY: Eighteen.

MEAD: I said, I don't care. The old ways of doing things are not my way, so if you want your job...get those things out on that table and get out on that sidewalk.

(*Sally is beginning to crumble*)

SALLY: But...lingerie isn't even my department...Arlene...

MEAD: Your department is whatever I tell you to work.

SALLY: But...but...

MEAD: There are no buts about it. This goes a lot deeper than just standing outside, doesn't it? (*Mildred and Tish are scared. Sally is about to cry*) From the time I came here, you've found it necessary to remind me, in one way or another, at least ten times a day, of how wonderful this store used to be. Right?

SALLY: It's a fact.

MEAD: But if you think you know so much, why aren't you the manager of this store now?

SALLY: I don't know.

MEAD: Well, I do. Because you don't know anything, Miss Banks. You just think you do. You're a good salesperson, but you don't know the first thing about how much something really costs or profit or loss or inventory control. You're full of opinions, but they're not based on any kind of knowledge...you don't understand the first thing about business, Miss Banks.

SALLY: (*Getting angry*) I understand I didn't go to any fancy college like you did and learn what I know out of books, like you did; but I've been here, learning what I know from directly dealing with my customers year in and year out for eighteen years ...knowing what shade of lipstick they like before they even ask for it, knowing people by name and treating them like they were special even if they're not...because everybody appreciates it, appreciates feeling like they're somebody even if they're just buying a lipstick. I've been here, out of duty to this store and my customers.

MEAD: But don't you see, they will buy the kind of things we sell without that kind of personal service. It doesn't matter.

SALLY: It matters to me.

MEAD: I'm already short one saleslady and I need you to do this.

SALLY: No, thank you.

MEAD: (*Getting angry*) God, I wish Arlene were here! But I told her last night, "Stay in bed or that back is never going to get better!" So just do this! No one is going to think a bit less of you, if for one summer morning you park yourself out on that sidewalk and sell a few items you think makes you look foolish.

SALLY: I can't do that.

MEAD: For God's sake, woman! You'd think I was asking you to take your clothes off and parade back and forth wearing one of these things!

SALLY: What would be the difference? It makes no difference to you if your wife parades around in a swimsuit.

MEAD: What does my wife have to do with this? God, what does it take to get you to just do your work and shut up?

SALLY: (*Really mad*) Don't you ever tell me to shut up! I will not see my life and my career...as little as it is...as pitiful as it has become...reduced to the final humiliating act of me...me, a respected person in this town for my entire life...me, the most loyal salesperson in this store...I will not see me or let anybody else see me sink so low as to think I can be ordered by you or anybody to do something I firmly believe makes a fool out of me. And, unlike you, I know when I'm being made a fool of and do whatever's necessary to prevent it!

MILDRED: Watch it, Sally.

SALLY: No...I'm going to see this out, because I'm beginning to see this clearly. Is it not a fact, Mr. Mead, that you and your wife are upstanding members of the Episcopal Church? That you are in the Lions Club, the Rotary, the Chamber of Commerce and the Republican Party? You did way you were at a Lions Club meeting last night, didn't you?

MEAD: So?

SALLY: So, Mr. Mead...could I speak to you privately for just a moment? Would you like to join me in the stockroom?

MEAD: What are you driving at? I am trying to run a business, Miss Banks, and I don't have time for games.

SALLY: Well, neither do I...but a lot of other people do. And if you'd like a further explanation, step this way, Mr. Mead. Believe me, this *is* private. I don't approve of airing anybody's dirty laundry in public anymore than I approve of selling lingerie there. After you.

MEAD: It's almost time to open the store, for God's sake, and I'm trying to deal with a nutcase!

(*He goes to the stockroom. Sally smiles at the others and then exits after him*)

MILDRED: (*Running around...almost hysterical*) Oh, God ...what am I going to do?

TISH: What is Sally going to do?

MILDRED: (*Running to Tish*) For Pete's sake, what are *you* going to do?

TISH: Me? It's Sally who's about to get fired.

MILDRED: (*Getting a plan*) Honey, could I ask you something?

TISH: Sure.

MILDRED: If you and Donny hadn't moved here, if you still lived back in...back in...where was that little place you came from?

TISH: Chatfield.

MILDRED: Chatfield. If you were there...what would you be doing today? I want a quick answer. (*She looks toward the stockroom*)

TISH: Well, I guess Donny would be working on his Daddy's farm, driving a tractor or something...and I'd be staying home waiting for him to come home for supper when I wasn't sitting around waiting for this baby to come.

MILDRED: Why, that sounds so lovely...and so simple. Doesn't it?

TISH: Yes, it does.

MILDRED: Now you yourself said you might have made a big mistake moving from there to here...to this place where Donny can't seem to find a job and you've got to earn the living? Right? Quick answer!

TISH: Yes...oh, yes, a lot of the time I wish we had never come here.

MILDRED: Then why not go back? Back to your roots...where you were loved, wanted, safe, happy!

TISH: Maybe we can. Someday.

MILDRED: (*All excited*) Why wait! Go! Go now!

TISH: What!

MILDRED: (*Pushing Tish toward the door*) Go right now! Get out of town! Quick!

TISH: Now?

MILDRED: Go get Donny, throw him in the car, race out of town and never look back!

TISH: What?

MILDRED: Where's your purse? Here it is! Get! Shoo! Go home!

TISH: Mildred, I don't understand this!

MILDRED: Don't you want to go home?

TISH: Yes, but...

MILDRED: No buts...just run...run away! Any girl who has an orange and black wedding certainly has a mind of her own! Go get Donny, if you love him...do you still love him?

TISH: More than anything.

MILDRED: Then fly...get out of here! Now! (*Pushing Tish out the door*)

TISH: But my job!

MILDRED: Take my advice...get Donny out of town!

TISH: Really?

MILDRED: Go away!

TISH: Okay...I'll go...I guess.

MILDRED: Go on! Get! Shoo! (*She locks the door leaving Tish outside. Tish stands there for a second...then knocks on the door*)

TISH: Mildred?

MILDRED: Go away! Run, Tish...run! (*Tish runs off . . . Mildred breathes a sigh...then runs toward the center counter, all the time looking toward the stockroom*) Oh lord. (*She pulls out the phone book, tries to find a number, does so, and then dials*) Donny, It's Mildred, down at the store. Yes, Mildred! Yes! Are you dressed? Never mind why...just get some pants on, pack a few things ...'cause Tish will be there in a few minutes, and I want you two to get in the car and go! Don't look back until you get all the way back to Chatfield! Do you hear me? Why? Because I know everything about that eyelash, Donny...so you'd better take care of that little girl and that baby and stop messing around...or by the time I'm through with you, you won't be half as cute as you used to be! I mean it...I'm one mean bitch! Just take Tish and go! (*She hangs up the phone because Sally is casually walking out from the stockroom*)

SALLY: It's all over. He'll never bother me again.

MILDRED: (*Losing it*) My God, you've killed him! You're going to go to the electric chair! You...murderess! (*She breaks into tears and flings herself on the stool*)

SALLY: Oh, don't be so dramatic, Mildred. Here he is.

(*Mead comes out of the stock room. He's very troubled. Mildred looks up*)

MEAD: Mildred...Tish...where's Tish?

MILDRED: I really don't know. Why?

MEAD: I have something I need to take care of, so I'm leaving

Sally in charge.

MILDRED: What?

SALLY: Michael's leaving me in charge.

MILDRED: Michael?

MEAD: I'll be back sometime. I don't know when. (*He starts to leave*)

MILDRED: Wait! Uh...uh...what about the summer sale?

MEAD: You handle it. What I've got to do can't wait.

(*He suddenly rushes out of the front door...Mildred runs after him, out onto the sidewalk, yelling*)

MILDRED: No! No! You can't go! Come back here! Don't do it, Mr. Mead! (*She runs out of sight*)

SALLY: (*Left alone, she is freshening her make-up, looking in her compact mirror*) Well, I guess that's settled. I'd better open up for business. Needless to say, I will not be selling any lingerie on the sidewalk today or any day, for that matter.

MILDRED: (*Rushing back in ...she slams the door*) I've known a lot of hard, selfish characters in my life but you...you take the cake! If I hadn't gotten Tish out of here and her and Donny on their way out of town...Lord, I only hope they get gone before Mr. Mead gets there! If Mead murders Donny, then you're the one who's going to have Tish's poor orphaned baby on your conscience. Not me! How could you have told him about Mrs. Mead running around with Donny?

SALLY: I told him no such thing.

MILDRED: What?

SALLY: I don't think Donny is running around with Mrs. Mead. And I would never hurt Tish.

MILDRED: But...but...but the eyelash! What about the Glamour-Lashes Mr. Mead wanted for his wife?

SALLY: You silly goose. It dawned on me, Mrs. Mead doesn't wear false eyelashes. I've seen her up close enough times to notice. I suspected he didn't want those eyelashes for his wife...but for someone else! Now about this sale...

MILDRED: Who were they for? Who? Who?

SALLY: Oh, Mildred, you're beginning to sound like some old hoot owl...who? Who?

MILDRED: Tell me what's going on! Please!

SALLY: Oh, honestly, Mildred...think! You don't wear false eyelashes. Mrs. Mead doesn't wear false eyelashes. God knows, I don't wear false eyelashes...but who does?

MILDRED: Who? Who?

SALLY: Suddenly, when Mr. Mead was yelling at me, it just all came together for me...like a vision of deliverance. I realized he wasn't keeping his story straight. You see, Mr. Mead said something earlier about being at the Lion's Club meeting last night. But the Lions never meet on Tuesday night. It's always Thursday. So where was he?

MILDRED: Where? Where?

SALLY: And something else didn't jell. When I first got in this morning, he said Arlene had just called in sick. But then he said later, he'd told Arlene last night to stay home from work today. So exactly when did he talk to her?

MILDRED: When? When?

SALLY: I didn't know...but I guessed he went over to see Arlene last night and maybe a lot of other nights, too. I mean, anybody who misses work as much as Arlene does and doesn't get fired ...well?

MILDRED: I'll be damned.

SALLY: Now I wasn't sure of anything, but I thought I might as well accuse him of his infidelity. What did I have to lose? He was all ready to fire me anyway. And sure enough...he was as guilty as sin. He just started bawling like a big baby. How could he be so stupid? With all his fancy education?

MILDRED: So where did he run off to?

SALLY: It was my suggestion he go talk over his problem with his minster or I'd just have to do it for him. Maybe in front of the congregation, and his wife and kids this Sunday.

MILDRED: My Lord, you are a regular Charlene Chan! I hope you don't have anything to use to blackmail me.

SALLY: Oh, no, Mildred, you're much too obvious. You keep all your secrets right out in the open.

(*They both laugh*)

MILDRED: Heavens, I can't believe I sent Tish out of here running back to her hometown.

SALLY: I think that was a stroke of genius on your part. Maybe she'll be happier there. And Donny was seeing Arlene, not Mrs. Mead. That explains the eyelash. Poor Arlene...I've gotten rid of two of her boyfriends in one day.

MILDRED: Her back might be so much better she'll be in to work tomorrow.

SALLY: I wouldn't count on it.

MILDRED: You didn't...

SALLY: Canned. It's just you and me now, Mildred. We can choose our departments...but as assistant manager...

MILDRED: Now wait a minute.

SALLY: It's an honorary title, bestowed by me on me...but I get to choose first. I'll keep cosmetics...take candy, costume jewelry and lingerie. You can have your better dresses and piece goods, and add in wigs, sportswear and shoes.

MILDRED: Shoes? You've given me all the hard ones. I'll trade you wigs for candy.

SALLY: Fine, I don't like candy anyway. And I'm going to move those Afros away fron the peanut clusters. It's not sanitary. Now these arrangements will just be temporary. Until we can find somebody new to work with us, we'll just have to do everything ourselves.

MILDRED: I've got an idea...what about Lothar?

SALLY: You've got to be kidding me?

MILDRED: Oh, please...give the kid a break! Give the kid a job! Get him out of my hair!

SALLY: I'll certainly think about it.

MILDRED: You know, you should get to know Lothar better. Sometimes, instead of just looking out the window at what we're doing down the block, you ought to come over and join in the fun.

SALLY: Me? Well, I just couldn't.

MILDRED: You like Dennis. You said so yourself. And there's always something going on over at our trailer. Usually not half as exciting as you suspect. Oftentimes we just get out the Scrabble board and play for hours. As smart as you are, I'll bet you could beat the pants off of us!

SALLY: I will not play "strip Scrabble" if that's what you mean! (*They both laugh, then Sally becomes quiet*) You know, Mildred, in all the years I've known you, you've never asked me over?

MILDRED: I know, and I just feel lousy about it.

SALLY: I'd really love to return the favor and invite you to our place, but Mama goes to bed so early. Oh, but maybe you and the boys would like to come over sometime for Sunday dinner. I always go all out on Sunday. Chicken and dumplings, fried okra, summer squash, cornbread and peach pie! I'm a real good cook. I know you all don't go to church, but you could come over after I get back.

MILDRED: Oh, Sally, honey...we'd just love that.

SALLY: But under no condition...no matter how friendly all of us become...will I let Lothar get his hands on *my* hair.

MILDRED: Some things are just too much to ask for.

(*They laugh*)

SALLY: Well, it's almost time. Have you checked the tape on your register, Mildred?

MILDRED: No.

SALLY: From now on...get a spare one ready so in case you run out in the middle of the day, you can just pop it in! Customers hate to wait.

MILDRED: All-righty!

SALLY: I think there are going to be a lot of changes around here. I'm going to tell those fancy bosses in New York, New York, we're not going to send them any money from our store until they drive down here and say "hi" to us.

MILDRED: Good thinking.

SALLY: Oh, it's ten o'clock! Time to open up! Snap to, Mildred. The day's just started. And...(*Mildred runs to her register. Sally goes and unlocks the front door*)...we're open!

MILDRED: Anybody coming?

SALLY: Yes! Oh, I can see our first customer coming down the walk! (*She is looking out the door*) It's Harriet Crumley...she's getting closer and closer...she's coming to our Summer Sale! She's going to buy a lot, I'm sure! She's getting closer and closer...and she just turned and went into the Roy Rogers!

MILDRED: I see it's going to be business as usual.

(*They laugh*)

SALLY: Come on, Mildred. Help me throw away all these shoe boxes. I'm gonna crush every one of them with my bare hands!

MILDRED: You'll ruin your nails!

SALLY: It'll be worth it! Don't be such a stick-in-the-mud, Mildred. You've got to learn to take a few chances.

MILDRED: But you're going to get yourself in trouble!

SALLY: No, I'm not!

MILDRED: Yes, you are!

SALLY: No, I'm not!

MILDRED: Yes, you are!

SALLY: No, I'm not!

MILDRED: Yes, you are!

(*They continue this argument as they crush the shoe boxes ...and the lights fade*)

The End

David Kranes

CANTRELL

David Kranes

David Kranes makes his second appearance in *Best Short Plays* with *Cantrell*, a suspense-filled character study of a hit man attempting to lead a reformed life. The play was first produced in March, 1988, by the Salt Lake Acting Company. Mr. Kranes was last represented in this series in the 1986 edition with *Going In*, a sensitive study of a physician's mid-life crisis involving his wife and son. An earlier play, *Drive In*, was published in the *Playwrights for Tomorrow* series, edited by Arthur Ballet. At present Mr. Kranes is working on two plays commissioned by the Philadelphia Festival Theatre.

Mr. Kranes is a graduate of the Yale School of Drama, where he studied playwriting with the late John Gassner, noted anthologist and theatre critic. Mr. Kranes' full-length play *The Salmon Run* was the co-recipient of the 1985 National Repertory Theatre Award, and the Manhattan Theatre Club presented one of his plays in their 1986-87 season.

The playwright also writes novels and screenplays. His novel, *The Hunting Years* (1984), received a laudatory review in the *New York Times*, and a new book of fiction, *Keno Runner*, was published in the fall of 1986. In 1986 his screenplay *Truants* was produced. Mr. Kranes has also adapted his novel *Criminals for Agincourt* into a screenplay.

A Distinguished Teaching Award has been given to Mr. Kranes by the University of Utah, where he teaches playwriting, dramatic literature, and theater history. In addition to his position as professor, Mr. Kranes is the artistic director of the Playwrights Conference at the Sundance Resort in Provo Canyon, Utah. This Center for Performing Arts at Sundance offers selected playwrights the opportunity to develop their skills and artistry. Ideas and concepts are explored in depth at the conference without the financial and critical pressures of the commercial theater.

Mr. Kranes lives in Salt Lake City with his wife and two sons, and continues to write for the stage, the cinema, and the reading public.

This play Mr. Kranes dedicates, "For Patrick Tovatt."

Characters:

CANTRELL, *forty-three, once a hit man*
THE HIT
THE MAN
COWBOY #1
COWBOY #2
UTAH STATE HIGHWAY PATROLMAN
BARTENDER
CHRISSIE, *fifteen, learning*
RUPERT, *thirty-seven, Chrissie's foster father*

Setting:

The back wall of the set is a scribble of neon. We are in—
among other places—Las Vegas, a cowboy bar, a motel in St.
George, Utah.
  Two levels. The upper level upstage, a full U-shaped thrust—
the partial arc of a bar and barstools stage right. A café table,
chairs and a jukebox stage left. To the rear of the raised platform is a motel bureau. At the front center of the upper level—
situated so that its footboard forms/flows into a car front-seat
back on the lower level—is a raked motel bed. The principal areas on the lower level are a golf green stage right and the re-
straining rail of a canyon overlook stage left. There is a public
phone somewhere on the periphery of all this.
  Characters move fluidly from space to space within all of
this—without interruptive blackouts. Modulations and transi-
tions are covered with current country and western music.

Time:

Last July

At Curtain:

Lights fade in on the scribble of neon on the back wall. The
sound of distant cars moving every once in a while, along
Sands Road in Las Vegas.
  A dim pool of light on Cantrell. He wears an extremely ex-

*pensive dark suit and is sitting on the front seat of this car,
polishing his gun with a silk ascot. The gun should gleam like
an emerald and look murderous. If Cantrell has the radio in his
car on, it plays Telemann. Beside Cantrell, on the passenger
side of the front seat, sits a portable fridge—plugged into the
cigarette lighter. Cantrell interrupts his polishing to open the
fridge unit and takes out a quality glass and a bottle of expensive Russian vodka. He pours himself a drink, sits sipping it,
checking the chamber of the gun. Cantrell will also slip two zip-
lock bags over his hands and tighten them.*

*We hear a particularly close vehicle. Perhaps some head-
lights even sweep by Cantrell. Whatever the effects—it is what
Cantrell has been waiting for. He sets the glass back into the
fridge, turns the radio off or lower.*

*While Cantrell makes his final preparations, we will hear a
garage door rolling up and a car moving into the garage. Cantrell is out of his car by the time the garage door begins down
again. In fact, he has moved forward, through the shadows into
the "garage space" before we hear the sound of the other car
door opening—then closing.*

*There is enough light now to see "The Hit." The Hit is a man
in his forties, also wearing an expensive suit.*

CANTRELL: This is a historic moment.
THE HIT: (*Seeing him, startled*) Whoa!
CANTRELL: (*Advising*) Still. Just...
THE HIT: (*In his way, he knows*) Wait, wait. Who are...?!
CANTRELL: This is my last.
THE HIT: Don't.
CANTRELL: I'm finished.
THE HIT: I'm serious.
CANTRELL: I do you—and then I don't do this any more.
THE HIT: Hey, let's talk. Who's paying?
CANTRELL: You can't kill people forever, it's wrong.
THE HIT: Really, we can...
CANTRELL: What's the future—you know?
THE HIT: Don't...
CANTRELL: Just relax.
THE HIT: Please—really—don't.
CANTRELL: And think of it this way...
THE HIT: I'll split town. I'll go away. I won't exist. It'll be the

same, you just won't have it on your conscience.

CANTRELL: Think of it this way: no more decisions: no more questions.

THE HIT: Really. Please. Don't. Wait.

(*Cantrell will fire three shots. We will see the flares of light from his instrument*)

CANTRELL: You can change your life. (*First shot*) A person. Usually I drink the vodka *after* the hit. Do the hit first...go back to the car...enjoy the vodka. But you can change. You can change the order. (*Second shot*) I found that! And if you can change the order, then you can change your life. No more killing. No more jobs. It's a wonderful day! (*Third shot*) Now I get in my car and change my life. I've always wondered what to do with the money (*Clip of bills in his hand*) that I get. An amazing thing happened. Today. I was at the MGM Grand...by the pool...watching what I call the "fish scales," light the sun makes on the pool water—and I started remembering all kinds of tiny pieces of when I was a kid. Time, once, I almost drowned. Now I get in my car and change the order of all the pieces. I drive east. My tank is full. I got my wheels aligned. I've never been east of here. Go to "Utah"! (*He laughs; says the word again: he likes its sound*) "Utah." Maybe I'll even throw my instrument totally away! It's a wonderful day! It's a historic moment! Cantrell will never again be the same! You can stop doing what you're doing. You can start doing *different* things. (*Leaning over the body of The Hit*) Thank you.

(*Fade the light on the garage. Bring up the Telemann; then modulate it into Willie Nelson. Slow fade up on Cantrell, sitting in front seat of his car, elbow out the window, singing along. Perhaps there's a band of turquoise blue sky high above.*

The red/blue turning of a patrol car light behind Cantrell. Cantrell checks his rear view mirror. He slows. He stops. From the very rear of the stage, a Highway Patrolman approaches— first silhouette, then full. Cantrell smiles)

PATROLMAN: Good morning.

CANTRELL: Absolutely...absolutely. How are you?

PATROLMAN: License and registration, please.

CANTRELL: (*Searching for license and registration*) That's a wonderful drive, down through the Virgin River Canyon. The air smells like fish. One time I went scuba diving. In Lake Mead. And it was like that. I bought the gear. And I used it once. And it was wonderful. But I let it go. I never got back. I think what you *need*, really, is lifetime activities. Well, now I'm ready for those. This is the first day of my life. I suppose you've heard that. I may take up golf.

(*Cantrell hands his license and registration to the Patrolman*)

PATROLMAN: I'll be just a moment.

CANTRELL: Take your time.

(*The Patrolman will walk back about ten paces and stand with his back to Cantrell. Cantrell will bellow along with whatever country and western song is on the radio. The Patrolman will return to stand beside the "car"*)

CANTRELL: It must be nice—having a uniform. That must be gratifying. It looks good. It fits well. Maybe someday *I'll* have a uniform. Who can say?

PATROLMAN: Are you aware, Mr. Cantrell, that you were going eighty-two miles an hour, twenty-seven miles in excess of the speed limit?

CANTRELL: I knew it was somewhere around there.

PATROLMAN: I'm going to give you this citation, Mr. Cantrell. You can mail it. Or I've included an address in St. George.

CANTRELL: "Utah"!

PATROLMAN: Yes, Utah. If you're there after nine, this morning, you can simply go to the court house and pay it. It's—I'm sorry—steep. But you were being very excessive in your speed. You've got to watch that.

CANTRELL: (*Handing it out*) Here's one hundred dollars.

PATROLMAN: I'm sorry, Mr. Cantrell. But you've got the wrong person. I have religious principles.

CANTRELL: I thought you were charging me for speeding.

PATROLMAN: No, sir, the *State* is.

CANTRELL: Oh. The State. Excellent. But don't you work for the State?

PATROLMAN: Yes, sir. But I can't take the State's money.

CANTRELL: Oh. That's fine. I didn't know. Listen…Listen, you have a brother?

PATROLMAN: I have *four* brothers, Mr. Cantrell. And three sisters.

CANTRELL: (*Squinting, appraising*) No. No, up close, I can see. I had a job once. My twenty-third, actually. But…no connection, no. I was wrong. Wrong eyes.

PATROLMAN: Mr. Cantrell—sir? Is that a respirator? Beside you? On your front seat and plugged into your dash? I'm sorry:

Are you on a respirator? Do you have a medical problem—I'm sorry if I caused any difficulty for you. It just didn't occur to me that...?

CANTRELL: (*Laughing*) No. No.

PATROLMAN: (*Backing away*) Good. Well...just keep your speed down, then.

CANTRELL: I will...I will. You watch. I'm ready. (*Fade down lights. Fade up music. When the lights and music cross fade again, we see Cantrell in his motel, at the bureau, on the phone. A piece of expensive luggage sits on the bed. Cantrell still wears his suit*) ...Hello, golf course? This is Cantrell: How are you? Good...Cantrell. Listen, I've just checked in here at the Globe Motor Lodge and I'm ready to take up golf. You open for business?...Cantrell. What do I owe you? You have everything I need for this new activity? Do you have everything that I'll have to use? Do you take major credit cards? Or should I bring a cashier's check? Or, if you would prefer, I have some unmarked bills. What does golf cost? If I do it every day for the rest of my life, what's it going to run me? (*The light begins to fade on Cantrell as he continues on the phone*) ...The Globe Motor Lodge...Cantrell...I just retired from my former line of endeavor...I hit people...What does golf cost? (*The light is down. The music is again up. The music fades down and we hear Cantrell's voice in the dark*) This is great! This is *it*! (*Very gradual fade up of light to bright sunlight*) This is great, man! Fuck hits! Fuck *those* assignments! Fuck *that* life! All right, *golf*! Someone should've told me. This is great!! I love it! (*Cantrell is on the course. He has no idea what he is doing, but he is having the time of his life.We have seen him take a swing in the dim light. He has followed the "ball" almost straight above his head with his eyes. By the time the lights are full, a golf ball drops just in front of him, and Cantrell roars with gleeful laughter. He is still in his suitpants, silk shirt with the sleeves rolled up, open vest, wingtip shoes*) (*Calling off*) Hey...!! Hey...!!

DISTANT VOICE: ...Yeah...?

CANTRELL: (*Pointing to himself*) Tom Watson!

(*Cantrell erupts again with deep, gleeful laughter. Fade the light on Cantrell, having more fun than he has ever had. Light in on the cowboy bar. Chrissie, a fifteen-year-old trying to be loose and thirty, is near the bar, flirting with two cowboys*)

COWBOY #1: C'mon home with us.

CHRISSIE: You mean—come to your pickup?

COWBOY #2: Home is where you hang yer hat, honey.

COWBOY #1: Haven't you heard that?

CHRISSIE: You guys wanna hang your hats on me—s'that it? (*The two Cowboys laugh*) Gimme some quarters, an' buy me another beer. Nothin's free, ya know.

COWBOY #1: Absolutely! (*To Cowboy #2*) Give Chrissie some quarters. (*As Cowboy #2 does, calling off*) Three more draft!

(*By now, the light is also up on the left side of the stage, the table next to the juke where Cantrell sits. He has still not changed—though his hair is slickly brushed. He looks strangely elegant, though very out of place. He is eating a steak. Cantrell has been watching Chrissie and her scene with the Cowboys. He watches her cross by him to the juke, watches the Cowboys lecherously watching her. Cantrell rises and crosses to Chrissie at the jukebox*)

CANTRELL: I want you to come over and sit at my table for a while with me. (*He crosses back to his meal. Chrissie looks at him, a bit mystified. She makes her last selections with her last quarter, moves, somewhat defiantly to the edge of Cantrell's table*)

CHRISSIE: So what kind of bullshit was *that*—just then?

CANTRELL: Sit down.

CHRISSIE: Yeah? Who are you?

CANTRELL: Cantrell. Just sit down. (*Silence*) Sit down. I want to talk with you.

(*A beat. Chrissie sits. The Cowboys, of course, will starting noting this*)

CHRISSIE: So? (*Cantrell nods*) So, I'm sitting. So what?

CANTRELL: What are you: sixteen?

CHRISSIE: What are you—my father?

CANTRELL: Fifteen? Seventeen?

CHRISSIE: I'm old *enough*.

CANTRELL: Look...(*The Cowboys are now in conference*) You think you're a pro? (*No answer*) You want to be a pro...Fine. Here's two hundred bucks. I'm buying you for the next hour. You think you're up to that?...Or are you just a mouth?

(*Cantrell slides the two bills across the table and under Chrissie's hand. She looks at them, unfolds them. Cowboy #1 has started across the space to Cantrell's table*)

COWBOY #1: This greaser giving you shit, Chrissie?

CHRISSIE: ...No.

COWBOY #1: I think he is.

CHRISSIE: Well, he isn't.

COWBOY #1: (*To Cantrell*) We protect our own, here.

CANTRELL: (*Picking up his steak knife and fork*) That's admirable.

CHRISSIE: (*To Cowboy #1*) Why don't you fuck off, Vern?

COWBOY #1: Don't...

CHRISSIE: We're having a conversation.

COWBOY #1: (*To Cantrell*) This girl's too young. She ain't accountable. She needs close caring for.

CHRISSIE: (*Standing*) Listen, Vern: I don't need fuckall! I mean it. So don't...

(*Cantrell clears his throat and holds his steak knife vertical in a gesture somehow hard not to attend to*)

CANTRELL: (*Essentially to The Cowboy*) I want you to watch. Do I have your attention? I want you to watch. (*With one hard-pressed stroke, he cuts the little finger from his left hand. The Cowboy gasps and steps back. Chrissie shrieks. Cantrell stanches the blood with his linen napkin. He has their attention*) You see...if I can do that to *myself*...I think you've got to think about what I could do to *you*—and to your *friends*.

(*Chrissie's breathing has almost a tiny hum to it in its expiration. The Cowboy's breathing seems to be through mucus*)

COWBOY #1: (*Backing*) ...Right...Right. I get...I see.

(*Cowboy #2 has been edging toward the exit. Cowboy #1 joins him—and they are gone*)

CANTRELL: (*To Chrissie*) Let's go for a walk. (*Fast fade down of light, crossing with music. Fewest necessary beats. Crossfade in again on the room at the Globe Motor Lodge. Cantrell has the stub of his finger taped and bandaged. He moves while he talks. Chrissie is on the bed, wide-eyed, watching him*)...Forty-seven people. Forty-seven assignments. This is not a good line of work. This is not rewarding. There's no pleasure in it. This afternoon, I started playing golf—and it's much better. Tomorrow...what's that building in this town? The round one. Just west. At the college. Near the library.

CHRISSIE: It's a "replica."

CANTRELL: "Replica"? What do you mean: "replica"?

CHRISSIE: That's just what it is, asshole. That's just what it's called. "Replica." Don't ask me those questions. "Replica." It's what we learned in school.

CANTRELL: "Replica."

CHRISSIE: It's a big thing here.

CANTRELL: "Replica."..."Utah."

CHRISSIE: It's called Shakespeare. Something Shakespeare. It's all famous. They do plays there. Don't ask me about it.

CANTRELL: "Shakespeare"...in "Utah"...in a "replica." (*Cantrell laughs gleefully*) I like it. I like it! I like it a lot!...So you mean the building's called "Shakespeare"?

CHRISSIE: No. I don't know. They do Shakespeare...that's all I know—whatever that is. Jesus Christ, Cantrell! In the summers. Like now. They do Shakespeare's plays.

CANTRELL: ...Then maybe I'll start doing Shakespeare. Work it in. Around the golf. They do that during the day—do you mean—or at night?

CHRISSIE: I don't know! Night...I guess...mostly.

CANTRELL: Good...here. (*He extends something to her*)

CHRISSIE: What?

CANTRELL: Keep this.

CHRISSIE: Your...? (*She touches her own little finger*)

CANTRELL: Put it somewhere outside for a couple of weeks. Then keep the bone. Save it. I want you to think about me. Stop trying to be something that you're not. It costs too much. People have choices. They can do Shakespeare. They can play golf.

(*Chrissie has no real idea why she is feeling what she's feeling. She will slip the stub into her Levi shorts pocket*)

CHRISSIE: ...This is so weird.

CANTRELL: ...What do you mean?

CHRISSIE: This is just so weird. That's all!

(*Chrissie does something, does its opposite, does the first thing again. Cantrell watches her*)

CANTRELL: ...What seems weird?

CHRISSIE: Fuck off! Just fuck off! Who do you think you are? ...one of my foster fathers?!

CANTRELL: What seems weird?

CHRISSIE: Just shut up!

CANTRELL: If you want to leave—then leave.

CHRISSIE: No!

CANTRELL: Stay, then.

CHRISSIE: God! You have... (*Chrissie hits or throws something*) *No* one gives me presents! Do you know that?! *No* one! You have really fucked up my life! You have really fucked up my life tonight—*badly*! (*Cantrell stares at her. Chrissie takes off one of her sandals and throws it at him*) Shit! (*Cantrell moves to where he's put his fridge on the bureau. Chrissie stares at him, in part afraid he's going to do something violent. Cantrell opens his fridge, takes out his glass, his vodka, pours himself a drink*)...So I don't get any?! I'm not here?! I don't get any vodka offered to *me*?!

CANTRELL: Would you like some vodka?

CHRISSIE: No! You stupid asshole. I've got an allergy! (*Cantrell puts everything back in place, precisely*)

My goddamn *real* father—whoever *he* is—gave me all these goddamn allergies! Everything I've got in this fucking world is all *allergies*! (*Chrissie starts crying, will throw herself face down on the bed. Cantrell studies her a moment. He stares out. From his suitcoat pocket he produces golf balls. He juggles them, three...then four. At some point, Chrissie looks up from her crying. She stops crying. She watches him*)...Holy shit.

CANTRELL: I grew up in a carnival.

CHRISSIE: Your parents worked in a carnival?

CANTRELL: I don't know. That's just where I was.

(*It would be ideal if Cantrell could now catch balls behind his back as part of his juggling*)

CHRISSIE: You...

CANTRELL: ...Young lady?

CHRISSIE: My name is Chrissie.

CANTRELL: I know.

CHRISSIE: You got a bloody rag taped to your hand—and you can still juggle like that?!

CANTRELL: That's the carnival. (*He juggles*) I had a friend in the carnival. We were both your age. (*He smiles*) Thirty-five. Torey Weathers. I haven't had a friend since then. I should get one. Torey had all the jobs that had to do with the hoses. He had hair that was always plastered on his head. Once he hosed down a field where they were going to set up the carnival. I was there. Some...like *lightning* jumped from the generator truck to Torey's hose. And Torey...rose up. He...lifted up...like he was something that the hose was juggling. I ran and turned off the generator. And Torey came down. He didn't die. That night, Torey and I ate pizza together. I have three knives I'd stolen from Rizcatto, the knife thrower. Torey said to me: "I'm the Loch Ness Monster!...I'm the Loch Ness Monster!" (*Cantrell smiles at the memory*)

CHRISSIE: You're in space. (*Cantrell nods*)...So close the curtain. (*Cantrell mimes the closing of his motel room curtain*)

...Flip the lights.

(*A beat. Cantrell flips the lights. Chrissie lifts her tank top off. Under it she wears a cheap satin bra*)

CANTRELL: What's that?

CHRISSIE: What's what?

CANTRELL: (*Indicating—by his own shoulder blades*) On your skin. The pink. Like tiny flowers.

CHRISSIE: It's my allergies. It's my goddamn allergies, stupid. How can you see them? It's dark.

CANTRELL: Training.

CHRISSIE: Shit! (*Silence. Cantrell doesn't move*) So...?

CANTRELL: ...Excuse me: What's the question?

CHRISSIE: Listen...you're a big boy. You've lived in Las Vegas. You know what's going on. You know what to do. (*Cantrell crosses to his bureau. He picks up two ends of a towel which is there with something in it and carefully carries it across, setting it down on the bed. He shines a penlight onto it*) What's that?

CANTRELL: What does it look like?

CHRISSIE: ...It looks like...all the parts of your gun.

CANTRELL: It's my instrument.

CHRISSIE: What do you mean...it's your "instrument"? It's your *gun.*

CANTRELL: It's all the parts of my instrument—broken down.

CHRISSIE: Yeah...*gun* pieces.

CANTRELL: Remember that.

CHRISSIE: Remember what?

CANTRELL: About the world....That everything in the world is just pieces—added up....Parts....Parts...I could juggle these...and entertain people.

(*Pause*)

CHRISSIE: (*Touching Cantrell's arm with her hand, running her finger*) So...

(*A beat*)

CANTRELL: No.

CHRISSIE: No?

CANTRELL: No.

CHRISSIE: Why? What do you mean..."No."

CANTRELL: I mean..."No." I jerk off in the shower. Put your sweater back on.

(*Blackout. Music. As smooth and swift a transition as possible. Light coming up on the golf course*)

CHRISSIE: This game sucks!

(*Light up now. Chrissie and Cantrell on the course—Chrissie with club*)

CANTRELL: Try it again.

CHRISSIE: I'm telling you: This game sucks! I hate it!

(*Cantrell points to where we imagine a ball. Chrissie swings. They both watch the ball soar*)

CANTRELL: Nice shot.

CHRISSIE: (*Proud*) Pretty good—huh?

CANTRELL: Excellent.

CHRISSIE: Not bad—for a little slut of a brat like me. (*Cantrell stares at her hard, reproachfully*) So...are you, you know...thinking about, like, *confessing*? You know, like...turning yourself in?

(*Cantrell is balancing a five iron on his chin*)

CANTRELL: Why? (*He adds a two iron*) Why?...Why do that? What's the future?

CHRISSIE: ...I don't know. (*Cantrell throws his chin into the air. The clubs rise. He catches them. He mimes putting a ball down. He addresses it. He swings. Chrissie's eyes grow wide*)...God: You're so fucking good!...How'd you get so fucking good so fast?

CANTRELL: Concentration.

CHRISSIE: I think it's fucking amazing!

CANTRELL: Don't say that word so much.

CHRISSIE: ...You could go on television. You could be a pro.

CANTRELL: If you're going to do something with your life—you should do it. I'm playing golf. I don't want to go on television.

CHRISSIE: Why not? Those guys make money!

CANTRELL: I've done that. I've made money. That's history. I went to Shakespeare last night.

CHRISSIE: Uh-*uh*.

CANTRELL: "Uh-*uh*?" What do you mean..."uh-*uh*?"

CHRISSIE: I mean...you didn't go. You couldn't have. It isn't open yet.

CANTRELL: I went to watch it rehearse. A woman let me.

CHRISSIE: So did it suck?

CANTRELL: You use a lot of words that end with those three letters.

CHRISSIE: Well...

CANTRELL: It was *Richard the Third*. That's what they said....I don't know. I think Shakespeare needs, maybe, to change his life.

At the end...the end of the play, this guy, this Richard...the Third—I never saw the first two; I don't know *where* they were—he comes out, and he says: "My kingdom for a horse!" Then he says it again. Then someone else comes in...with a sword...and kills him. And this other guy says, "The bloody dog is dead!"

CHRISSIE: ...So...

CANTRELL: So I don't know...horses and dogs...horses and dogs. The guys were animals...Then, at the *very* end, the same guy, the guy who hit Richard says: "God say amen!" And somebody, somewhere in the place, did a number on a trumpet...Here—I'm going to use one of your words: Fuck that life! You know? I *did* that. People saying "God say amen," after they hit people. I'm sorry. I'm not doing Shakespeare. Shakespeare needs to play golf. (*To Chrissie*) Put your club on my hand there. (*She puts her club on the extended fingertips of one of his hands*) Good. Thank you. Now put *my* club on my other hand. (*She does*) Thank you. (*Cantrell balances both clubs*)..."Replica"... "Replica"...

(*The lights fade. Country and western music. Dim light on one of the Cowboys at the bar. Fade in the sound of at least one car honking on a street*)

RUPERT'S VOICE: I'm not movin'!...I'm not movin'! Go ahead! Why don't you just drive on over me, asshole—with your fucking Seville!

(*Light up at the front of the playing area, center. Rupert, a hairy and unruly man in a Hawaiian shirt, down vest, khaki pants and combat boots, faces his wheelchair into the car seat that Cantrell used in the early scenes. He is kicking with his boots at the front of the "car." Lights also up on Cantrell, eating at bar/café table. He is hearing the ruckus outside. By the time Rupert is through, Cantrell will be outside*)

RUPERT: No! I *won't* move. No, I won't move, man—tough shit! ...Hey! Hey—I went to fucking *Nam* for you, man. I slept with fucking *snakes*! I fucked my body up with *chemicals*! Charlie took my *legs*! You got some extra legs for me? You got some legs you want go give me, Rich-man? For doing that for you? For puttin' my life on the line for you? I'm a fucking *hero*, man! I'm a fucking crippled *hero*. Get your Seville out of my way!

(*Cantrell takes the back of Rupert's wheelchair and starts to wheel him out of the "road"*)

CANTRELL: Let's go.

RUPERT: Hey! What the fuck do you...?!

CANTRELL: Light just turned green.

RUPERT: Watch it, man!

CANTRELL: I'm saving your life. It's a dangerous intersection.

RUPERT: All right, Jerko!—you got warned!

(*From somewhere, Rupert produces a piece of metal tow cable and swings it at Cantrell. It strikes Cantrell on the face. In a flash, Cantrell has grabbed the cable and has it tight around Rupert's neck. Cantrell and Rupert face directly into the audience. We should see Cantrell's cracked open face...and the thread by which Rupert's life hangs*)

CANTRELL: (*Very calmly*) I would like to say something. I would like to give you some information, it's important. This is nothing for me. This is like watching television...or driving up and ordering a Quarter Pounder and fries. You see—your head is just a head—that's all. It's just a head; it's just another head. And I've kept three heads in the air. At one time. Like medicine clubs...Same time—balanced someone's cock on my chin. But the point is...the point is, you see—the carnival's over. The carnival's over, Jack. It left town. Yesterday. So the both of us...need to remember that. Especially you. (*Cantrell relaxes the cable on Rupert's neck. He removes it. Rupert, wide-eyed, turns to look at Cantrell. Cantrell nods to him*) Get a job as a receptionist. You could excel. Give up kicking cars and excel at the trade of receptionist. I feel confident that you could do it. You just need to apply yourself. (*Silence. Tableau. Fade light. The ringing of Cantrell's motel telephone. Dim light on a Man in a suit at a public phone*) Yes?

MAN: Cantrell?

CANTRELL: Hello?

MAN: Cantrell?

CANTRELL: Hello?

MAN: You know—I don't know a person likes to work as hard as I had to work to *find* you. (*Light, by now, up on Cantrell in his motel room. Chrissie is in the room, trying to juggle two golf balls. Every time one drops, she says, "Fuck!"*)...Cantrell?

CANTRELL: Hello?

MAN: I said—I don't know a person likes to work as hard as I...

CANTRELL: Hard work's good for everyone.

MAN: They say you take assignments. You do work.

CANTRELL: I took my name out of the yellow pages.

MAN: I've got an assignment.

CANTRELL: I'm out of business. I lost my lease. I had my "prices slashed to rock bottom" last week.

MAN: I don't think so.

CANTRELL: Well, then read it over one more time, and you can take the quiz again tomorrow—I'm out of business. I lost my...

MAN: From what *I* hear...you can't *afford* to be out of the assignment business. I hear—anyone gets out, people start to worry. People start to worry...then the assig*nor* gets to be the assig*nee*. You understand what I'm saying?

CANTRELL: ...Call up Shakespeare.

MAN: Listen, Cantrell—I'm calling from a pay phone on Paradise Road. I don't have a lot of spare change in my pocket to bullshit and humor you.

CANTRELL: I'm in golf now. I'm in dog-legs and traps.

MAN: You're in the *ground*, smart guy! That's where *you're* going!

(*The man hangs up. Light fades on his phone. Cantrell hangs up*)

CHRISSIE: Who was that?

CANTRELL: Used car salesman. He wants me to trade in my Audi.

CHRISSIE: Are you ever serious? (*Cantrell doesn't answer*) ...Why won't you tell me how that [*His slashed face*] happened?

(*Cantrell is looking out the window. Rupert is there, in a pool of light, in his wheelchair*)

CANTRELL: Looks like the golf course is "under siege."

CHRISSIE: You're *insane*.

CANTRELL: Looks like golf may be tougher than I thought.

CHRISSIE: What're you talking about?

CANTRELL: Just the pieces.

CHRISSIE: Why won't you tell me what happened?

CANTRELL: You don't like my face?

CHRISSIE: I think it's *ugly*!

CANTRELL: I had it sewed up—just for you. Should I take the stitches out?

CHRISSIE: No! Yich! Come on—what happened?

CANTRELL: I was in the library—a book bit me. That's where I read those words "under siege." Like them?

CHRISSIE: I think someone forgot to lock your door! (*The phone rings again. Dim light on Man at the public phone*) You're popular!

CANTRELL: How's the juggling coming?

CHRISSIE: It's stupid! I'm terrible! When're you going to fuck me, anyway?

CANTRELL: (*Pointing to the golf balls on the bed*) Practice. (*Answering*) Yeah.

MAN: Cantrell?

CANTRELL: Here we go again. Hello?

MAN: Cantrell—I'm gonna give you one more chance. I have an assignment. It's forty thousand. Guy who's skimmed quarter of a mil in black chips over the last year. From a baccarat pit. At the Trop. And we both know that that's not in the rulebook. So...the access is nothing. No risk. Piece of cake. You take the assignment...or I call someone else and give them *two* assignments. Are we clear about what's being described here?

CANTRELL: ...Is this the guy who keeps saying, "My kingdom for a horse?"

MAN: Cantrell—what're you talking about?

CANTRELL: I'd use a six iron. (*Cantrell hangs up*)

MAN: Cantrell?!...Asshole!...All right...!

(*Blackout phone and Man's light*)

CANTRELL: (*To Chrissie*) You know what I learned this morning? In the library? I learned the following things: (1) "Methyl salicylate, occurring naturally as wintergreen oil, is the most widely used counterirritant." (2) "The right lens for a man prowling at dusk for moody pictures of wildfowl in swamps will have to be a fast one in order to provide him with enough light to make his pictures." (3)...

CHRISSIE: Stop it! I mean it—stop that shit—it scares me! You can get so fucking off the wall that it isn't funny! And it scares me. I mean—why are you telling me these things?! Why are you going to the library and learning that shit!

CANTRELL: It's interesting.

CHRISSIE: Yeah, well...

CANTRELL: I never finished school. I never went to the library. Now I'm doing both. (*Chrissie sulks*) I'm sorry if I scared you.

(*Silence. Cantrell goes to his bureau, gets a small gift wrapped box and brings it to Chrissie*)

CHRISSIE: (*In her sulking*) I don't even know why I talk to you. You are the most weird fucking man I have ever met.

CANTRELL: So how's my hand?

CHRISSIE: Your what?

CANTRELL: My hand.

CHRISSIE: It's not hour hand! Your hand's still *on* you, stupid! It's your finger.

CANTRELL: How's my finger? (*Chrissie doesn't answer*) How's my finger?

CHRISSIE: I had it outside on a rock. A dog got it. I *hate* that dog. I chased that dog for a year and finally got it. It's pretty much bone.

(*Cantrell brings the small white box out from behind his back*)

CANTRELL: Don't look that way.

CHRISSIE: What's that?

CANTRELL: Open it.

CHRISSIE: What is it?

CANTRELL: It's whatever it is. (*Chrissie takes the box, opens it, removes a gold chain, holds it up. In spite of herself, as usual, she is moved*) It's got the name of the jewelry store. On the top of the box. The guy will put the bone on…It's like Indian jewelry. It's all set up.

CHRISSIE: …I told my mother I was dating a forty-four-year-old guy who'd killed twenty-seven people and cut his finger off and given it to me. She didn't believe me. She sees that bone on this chain, she'll freak out.

CANTRELL: What's your mother do?

CHRISSIE: She's a receptionist.…J.B.'s Big Boy.

(*Cantrell walks to where he can look out and see Rupert again*)

CANTRELL: "Cedar City, Utah!"

CHRISSIE: Yeah—la-di-da! That's where we are!

CANTRELL: I wonder what ever happened to my friend, Torey Weathers. I wonder where he would be. Where he lives. If he's alive. What he's doing. If he remembers flying at the end of the carnival hose.

CHRISSIE: Would you take me somewhere?

CANTRELL: Where?

CHRISSIE: It's a great place to drive. It's by Brian Head. It's called "Cedar Breaks."

CANTRELL: "Cedar Breaks."

CHRISSIE: It's, like, this hundred-mile-high *cliff*. (*Cantrell nods. He's watching Rupert. Chrissie holds up her chain*) Thank you.

CANTRELL: Right.

CHRISSIE: Thank you, Cantrell.

(*Fade the light. Hold the light, a beat longer on Rupert, have him wheel himself out of it. Crossfade the sound of a car on the road, the car radio playing low. Crossfade that after some beats with night sounds. Fade in dim, moonish light on overlook area. And on Cantrell's car: same light. Cantrell and Chrissie are staring far out and away)*

CANTRELL: ..."Scenic Overlook."

CHRISSIE: This is so fucking cosmic!..."E.T.—Call home!" *(Chrissie laughs. Cantrell opens his door)* Where're you going?

CANTRELL: To the edge.

CHRISSIE: Wait! *(Chrissie opens her door and joins Cantrell. They walk together to the guard rail. They stand there. Chrissie is hugging Cantrell's waist. Several beats in silence)*...See that light? *(Pointing)* Hundred and thirty miles! No shit. From an oxide plant. This guy my mother saw worked there. They got so many, I heard, what-they-call *fossil fuels* in all this stuff, this place—if you *lit* them, you could lift the whole fucking planet like a rocket. Why don't you want to lay me?

CANTRELL: ...You know what I think?

CHRISSIE: Why don't you want to lay me, Cantrell?

CANTRELL: I think...that if your mind was strong enough...you could juggle yourself. ...You could just...jump over this railing here. And juggle yourself. Keep yourself in the air. And never fall. *(Cantrell makes the juggling motions with his hands)*

CHRISSIE: ...I told this girl I know...Crystal? She's almost a friend...That I had a lover. I said my lover killed people. I said he was a criminal.

CANTRELL: I'm not a criminal.

CHRISSIE: Really. Tell me about it.

CANTRELL: I'm not a criminal. Criminals are bad. I'm not a bad person.

(A beat. Chrissie stretches and kisses Cantrell on his suture)

CHRISSIE: I know.

CANTRELL: I have an entertainer's heart.

CHRISSIE: I know.

CANTRELL: Once...

CHRISSIE: ..."Once"...?

CANTRELL: *(Saying it for himself, looking straight and far out)* I have an entertainer's heart.

CHRISSIE: I can't figure you.

CANTRELL: One time...I pulled three people from a rolled-over "Z." It was on the Tonopah Highway...and I broke the back windshield with a rock. And I pulled the three people out...It was two men and a woman. Twenties. One guy was dead. The other two were alive. It was dark—like now. Raining. The one guy who was alive was saying, "It wasn't me...it wasn't me"...but his voice was...something was in the way of his voice. He wasn't conscious. The girl was out too; she wasn't saying anything. The dead guy I rolled over into a gully—he was dead. The other two...I took their clothes off to see if there were bad places that they were bleeding. On the girl, something had gone into her chest. So I ripped my shirt and did the best I could—stopping the blood. I keep a blanket in my Audi. I just keep it. I wouldn't drive without a blanket. So I wrapped the two, the guy still saying in his voice that something was in the way of, "It wasn't me," and I got them back to a truck stop south of Austin. I'm not a bad person. When I was thirteen, thumbing in California near the border, this guy who said, "I own three casinos," picked me up, then made me suck him off. He held a gun to my head. That pissed me off. It pissed me off for a lot of years. But lately—this week—it's only parts. I can remember it. I can think of it. But it's just...pieces. Pieces of what happened...at the side of the road: the guy's car—the dust...the light...his cock...my mouth...his gun. And all those pieces, even...are pieces. Like *my* instrument, now. On the towel. Like you saw. And it doesn't piss me off anymore. It's just...pieces of something... pieces of pieces...pieces of pieces of pieces all that happened when I was thirteen.

(*Cantrell takes a deep breath. He stares out*)

CHRISSIE: (*Head against his chest*) I can hear your heart beating.

CANTRELL: If you couldn't, I'd be in trouble.

CHRISSIE: It's like a drum.

CANTRELL: No—a *pump*. I read that.

CHRISSIE: Cantrell?

CANTRELL: (*Spelling*) C-A-N-T-R-E-L-L, Cantrell.

CHRISSIE: Would you kill someone who'd really done a shitty thing to me? (*Cantrell doesn't answer. Light up on Rupert, sitting on a bar stool, his wheelchair behind him, drinking at the bar*) 'Cause someone did....And he did it again. And he did it a lot. And it made me feel kind of like...puke, you know.

CANTRELL: Like a "cipher." It means: "something of no value or importance." "Zero." I learned it yesterday. It means: ...

CHRISSIE: (*Nodding agreement*) Yeah, and it scared me. And it hurt. He was one of my foster fathers. And I guess—I don't know—maybe I liked it too...a little bit. He said I did. Maybe. I don't know. Maybe I'm sick. Maybe he should've killed me or something. Once...

(The phone in Cantrell's motel room starts to ring. Dim outlining light on The Man at the phone. In the bar we see Rupert, picking up the dead soldiers of beer and hurling them, one after the other, at the bar mirror. We hear the series of shatterings in counterpoint with the phone ringing)

MAN: Okay, Bozo...! That's the way you want it: Fine!

(Fade the light on the phone. Rupert emits a bizarre animal roar in the bar)

CHRISSIE: *(Closing out whatever story she's been telling Cantrell)* So would you do it, Cantrell? Would you kill him?

CANTRELL: Angel...

CHRISSIE: Jesus Christ...Jesus Christ, Cantrell, I wish you would.

CANTRELL: Honey, I'm out of the business.

CHRISSIE: I know, but...

CANTRELL: I'm retired. I told somebody else that, earlier today. I just better not see him *do* anything.

CHRISSIE: Yeah? Well, you *might*. You just might. 'Cause he's still able to...Rupert's still able to do *a lot*. Even in a wheelchair.

CANTRELL: ..."Rupert?"

CHRISSIE: Rupert!

CANTRELL: "Rupert."

(Fade the light on Cantrell and Chrissie. We see Rupert, in the bar. He has been wheeling his chair...forward...then back. Now he starts a move that takes him, at first, just outside Cantrell's motel room, where he pauses. Then he moves into it. He waits.

Fade the light on Rupert. Music. Fade the light up on Cantrell's car. Chrissie sits beside Cantrell. She has his blanket around her, rests her head on his shoulder)

CHRISSIE: I feel safe with you, Cantrell. Like I'm okay. Like I'm not a...what was the word?

CANTRELL: "Cipher."

CHRISSIE: Yeah.

CANTRELL: I need to practice my approach shots.

CHRISSIE: It's so weird. I've never felt safe with anybody before.

CANTRELL: I used to walk out...on the Desert Inn Country Club course—five, six A.M.—when the light was like this. The dark. I didn't know why. It was just some place that felt good. Maybe I knew that I'd stop taking assignments. Maybe I knew that my life would change.

CHRISSIE: ...We're home. (*Cantrell checks beyond the windows of the car apprehensively*) We're home. Turn the car off.

CANTRELL: No.

CHRISSIE: "No." Whadda you mean?

CANTRELL: Something's wrong....Something isn't right.

CHRISSIE: Hey, I thought I was spending the night for once!

CANTRELL: The night's over!

CHRISSIE: You bastard!

CANTRELL: Never trust a hit man.

CHRISSIE: You son of a bitch! Goddamn it! I was having a fantasy about us all the way back from Cedar Breaks in the car!

CANTRELL: Look, I just said you could spend the night. I didn't say you could have a fantasy.

CHRISSIE: *You're so fucking weird*!

CANTRELL: Come on.

CHRISSIE: Where're we going?

CANTRELL: It's called a truck stop. You see the trucks? You see them stopped? The trucks are all stopped here for food. This is where they feed the trucks...while they're stopped. Sometimes they feed a car too. So that's what we're going to do. We're going to go inside...and get fed. It's time for breakfast. (*Reaching into the "back seat," producing a box*) Oh, and take this with you. Open it when you feel like opening something. Sometimes things need to be opened.

CHRISSIE: What's the matter with you?

CANTRELL: Nothing's the matter with me. I learned another word yesterday. In the library. "Intuition." I'm having an "intuition." This is Cantrell having an "intuition," that's what you're seeing here. Cantrell, stopped at a truck stop, after having had an "intuition." "God say amen!"

CHRISSIE: You need a caretaker.

CANTRELL: (*Getting out*) "Thank you, Cantrell. Thank you for the package you just gave me to open." Come on.

CHRISSIE: You need a keeper, who'll come bring food to your cage.

CANTRELL: Good. Now...up the stairs...and open the door—don't act like a "cipher"—and we'll be in the truck stop. Good. Excellent. (*They are by the café table*) Good. Now order me an omelette. (*Cantrell moves off*)

CHRISSIE: So, okay, but what kind of...?!
(*But he's gone. The phone starts ringing in Cantrell's room. Rupert watches it ring. Finally he picks it up*)
RUPERT: Yeah?...Hello?
(*We see Cantrell in a dim light at the pay phone. He hangs up. Rupert hangs up*)
CANTRELL: (*As he strides back to where Chrissie sits*)
..."Intuition"..."Intuition!"..."Intuition!"... (*Arriving*)...Tricks!
CHRISSIE: I ordered your omelette.
CANTRELL: Somebody thinks they're Einstein!
CHRISSIE: Cantrell?
CANTRELL: Somebody thinks they can teach me lessons. Well, I got my *own* school now! So...
CHRISSIE: I ordered your omelette.
CANTRELL: I hate my instrument—do you know that?!
CHRISSIE: Well, I...
CANTRELL: I hate it put together. I hate its parts. Tricks! "Intuition"! "Replica," "Rupert," "Cedar City, Utah"! Well, things own their parts...Okay?
CHRISSIE: Sure. Fine. I guess. I don't...
CANTRELL: Things own their parts.
CHRISSIE: I ordered your omelette.
CANTRELL: Good. Thank you.
CHRISSIE: You're welcome.
CANTRELL: Now, when it comes—I appreciate it—eat it. I'll be back in an hour. (*He leaves*)
CHRISSIE: (*After him*) Cantrell...?!!
(*Fade to half-light. Music. Phone ringing in Cantrell's room. Light on Cantrell at the pay phone. Rupert answers the phone*)
RUPERT: Yeah?
CANTRELL: Cantrell?
RUPERT: ...Who's calling?
CANTRELL: Cantrell?
RUPERT: Who's calling?
CANTRELL: Cantrell—it's *over* for you.
RUPERT: Hey—maybe this isn't even...!
CANTRELL: Your ass is grass. Your blood is mud. Your breath is death. (*Cantrell laughs. Silence*) God say amen!
(*Cantrell hangs up. The phone starts ringing in the bar. Cowboy behind the bar answers it*)
COWBOY: (*Across to Chrissie*) It's for you!

(*Chrissie runs across to the phone*)
CHRISSIE: ...Hello?
CANTRELL: How're you doing?
CHRISSIE: Where *are* you?
CANTRELL: How're you doing?
CHRISSIE: I finished your omelette.
CANTRELL: Good. Excellent!
(*Cantrell hangs up. He moves to the center front area, pacing, gathering himself. As Chrissie hangs up the phone, the Cowboy grabs her arm, smiles a shit-eating grin at her*)
CHRISSIE: Hey, Verl—I mean it—let go. (*He doesn't*) Let go. (*He doesn't*) I got friends. I'm a person. I'm not a cipher, so watch out. Let go of my arm. (*A beat. He lets go. Chrissie crosses back to the table*)
CANTRELL: (*Pacing*)...Okay...Okay. "Methyl Salicylate." Hello? Cantrell? Cantrell, are you listening? Stay alert! Pay attention! If someone picks up a thirteen-year-old hitchhiker and takes away some part...do you quit the carnival? Pieces! Pieces! Pay attention, Cantrell! Keep your mind on things! Someone takes away your balls...you juggle clubs. You juggle...clubs. Okay. Good work! Keep your head down! Follow through! Concentration! Don't look back! Concentration!
(*In the truck stop, we will see Chrissie opening her package, and we will see that it is a white silk scarf with fringe. Cantrell moves off to the phone with purpose. Dials. The phone rings in the motel room, Rupert snatches it up*)
RUPERT: Hello! (*No response*) Hello!! (*No response*) Okay, asshole—who *is* this?!
CANTRELL: Chrissie?
RUPERT: No—this isn't Chrissie.
CANTRELL: You're right! You're on your toes! Good. This is Cantrell. Himself. Why don't you meet me on the first tee. Of the golf course. In an hour. My room's a mess.
RUPERT: Your room's not a mess.
CANTRELL: My room's a mess. Take my word for it. There's somebody there.
RUPERT: It's me.
CANTRELL: Right. Exactly. First tee.
(*Cantrell hangs up. Fade his light. Fade Rupert's light. Light up slightly on Chrissie, sitting alone at the table in the café*)
CHRISSIE: (*Holding her fork in front of her—a microphone; she*

*feels beautiful draped in her scarf)...*And now...!...The girl you've all been waiting for...! Miss Chrissie Lane!...Singing her own rendition for you now of..."Motel Memory"! *(She moves to the juke, plays the song and gets deeply into singing along as though she were, in fact, the artist.*

*This activity should continue throughout the following golf course sequence—as a muted background: Chrissie introducing herself and then singing along with the numbers. One of the numbers, of course, should be "Stand By Your Man." In her self-introductions, Chrissie should say the following sorts of things...in no special order)...*And now...the little girl you've all been hoping to see...the girl who's come so much into her own of late...And now...the girl whose star is clearly on the rise...the girl who's rising out of obscurity and is movin' right up the charts...Here she is—the girl who's been knockin' 'em all dead in Las Vegas...And now...the little gal, who's clearly been doin' it *her* way...! Chrissie Lane! *(One one occasion)* Crystal Lane!

(Light up on Cantrell on the golf course. It is a "new" Cantrell. He wears madras pants, a golf shirt, a white visor, golf shoes. He is whistling...perhaps the song that Chrissie was singing...and practicing his shots)

CANTRELL: ...Elbow straight...elbow straight. *(We see Rupert— hairy and unruly as ever—approaching in his wheelchair. When he is close enough, Cantrell senses his approach, continues his activity without looking up, but speaks)* ...Practicing my approaches.

(Rupert takes a squared pistol from the pocket of his down vest)

RUPERT: I don't like you with my daughter, man.

CANTRELL: Loft...and backspin. Loft...and backspin. That's what they tell me. It isn't easy. *(He takes another shot, is pleased with it)*...Loft and backspin. It's coming. *(Rupert fires—a shot that goes past Cantrell. Nodding to Rupert)* Rupert. *(Cantrell smiles, picks up his seven iron and balances it on his chin)* "Ru-pert."

RUPERT: Stay...the fuck...away...from Chrissie, man.

(Cantrell hikes his chin, sends the seven iron into the air, catches it)

CANTRELL: Chrissie tells me stories.

RUPERT: Get someone else!

CANTRELL: With Chrissie's stories?

RUPERT: You had a call, Scarface. *(Rupert laughs)* When I was in your room.

CANTRELL: Right—I called *myself.* I *do* that. Sometimes I

answer. Sometimes I don't. But I think it's good. To check in. Don't you? ..."Ru-pert."

(*Rupert fires again. This time the shot grazes Cantrell's shoulder*)

RUPERT: I *hate* that name! I *hate* that name—"Rupert." I hate it!

CANTRELL: Should we play a round?...Rupe?

(*From the neon scribble at the back of the set, we see The Man begin to make a slow approach. He wears the suit and perhaps hat that we've seen him wearing when he placed his phone calls to Cantrell. Rupert fires again. This time the shot enters Cantrell's foot. Cantrell makes a sudden, involuntary sound of pain*)

RUPERT: Guy who called...guy who called just said *one* thing, man. Guy said—"One last chance." So I guess that's the fucking message. Right? You understand what I'm saying? I guess that's the fucking message of the morning—"One last chance"...for old Cantrell.

CANTRELL: Let me get that down. (*Cantrell pulls a tan leatherette notepad from his hip pocket, plucks a golf pencil from his shirt. He is smiling but at the same time wincing*) "...One...last..." What came next?

RUPERT: You're dead. I was gonna kill you, but...you are, I mean, a dead man.

CANTRELL: (*Writing on his pad*) Just a second. You're going too fast.

RUPERT: You're being *marked*. You're being *hunted*. I saw *The Godfather*. Someone's on a *strike*, Baby...for an asshole named Cantrell. They got their zoom lenses and their scopes looking for a man with a gun.

CANTRELL: Man with a...I think that's possible. I think, actually, that's very possible.

RUPERT: Yeah, and, like, very soon.

CANTRELL: How about—just nine holes then? Since time is—how do they say that?—"of the essence"? A dollar a hole. What do you say? "This is the winter of our discontent...made summer by the glorious sun of York.",...Agree? I just learned that. "A horse!...A horse!...my..." Should we get a cart, do you think? Or can we use your wheelchair? A man with a gun. Listen—let me use your wheelchair. You caddy. Disabled's just a state of mind, really—don't you think? Here—you stand. Let me sit. Nine holes. A dollar a hole. I say—we go for it.

(*Rupert smiles, starts to laugh. He pushes himself, shaking, from the chair, stands on his braces. He nods for Cantrell to sit. Cantrell sits*)

RUPERT: Now I'm you and you're me.

CANTRELL: Can you feel the grief? Feel the regret? Does it seem a terrible waste to you that you've...?

RUPERT: Hey—now I'm the dude who cools people, man. And you're the schmuck in the chair.

CANTRELL: (*His notepad again*) Excellent! Good! Let me get that down. "Now I'm the..." what was it—"dude"?

RUPERT: Yeah—I'm the *dude!* I'm the dude who wastes other people's lives.

CANTRELL: God—your mind is like *lightning!*

RUPERT: And now, baby, you're gonna know just what it feels like—to be a cripple...to be "Rupert"...'cause I'm gonna shoot both your fucking kneecaps out. And then I'm gonna leave you for whoever's...

CANTRELL: "Now I'm the dude with the gun!" *That* was what you... (*The Man, still some distance away, has lifted a gun with a silencer on it. He has fired—each shot a kind of "pop." Rupert, with a look of immense surprise on his face, jolts and falls forward over Cantrell. Chrissie is still singing and doing her own private routine in the background. The Man turns and will exit to the back. Cantrell lifts Rupert off and lays him out on the ground. He checks his notepad, reads from it*)..."One last chance." (*Cantrell looks at Rupert...nods*)..."So, the bloody dog is dead!"..."I'm you—you're me."...Cantrell is dead. Long live Cantrell..."My kingdom for a horse." "God say amen."

(*The light fades slowly on Cantrell and then slowly on Chrissie—singing along with the juke in the background. When the light comes up again, it comes up on what was the "overlook" area, upstage right. Cantrell is still in his golf clothes, still in Rupert's wheelchair. There is a police officer with him*)

OFFICER: Cantrell.

CANTRELL: Cantrell.

OFFICER: Two "l"s?

CANTRELL: Exactly. After a "c" and an "a" and an "n" and a "t" and an "r" and an "e."—two "l"s.

OFFICER: Well, if we need any more information, Mr. Cantrell, we'll call The Globe.

CANTRELL: Call the golf course. I'm giving golf my best shot.

OFFICER: (Shaking his head) ..."Random violence."

CANTRELL: Well...

OFFICER: This is not our normal circumstance—that's all I can say. We are not a town known for our random violence.

CANTRELL: Check the Shakespeare. I think maybe...

(*In the background, in Cantrell's motel room, we see Chrissie "dancing" to a slow country and western song, holding her scarf out like wings*)

OFFICER: I mean Rupert was a cruel son-of-a-bitch. Viet Nam took his head apart: we could see that. But this kind of sudden thing...in broad daylight...on a public golf course...I mean—I don't mean to say that everybody here in Cedar City is a saint. Just because it's Utah. Or because our people are LDS, most of them—you know L-D-...? (*Cantrell nods*) But this is not a place where...

CANTRELL: Listen...uh, my... (*He points to his foot*)

OFFICER: I mean, Rupert had his...do you call them "tics?"...anyway: "quirks." That was reasonably common knowledge—that he hit women.

CANTRELL: My...

OFFICER: He had this...it was like a length of tow cable. Did you ever see it? Couple of times we've had to sew up...one of the local docs...we get reports. And he burned a couple of young girls...like with matches, or car cigarette lighters, that stuff.

CANTRELL: My foot, I think, is still...

OFFICER: Almost blinded—I guess that *was* pretty bad—this foster daughter of his with a...when he was out living with...But this random violence that we've got happening around this country...and now here. It really makes me want to...I mean, I'm not forgiving Rupert for what he was—which was pretty much a kind of local monster...But we all, still knew him; he was one of us; this is the town, after all, he'd grown up in...been a pretty good tailback for two years, not a bad sixth man off the bench either in the clutch...except that, most times, he'd foul out. (*Shakes his head*) I really hate to see this kind of incident come to Cedar City.

CANTRELL: My foot's still bleeding. Could I fix it?

OFFICER: Oh...yeah...sure. I'm sorry. You told me before. I didn't...

CANTRELL: It isn't...

OFFICER: When I started the questions. That was Rupert—right?

CANTRELL: Right.

OFFICER: Just before the shots came from behind the bunker.

CANTRELL: Right.

OFFICER: Right. I should've remembered. I should've paid closer attention.

CANTRELL: It was all the random violence, I think...distracted you.

OFFICER: ...You're right.

CANTRELL: I know...but I think I've lost a lot of blood. (*Fast fade of the lights on this scene. Lights up more in the motel. Chrissie is putting her piece of jewelry around her neck—bone and all. It makes her feel strangely adult and beautiful. And those feelings confuse her. She sits on the bed. She lies on the bed. She cries there. The country and western love song that has been playing cross fades with the sound track for "Three's Company." Cantrell approaches the bed from far downstage—from the scribble of neon. His foot is bandaged*)...It wasn't me....I didn't shoot him. Someone else shot him...It was "random violence."...I thought you *wanted* him dead...Are you crying because it actually happened?

CHRISSIE: (*Into the bed*) Shut up!

CANTRELL: "Shut up, Cantrell." "You talk too much." "You put your foot in your mouth"...although it's harder these days.

CHRISSIE: (*Into the bed*) Just keep quiet!

CANTRELL: Jack Tripper just did a forward roll...over the couch. You should see it. It's very funny. (*No response*) People stop living when they die. It's amazing that it takes us as long as it takes us, sometimes—maybe I'm just speaking for myself—to realize that...Jack Tripper's a funny guy, I think—whatever his name is—not Jack Tripper but the guy who calls himself Jack Tripper in this show...He has an entertainer's heart...You should watch me—I'm juggling three naked women. (*Chrissie looks up fast from her crying*) Then I made them disappear. Great trick—huh? If I ever go back to Vegas, I'm going to do warm-up for...who?...who would be good?...Ann Margret! You like Ann Margret? You ever seen her? You want me to call her up and have her come over here? She has an entertainer's heart too. You should see her sweat when she's dancing. You look extremely pretty—wearing that. With the scarf too. You look almost as old as you were trying to be ten days ago when I first met you. You look like someone someone could live a lifetime with. What are you crying about?

(*Silence. Chrissie's taking in Cantrell's barrage*)

CHRISSIE: (*After thinking about it*) Shut up.

CANTRELL: That's good. That's original. That'll be in the library in a couple of hundred years, I'm sure.

CHRISSIE: *I'm confused*!!...I'm confused, you stupid off-the-wall asshole! *That's* why I'm crying! I'm confused!

CANTRELL: Good.

CHRISSIE: Yeah—"good." Right. Terrific.

CANTRELL: No—good. You should be. It's a confusing place.

CHRISSIE: *What's* a confusing place?!

CANTRELL: This room. This motel. This world. The television program.

CHRISSIE: You are so fucking weird!

CANTRELL: Some things never change. Be grateful.

CHRISSIE: (*Slugging him with a pillow*) I'm *mad* at you.

CANTRELL: Why's that, Doll?

CHRISSIE: I just AM! (*Chrissie hugs the pillow and starts crying into it again. Cantrell rubs her shoulders or strokes her hair. Chrissie suddenly rips the pillow from in front of her face*) BECAUSE FOR A WEEK AND A HALF I'VE WANTED YOU TO TAKE ME TO BED! I'VE REALLY WANTED IT. I'VE REALLY PLANNED ON IT. AND NOW I DON'T WANT YOU TO TAKE ME TO BED ANY MORE! BECAUSE IT'S DIFFERENT! AND IT'S JUST CONFUSING—THAT'S ALL. AND IT MAKES ME MAD!

(*Chrissie collapses again flat onto the bed. Cantrell slowly rubs her back. With the fingers of one hand, he traces the suture on his face*)

CANTRELL: ...It's just pieces....It's just pieces, honey—that's all....Some day they'll all be in the air...and you'll understand... It's just a trick that you have to do...using pieces.

(*Slow fade*)

The End

Sheila Walsh

MOLLY AND JAMES

Sheila Walsh

An actress turned playwright, Sheila Walsh makes her debut in this series with the charming character sketch, *Molly and James*, a fanciful account of James Joyce's encounter with his memorable creation—Molly Bloom. First produced by Will Lieberson in New York's Quaigh Lunch-Time Series in 1985, the production was repeated at the TOMI Theatre by the Double Image Theatre organization. Ms. Walsh's play was then presented in the Tenth Annual Off-Off Broadway Original Short Play Festival, which the Double Image Theatre also sponsors. A second short play written by Ms. Walsh, *Joanna's My Name*, was presented in the Eleventh Annual Short Play Festival in 1986.

Ms. Walsh's first full-length play, *Within the Year*, was produced Off-Off Broadway in 1984, and another play, *Absolution*, received a reading at the Circle Repertory Theatre the following year.

Born and raised in Cambridge, Massachusetts, Ms. Walsh received her college degree from Boston University. She is now a member of the Dramatists Guild.

Her most recent full-length play is entitled *Tea with Mommy and Jack*. Ms. Walsh dedicates *Molly and James* "To David."

Characters:

MOLLY BLOOM, *early thirties, Irish, healthy good looks*
JAMES JOYCE, *thirty, Irish, slender*

Setting:

We're in the bedroom of Molly Bloom in Dublin, Ireland. It seems as if flowers are everywhere. Flowers on the wallpaper. A flowered spread covering the brass bed. Fresh flowers on the vanity table and washstand and flowers on the mahogany chest. A chair and stool are near the vanity. A tall window with lace curtains is at the rear of the room. The entrance to the bedroom is stage left.

At Curtain:

It's a hot evening in August, 1912. The light from the window is catching that very moment day slips into night. The door opens; a man's face pops in. It's James Joyce. He closes the door gently, crosses to the vanity and examines the jars of creams. He writes in his notebook as he roams the room. As he crosses to the washstand to feel the water, we hear Molly's vibrant voice.

MOLLY: *(Offstage)* I have enough to do. *(James panics and crawls under the bed. Molly enters and leans her hips against the door)* I can keep myself occupied. Just try not to lose. Bad luck arse. Toodle-oo. *(She closes the door, rushes to the window and pulls the curtain aside)* Bye-bye. (What good do you do me when you're here?) Bye. (Stink up the place with your smelly tobacco. Hide behind papers with your BIG THOUGHTS!) Good-bye! *(She pulls the curtain closed, crosses to the bed and flops down into it)* DAMN!...Not fair!...It's not fair! *(She moves from the bed, takes off her blouse and flings it onto the chair)* No need to get at a loss. By no means found with himself around. Being wed to a man is like living a half-baked life if you ask me. *(She crosses to the vanity table)* Well, it's not fair. Him free to go—me stuck the prisoner here...Ack, look at the lines! Now come Molly, not nearly as bad as most. You've been blessed with the looks. Fine lot he notices.

Might as well be married to a blind man. Wonder what that would be like. (*She closes her eyes and fumbles with the jars on the table*) Keen sense of the touch I bet. (*She opens a jar and creams her neck*) Sure this is considered a sin. All the good feels are sins. But which sin? Doesn't cost much. No real abuse there. Does no one harm. No one even knows. So which one?...Ack, got it! The sin of pride! The big one! Made the angels fall so they say. Well, what would they have me do? Walk around oblivious to my obvious advantages? Not my fault I was given more than most. Fault's in a barbaric law saying I'm not to share it with none other than my husband. (*She creams her arms*) Well, what if the husband long ago lost that desire? Abandoned to the higher cause of morals and politics...Lame excuse if you ask me for them that no longer get it up. Lack of the imagination. Ay, that's what it takes after the first few times. Imagination! (*She creams her breasts*) What's a higher cause than pleasure? Answer me that. Should have been a priest, the lot he cares for these. And him telling me my point of view don't count. (*She senses "something"...pauses for a moment, decides there is nothing, continues her creaming*) Himself saying pleasure's a minor pursuit. "Proof: Pleasure doesn't last." Well, what does? But the sea, sky, the things of Nature. Ack, that's the really tragedy. All of my wonder won't last, and him so dumb it goes to waste in the here and now. You want your social injustices to rant and rave about? Well, this is one for you! The waste of me! (*She examines her face*) Wonder what pack of lies I'll be telling the face when I'm sixty? "Go on girl, you're not nearly as shrivelled as the rest of them." (*Convinced there is someone in the room, she puts on her night-shawl and picks up the mirror*) Good thing Sally plans on visiting me any moment with that big lug of a husband, Gerald. He could have been a professional boxer with those hands of his. (*She opens the door, then pulls up the bed covers*) All right you weasel, crawl from under.

JAMES: (*From under the bed*) I can explain.

MOLLY: And you will, to the bobbies.

JAMES: I seem to be stuck. (*He struggles to get up*)

MOLLY: What kind of a robber are you? Stuck.

JAMES: I'm no robber. I assure you. Here, take the bottle. We don't want it broken.

MOLLY: Not altogether stupid. (*She takes his whiskey bottle*)

JAMES: Could you give a pull?

MOLLY: Why should I?

JAMES: Yes, indeed. Good question. You shouldn't.

MOLLY: Think you're pulling the wool over my eyes with your agreeing? I know your type. Square is filled with you "Yes" men. Give me your hand. I can't stand seeing anyone crushed down.

JAMES: Thank you.

MOLLY: (*She pulls him from under the bed*) Remember, this strong arm can just as easily defend itself.

JAMES: I'm not here to do you harm. Please believe me. (*He brushes his clothes and adjusts his hat and eyeglasses*)

MOLLY: You think it's helpful trespassing and scaring a woman? Do you? You think it's fit amusement? What will you sit with your mates playing the funny one? Hahahaing into the night? Well, I'm no man's joke, mind you.

JAMES: You have every right to be angry with me.

MOLLY: Well, thank you, sir. Dumb that I am, I need you to tell me how I feel. Go on with you before I blue your arse like your mother forgot to do.

JAMES: You're exactly as I knew you'd be.

MOLLY: None of your lip. Move on, laddy.

JAMES: You're absolutely right. Please keep the bottle. I apologize for my lack of consideration. How foolish to think I could slip under your bed and actually be welcomed. It sounds ridiculous even to me. (*He giggles lightly, then grows serious*) My truth is, I was driven to know you.

MOLLY: Are you one of the nut-nuts from the asylum? Mother of God, Preserve us!

JAMES: No, Molly.

MOLLY: First name basis. Rude on top of all your other faults.

JAMES: Mrs. Bloom, my name is James. James Joyce. I'm a writer.

MOLLY: So?

JAMES: Of course, "So?" Do you think...a drink? It would help to help me explain.

MOLLY: I'm not interested in your explaining. I just want you out. I don't appreciate the intrusion. I'll keep the bottle. I earned it with me horrors.

JAMES: Out of desperation I came here tonight.

MOLLY: The door's to the right, Mister...

JAMES: I need you.

MOLLY: And don't slam it.

JAMES: I'll stop time for you. All your beauty, I'll chisel into clay of words. As you are now, Mrs. Bloom, I'll make you for eternity.

MOLLY: What goo are you slurping out?

JAMES: I want to write about you.

MOLLY: You mean you want to use me.

JAMES: I don't see it that way.

MOLLY: Sure, why should you? It wouldn't help you any. Why should you see it any other way but your own?

JAMES: Are you suggesting I want to profit from you?

MOLLY: What else? I don't know you. Don't want to know you. Have no need to know you. You come here...If I weren't the type of woman I am, do you know what a fright hiding under the bed could bring? Do you?

JAMES: I didn't think about it.

MOLLY: That's right. Now if that's not using me for your own ends, what is it?

JAMES: Good question.

MOLLY: Stop telling me that. I don't need you to tell me what comes out of my mouth is good or not good. (*She crosses and puts away her dress and blouse*)

JAMES: Remarkable! (*He gives a deep sigh of pleasure*) May I ask you something?

MOLLY: What?

JAMES: Have you ever desired anything passionately? Of course you have.

MOLLY: What are you asking me questions then answering my mind? What's your point, Mister?

JAMES: What's my point? Good ques...

MOLLY: Aaa...(*She shakes her finger in protest*)

JAMES: You win. Excuse me?

MOLLY: You're excused. (*She smiles*) It's no fun drinking alone. You still want that wee drink?

JAMES: If you'd be so kind.

MOLLY: (*Motions for him to move a chair to the vanity. She pours the whiskey into "short" glasses*) Had a few tastes this evening. This will be in keeping. You know, I have artistic talents, too. Not with the words on a page, but I've been known to hit many a good note.

JAMES: Would you please sing for me?

MOLLY: Go on with yourself. I'm no nightingale for strangers. (*She puts the glass down. He moves the glass slightly away from himself*) A wee bit of the superstitious?

JAMES: A wee bit.

MOLLY: (*Puts her glass down and, like James, she moves her glass. Then they raise their glasses*) Sláinte.

JAMES: Sláinte. (*They drink the whiskey with one swallow*)

MOLLY: Once I got a hundred roses. Wild! Picked from the woods...not store bought, but roses none the less...(*She closes the door*)

JAMES: Yes?

MOLLY: From a boy of nineteen. He heard me sing. He watched me sing. He gave me roses. Ah, what pleasure knowing one brings pleasure!

JAMES: I'd be honored if you'd sing.

MOLLY: You think because we share this drink, all's forgiven? You've still to tell the nature of your visit. (*She laughs*) It really is a howl come to think of it. Hiding under the bed! Grand whiskey we're drinking.

JAMES: I'm so pleased you're enjoying it. See, I have an idea for a book, Mrs. Bloom.

MOLLY: Molly, for heaven's sake. Make me feel like a crone with that Mrs.

JAMES: Thank you. Molly.

MOLLY: You're an odd combination. Courage to hide under me bed and the other side filled with apologies. Odd combination indeed. For a man, that is. So go on about the book. Another wee taste?

JAMES: Please. (*Again the ritual of pouring the drinks, placing the glasses down, moving them slightly, then raising the glass to toast*)

MOLLY: (*Sings*) "C'ead M'ile Failte, C'ead M'ile Failte, C'ead M'ile Failte."

JAMES: Lovely.

MOLLY: One hundred thousand welcomes! To your mind, your body, to your soul.

JAMES: Thank you. Thank you. Thank you.

MOLLY: "C'ead M'ile Failte." There's a tale it's the angels' language. Now, what of the book?

JAMES: What book?

MOLLY: Ack, you've got some mind for a writer. Your book. (*They laugh*)

JAMES: Oh yes, my book! There will be a part in my book?

...How do I explain?

MOLLY: You open your mouth and say your truth. I'm no dumbbell. You can talk to me, like you talk to anyone...like you talk to your mates. You don't have to change your talk for me. I can understand. I'm listening, James.

JAMES: Yes indeed. I want to write about a woman like you.

MOLLY: Like me? I'm me. There are no like me's.

JAMES: So right. I stand corrected. I want to write about you.

MOLLY: For what purpose need you come to my bedroom?

JAMES: The purpose of accuracy.

MOLLY: Close your eyes then. Quick! (*James closes his eyes*) Describe the room. What objects in your recall? What have your eyes seen?

JAMES: A garden of flowers!...Flowers everywhere...drenched, clinging, falling...to walls, covering bed, petalling table tops. Brass bed shined newly, detected by sojourn under Molly's spread. Rug—fringed...plucked from foreign soil...blotched with oil, dust and heel. Old mahogany...nicked, chipped, flowered...holding, sagging, leaning into leaves of wall. And washstand all pink, pinky, pinkiest of coral...cold, ocean coral...holds basin with flowers in warm, worn water. Plump jars...finger spotted...line vanity swept in night's fading shadows...emptying creams...round, mushroomed, glazed...squat by silver monogrammed brush... silver monogrammed comb...as weaves of Molly's hair cling to bristles...clutch to teeth. Stump of stool sitting angled west...near cane of chair warmed by sweet, smelling dress...stand opposite entrance to Molly's room.

MOLLY: Your mouth really runs on, doesn't it, James? But you've got the gift of observation. That's clear. Well, why not Carmel, the real beauty down the road? Why not hide in her bedroom? Write of her?

JAMES: She wouldn't do for my story.

MOLLY: If she wouldn't do, and you know I would, you must know me. If you know me, why hide under my bed? Answer me that. Another?

JAMES: Yes, please. (*Again the pouring and moving of the glass*)

JAMES AND MOLLY: SLÁINTE!

JAMES: Until I saw you...(*He removes his glasses and rubs his eyes*)

MOLLY: A speck of dirt in the eye?

JAMES: Nothing. Nothing.

MOLLY: No need to get on your high and mighty. I was asking out of courtesy.

JAMES: Forgive me. (*Molly gestures for him to continue*) What was it?...

MOLLY: The why of writing me. You can paint the whole room from your mind and not remember a second ago sentence! Why me and not Carmel was the topic.

JAMES: Yes...until I saw you, you were in my imagination like...What it must feel like to have a baby in the womb. Felt. Alive. Yet not known.

MOLLY: I understand. I know that mysterious feeling of the womb...Once alive...Your way of expressing yourself suits me fine.

JAMES: So follow.

MOLLY: I'll thank you not to tell me what I'm to do. (*He smiles*) And just because you've got a clever grin doesn't mean you've won me, James. My days of being won by merely a grin are long gone. (*They smile the smile of understanding...this "two-of-a-kind"*)

JAMES: May I continue?

MOLLY: Yes, you may.

JAMES: It was as if out of nowhere, you appeared...(*He takes out a notepad*) I was approximately twenty feet away that first time. Here we are...August 12th.

MOLLY: 12th of August?...St. Clair's feast day. She's the patron saint of sore eyes. So what did you say?

JAMES: (*Reads*) Woman medium height.

MOLLY: If you're referring to me, I'm taller than most.

JAMES: Walks, struts, swirls, this woman of warm, brown hair... First impression—she walks in freedom of her body.

MOLLY: You got me there. Go on.

JAMES: Fine breezy day with wind moving northeast at fifteen miles, rustles hair. She—pauses...as if water rushing down hair... plays head inside wind.

MOLLY: Make me sound like a masterpiece. Probably on my daily stroll, nothing more. What was I wearing? You got that?

JAMES: Dress of sky blue, speckled with dots. Doesn't she know? Petticoat swooning beneath swaying blue skirt? (*They exchange a "look"*) She knows. Shawl of gray slipping slightly off shoulder...far from finest...shawl of wool. Right shoulder dips three-quarters of inch. Neck four inches of unlined skin.

MOLLY: Couldn't you say something like I've got white swan skin? I think that sounds...

JAMES: Sh! Her face!...Eight inches from forehead to chin of pink, ripeness shining. Sea-colored eyes lead to high chiselled cheeks holding full pouting lips.

MOLLY: Ack, that's nice. And what of these? (*She waves her hands*)

JAMES: Gloved in ink, puddled, bruised of a blue...she's gloved.

MOLLY: And these! (*She kicks up her feet*)

JAMES: Moves her black boots...her old kept new boots... moving her blue, white, gray into the wind...moving, moving, my mountain woman of pleasure moving.

MOLLY: (*Interrupting*) What day was that?

JAMES: August 12th.

MOLLY: You got the dress and all. That was me all right. But I don't like the conversation about the shawl. Not the best wool! Cheeky lad! What, did you follow me about?

JAMES: No. I made my notes. Thought nothing more of that first time. Planned on combining you with a number of other women.

MOLLY: Part of a recipe, you mean?

JAMES: Correct.

MOLLY: And me? I hope the cream!

JAMES: ...Yes indeed.

MOLLY: Who else you throw into the pot? Any I know?

JAMES: That's just it. I can't match any with you. I had to find out your name...I found out your name.

MOLLY: How?

JAMES: The butcher.

MOLLY: No man's to be trusted.

JAMES: Listen! Please. (*He reads*) August 21st. That's my next entry...Cannot complete character sketch of female. Must find subject from 12th of month. Examine her regarding how she speaks, her likes, dislikes. What are her dreams? Her passions? Her fears?...It didn't take long to realize the most likely place to inquire of you would be the butcher.

MOLLY: So posthaste to himself.

JAMES: Not so fast. First, how do I inquire without seeming out of place?

MOLLY: Respectability enters its head.

JAMES: For both our parts.

MOLLY: What a nice gentleman. Thoughtful you are. So you go

to the butcher. Mr. Buckley or his quirky brother, Tim?

JAMES: Mr. Buckley.

MOLLY: Good. He's the good one. Not all foaming at the mouth like Tim. Fishmonger that one. Nothing more pleasurable than spreading some hard luck about another. People are that way, you know. All kinds of ways, people. So what tall tale did you tell Mr. Buckley?

JAMES: I decided the most appropriate way was to suggest I needed to return something.

MOLLY: You think he'd fall for that?

JAMES: He did.

MOLLY: How some men stay in business!

JAMES: He gave me your name straight off. Told me your address in the same breath.

MOLLY: I like that! So what next?

JAMES: I began knowing you.

MOLLY: How do you mean? In what sense of the word? What are you talking? I'm getting uncleared.

JAMES: I started passing your home.

MOLLY: I saw you last week on a bicycle, didn't I? I was out in the yard with the wash.

JAMES: Yes.

MOLLY: You turned and looked. Almost went into the ditch. Made me feel good for an instant…the attention.

JAMES: Good.

MOLLY: For an instant. Wasn't like you changed my whole life. I didn't think anything of you. Knew there was a group over from America. The cut of your coat told me you were a stranger.

JAMES: I've been living abroad.

MOLLY: Have you been to Paris?

JAMES: I have.

MOLLY: Is it true the women drive automobiles there?

JAMES: Some.

MOLLY: Lovely! Do you have any of those picture postcards? The ones that show the women off?

JAMES: No I don't. I've seen them though.

MOLLY: And do the women drink in public and flirt as they please?

JAMES: Some do.

MOLLY: Isn't that grand! Then Ireland can't be far behind. (*Molly and James laugh*) Your talk, why even your laughter, has our ring to it.

JAMES: I'm born from here. I've returned...to publish a book.

MOLLY: Well wishes with your ventures.

JAMES: Thank you. Now do you understand why I came here, to your bedroom? I needed to hear you speak.

MOLLY: I do have a way with words all right. Least I think so, and I've been told by more than a few. Bloom, the husband, doesn't like the flow. Him and his world of men's mutterings! You might find him a curious sort, being such a curious sort yourself.

JAMES: First you, then perhaps...what's his first name?

MOLLY: Leopold. That's L-E-O...Ack, you being a writer must know how to spell. (*James jots down the name. Molly pours herself a drink*) The sound of my words not educated enough for his grand ears! Isn't it a sorrow? A pity? A lament? So many marry the very person who doesn't like the sound of their words.

JAMES: A real sorrow.

MOLLY: What do you know of sorrow? You a man. I'm not so easily won, Mr. Writer. Don't think your needs become my needs. I've served well enough the needs of others. I've been a wife and mother. Why would I want you to write of me? For why? What need have I?

JAMES: To hear your song sung.

MOLLY: It's your song they'll be hearing. Not mine. You'll take what you can use, reshape whatever idea your head has of me. I hear already my words. You'll bend, twist, force till they come out the rhythm of Mr. Joyce—not the rhythm of mine.

JAMES: You have every right to be suspect of me.

MOLLY: You smell like a priest. Anyone ever tell you that?

JAMES: No.

MOLLY: All you men of the creative bent...distorters! Once a fellow painted me...rotten end. When I accused him of missing me in his picture, he claimed he was doing an impression. Well, what did he need me sitting under the sun for hours and days, boiling the head like a turnip, if it wasn't me, only the impression he needed?

JAMES: That's precisely why I came. I want to write you as you are, not as I think you might be.

MOLLY: You feel this brief visit on this one summer's eve will tell you who I am? Why what kind of a woman do you take me for? Even the moon changes from night to night.

JAMES: I'm trying to capture the very breath of you.

MOLLY: Even the breath of me changes...Why the sad face,

James Joyce?

JAMES: I'm caught in your web. Wanting you and only you, and I'm afraid I won't get you.

MOLLY: For your writings you want me?

JAMES: Yes of course. Why else?

MOLLY: I'm a little too beneath your starched shirt?

JAMES: *(Confused)* What?

MOLLY: Forget it. You priest-smelling men are all the same... You don't know the nature of joy, so you've come to me?

JAMES: Yes.

MOLLY: For it's joy I know about...not paper-thin feelings like pleasant, nice, comfortable. Angels sing about it...such a rare thing, this joy I know about.

JAMES: Yes.

MOLLY: And why should I tell of such joy to you? Why? What's in it for me?

JAMES: Didn't I overhear your sadness that your beauty won't last? Let me write your story. Molly, your wonders will last for as long as men read.

MOLLY: You're full of your importance as a writer, aren't you?

JAMES: Yes!

MOLLY: What good is it gonna do me, some reader I'll never know, reading of me? What good indeed when I'm gone?

JAMES: I'm telling you, Molly, you'll never go. I'll count the strands of hair on your head and write of them one by one, and as long as the sea, as long as the sky, that's how long you'll be Molly!

MOLLY: Dribble! You're offering me dribble.

JAMES: Dublin is filled with women who would want me to write of them.

MOLLY: But you want me? Isn't that so, Mr. Joyce?

JAMES: Yes, I want you.

MOLLY: All the compliments in my life, and believe me, James, there's been plenty...all the compliments got me nowhere. Vain idolatry is not enough. *(She brushes her hair)* Some of the same things have to be gained by me as you will gain.

JAMES: Such as?

MOLLY: Money.

JAMES: That's impossible.

MOLLY: No, it's not.

JAMES: You're turning this act...this act of poetry into a business venture?

MOLLY: That's correct. How about another taste? (*James nods "no"*)... She pours herself a drink.

JAMES: I don't know what to say. I wasn't expecting this. I thought possibly you might not want me to write of you, but this...

MOLLY: Full of surprises, aren't I?

JAMES: It's not money that moves me to write.

MOLLY: I told you, your needs are not mine.

JAMES: What about the truth? Art? Creativity?

MOLLY: Don't waste your wind. My mind won't change.

JAMES: I don't know if the book will sell. I'm a poor man.

MOLLY: I'll take a promissory note. With me in it, it's bound to sell.

JAMES: What makes you think a promissory note signed by me would hold up?

MOLLY: (*Sits at the vanity and writes*) Mr. Buckley, the butcher? ...a dear, a close, a very close friend of mine. I'm writing here how you're the same man who inquired of him about me. Tomorrow, I'll have him witness and sign it. It will hold up. Mr. Buckley's cousin, Paddy McQuire, the bailiff? ...another dear, close friend of mine.

JAMES: How can such a pretty woman even think this way?

MOLLY: Let me tell you, James, when pretty is your currency, you take precautions, for pretty leaves.

JAMES: I find this whole discussion not conducive for writing.

MOLLY: You're not writing now. You're discussing a few minor alterations to enable you to write.

JAMES: I'm known as a fair man.

MOLLY: A virtue of mine also—fairness.

JAMES: Well, what do you consider fair?

MOLLY: What part of the book do you think I'll comprise?

JAMES: Offhand, I'd say less than ten percent.

MOLLY: Then that's my worth. Ten percent! Book would be better with more of me in it.

JAMES: Ten percent of what?

MOLLY: Of every amount you make on the book. I get ten percent.

JAMES: NO! I find that exorbitant! Greedy! Unladylike!

MOLLY: Too bad.

JAMES: It's unbefitting this bargaining from you. It has no place in my book on this woman of pleasure.

MOLLY: And how am I to purchase my pleasures? They're

getting more and more expensive every day, my pleasures.

JAMES: I can't believe I was so wrong about you. What a regrettable end.

MOLLY: Now no need to break your heart, Jamie boy.

JAMES: Should I go out the back?

MOLLY: Walk out the front! Give them something to talk about coming home from Mass. (*She extends her hand*)

JAMES: (*He hesitates, then shakes i*t) It was a pleasure.

MOLLY: That's what they've all said. (*They smile. James exits. Molly closes the door*) What a sad squash of a man, but he gives grand whiskey. (*She has a quick drink. She hums and brushes her hair*)

JAMES: (*Enters*) I was thinking, Molly…ten percent seems fair.

MOLLY: Ack, good, I'm happy.

JAMES: You are?

MOLLY: Yes! See, I've always had a superstition someone would write my story. As well you as another! Sit at the table. We'll have to work fast before Bloom comes home. You're to write, no leaving to your mind to remember. I want none of your impressions.

JAMES: As you wish. (*He sits at the vanity table*)

MOLLY: If you distort, I'm warning you, James…

JAMES: I promise Molly, I'll tell it your way.

MOLLY: Good. That's a good lad. Another?

JAMES: Not while I'm writing.

MOLLY: Me? I've always liked that little extra something to drink when I wander into the territory the Church warns against.

JAMES: What territory be that, Molly?

MOLLY: Where a man and a woman find pleasure in one another. (*James watches as she fluffs herself up on the bed*) Ah, James, wait till I tell you about the rhododendrons, and him in his tweed, and how he tilted his hat! You'll love that part. But first… Once upon a time I said, "Yes"… (*The lights fade*) "Yes because he never did a thing like that before as ask to get his breakfast in bed with a couple of eggs…"

The End

Hugh Leonard

PIZZAZZ

Hugh Leonard

Well known in this country for his 1978 Tony Award-winning Broadway play, *Da*, Dublin-born and educated at Presentation College, Hugh Leonard has an impressive career writing for theater, films, and television. With *Pizzazz*, Mr. Leonard makes his debut in *Best Short Plays*. Regarding this play, first performed at the Dublin Theatre Festival, the playwright reports, *"Pizzazz* was originally the second half of an evening of short plays each with a twist in the tail. I had always wanted to created a Chinese box in dramatic form: a toy that is simple to look at but drives one to near madness when played with. And I utilised one of my favourite places in Ireland: the River Shannon, at the northern end of the most beautiful of its lakes: Lough Derg...To judge by the reviews, it put its two accompanying one-acters to shame, and now I am trying to write a worthy companion piece for a production in London's West End. Until that happens, I have half a smash hit."

Other plays by Mr. Leonard include: *The Poker Session, The Au Pair Man, The Patrick Pearse Motel, Time Was,* and *Summer.* His latest stage play, *The Mask of Moriarty,* played in London's West End in June, 1987. From 1976 to 1977 he served as Literary Editor of the Abbey Theatre in Dublin and has been Director of the Dublin Theatre Festival.

His screenplays include: *Great Catherine, Interlude* and *Da,* based on his stage play, produced as a film in 1986. Mr. Leonard's television credits are extensive. Among his television adaptations are: *Wuthering Heights, Father Brown, The Moonstone, London Belongs to Me, Strumpet City,* and three Dickens' adaptations, *Great Expectations, Dombey and Son,* and *Nicholas Nickleby.* Other dramatizations by Mr. Leonard include works by Saki, Maupassant, Simenon, W. Somerset Maugham, as well as Granada's *Country Matters.* Mr. Leonard's television play *Silent Song* won the Italia Prize.

More recently Mr. Leonard dramatized Molly Kean's *Good Behaviour* in three parts for BBC Television and contributed to England's Channel Four's acclaimed series, *The Irish R.M.* He has continued his association with James Mitchell, the producer of that series, by writing scripts for a four-part series based on J.G. Farrell's novel, *Troubles.*

In 1979 Mr. Leonard published the first part of his autobiography, *Home Before Night.*

Characters:

MARION
OLIVIA
ROONEY
CONROY
MRS. HAND

Scene:

A reception area. Afternoon.
    The Royal Brosna Line is one of the companies which hire
out cabin cruisers on the River Shannon. The reception area is
a bright, functional room with a small desk, a sofa and chairs
covered in matching patterns of green and saffron, and tables
on which there are brochures and boating magazines. On the
walls there are plans and elevation drawings of various types of
hire craft. Most prominent is a large simplified map of the
Shannon showing channels and markers. In a corner of the
room the holiday baggage of two people is heaped up. There
are two doors, one behind the desk, marked "Private," and another, the main entrance, alongside which runs a jetty. Mooring
rings and cleats are visible along the length of the jetty.

At Curtain:

    Marion is seen at the end of the jetty. She is American: mid-
dle-aged, vivacious, curious, boundlessly energetic. She is
dressed in chic yachting clothes, including slacks, a blue windcheater with red lining and inflatable pockets, and a trim
yachting cap. She is looking out across the lake.
    There are two people in the reception area. One, behind the
desk, is the dispatcher, Fergal Rooney, a young man who radi-
ates lack of enthusiasm for anything in sight. He is reading a
newspaper, his lips moving as he does so. The other person is
Olivia Gaynor. She, like Marion, is dressed in boating gear, but
with less emphasis on seeming the Compleat Yachtswoman. She
is in her mid-thirties, attractive, capable. She is leafing through
brochures with the air of one who has unwanted time on her
hands.

There is the sound of a cruiser's diesel engine. Marion waves energetically.

MARION: *(Calling)* Hi, there...hello. I mean, ahoy...avast or something. *(In the manner of a New York telephonist)* Come in, Number Fi-ev, your ti-em is up!

(There is no response from the crew of the unseen cruiser. The engine noise fades as the vessel moves further out. Shrugging) So be like that, see if I care. *(Shouting)* Bon voyage, Titanic! *(She walks back to the reception area as if the jetty were a walkway for a parade of fashion models. Lilting)*

"A pretty girl is like a melody

That haunts you night and day..."

(Entering the reception area, to Olivia) It beats me. They just keep going round in circles out there as if they were looking for a body. And all the time clockwise...why is that? *(To Rooney)* Is it a union rule of some kind? Sir?

ROONEY: Pardon me?

MARION: Those boats of yours...the six boats?

ROONEY: Cruisers.

MARION: Thank you. They keep going in a clockwise direction. If viewed from above. If you were in the lake and drowning—looking up, I mean—it would be anticlockwise. Is there a reason for that?

ROONEY: Don't ask me.

MARION: I thought I *had* asked. *(To Olivia)* How's about it, Olly...you want to play some more Scrabble?

OLIVIA: No, thanks. You always win.

MARION: I *play* to win. Tell you what I'll do. I'll give you the J, the X and the Z and throw in a blank. It's verbal suicide, but they don't call me Last Chance Lola for nothing. Penny a point?

OLIVIA: Will you promise to use English spelling instead of American?

MARION: Never!

OLIVIA: Then no.

MARION: *(Echoing)* No. It's idiotic. "Harbour"...h-a-r-b-o-u-r. Why do you people take a perfectly simple word and stick a "u" in it?

OLIVIA: We didn't stick it in. It was already there, and you people threw it out.

MARION: Americans believe in simplicity of language.

OLIVIA: I know. Like "faucet" for "tap" and "elevator" for "lift."

MARION: I could order you to play Scrabble. As my employee. (*Olivia gives her a steady unintimidated look. Wheedling*) So how's about a little backgammon? Two-handed bridge? Five-card stud? Pinochle? Craps?

OLIVIA: Gin rummy?

MARION: You got it. (*She tears her windcheater off and finds a pack of cards in her bag. To Rooney*) Sir, do we have time for a little gin? Young sir?

ROONEY: (*Without looking up*) I'm not here. Drink away.

MARION: Pour. Make a note of that, Olly. East Galway colloquialism for to deal or distribute. Cut for drink. (*They cut the cards*) Mine...oh, goody. Tell you what we're going to do to make it interesting. While we play, you tell me your life story. The works.

OLIVIA: You got that out of me the first day I came to you. Three years ago.

MARION: So give me the three years. Come on, Olly, be a pal and dish the dirt...we could be stuck here all day. (*To Rooney, who does not react*) Right? Right. You think those are just boats... cruisers out there? They are Flying Dutchmen, doomed to sail in small circles for eternity. They are never coming in. So give me a break. Who are you laying? What's his name? Is his wife pretty?

OLIVIA: Marion, you are the most inquisitive...(*She breaks off as G.P. Conroy arrives. He is a professional man of Marion's age: Irish, probably more attractive now than when he was younger. He is dressed in well-cut casual clothes. Marion looks at him with immediate interest*)

MARION: Whoops.

OLIVIA: Your play. Marion?

MARION: Down, girl. There are more exciting things in life even than gin rummy.

(*Conroy stands at the desk waiting for Rooney to take notice of him. He coughs. Rooney continues to read his paper*)

CONROY: Are you in charge here?

(*Rooney looks up*)

MARION: Pardon me, but...

CONROY: Do you mind? I was here first.

MARION: You want to bet?

CONROY: (*To Rooney*) I asked if you're the person in charge.

ROONEY: Yis.

CONROY: Is it possible to hire a boat?

MARION: (*Helpfully*) A cruiser.

CONROY: (*Ignoring her*) I mean, today.

ROONEY: It might be.

CONROY: Well, is it possible or isn't it? (*As Rooney looks at him*) When you've quite finished counting both my heads and arrive at a total, might I have an answer?

ROONEY: There's industrial action.

CONROY: Do you mean a strike? You're telling me that I cannot have a...(*Aware that Marion is listening*)...vessel?

ROONEY: I'm saying nothing, but ye might if ye wait.

CONROY: For how long? (*Ranting*) Christ, what a country. It has precisely two of everything. One is the wrong size, and the other one is due in on Wednesday.

MARION: Careful...blood pressure.

CONROY: Madam, I happen to be a doctor.

MARION: Gravediggers also die.

CONROY: (*To Rooney*) I asked you, for how long?

MARION: He's not here.

CONROY: What?

(*She takes his arm and leads him to the door*)

MARION: Doc, allow me. You see those white cruisers out there? Circling? Well...(*As he turns back to Rooney*) No, you stick with me, it'll save time. It seems that today all over this beautiful country of yours—and of mine by adoption—there are marches protesting against the level of unemployment. It seems that when your people complain about having no work to do, they mark the occasion by doing no work. Well, those cruisers are protesting.

CONROY: (*Pointing*) *That* is a protest march?

MARION: Give the man a cigar.

CONROY: Good God.

MARION: And just as soon as they quit marching in Dublin and points west, that phone will ring and we'll get our cruisers. Until then, I guess we're all in the same...(*Catching herself in time*) Oh boy. (*Now that Conroy has his information, he walk away from her brusquely. Murmuring*) "Why, thank you, kind lady, for your assistance." "Think nothing of it, sir, have a nice day."

CONROY: Bloody incredible. (*To Olivia*) Are you affected by this walk on water?

OLIVIA: Afraid so. We've been waiting these two hours.

CONROY: An Irish accent...praise be. There seems to be nothing in this wilderness excepted damn Germans and (*Lowering his voice*) bloody Americans. (*Glowering at Rooney*) Deplorable state of affairs. It's this sort of bolshie attitude towards visitors that's ruining the tourist industry.

OLIVIA: (*Politely*) Isn't it!

CONROY: Tell me...it's my first time for hiring one of these... (*Deliberately*) boats. Are there cooking facilities?

OLIVIA: Oh, yes. I mugged up on it: there's a cooker on board with an oven and gas rings.

CONROY: Good. Thank you.

OLIVIA: The Shannon is such a beautiful river. And you can just meander along at your own pace.

CONROY: No doubt. Well, I don't intend to meander anywhere. I'm going to be right here, attached to this quay.

(*Marion, listening, is keenly interested*)

OLIVIA: In a cruiser?

CONROY: That *is* permitted?

OLIVIA: I assume so. But...(*It is none of her business, she lets it go*)

MARION: (*Drifting past; sotto*) Ask him why.

CONROY: From here I do not move.

OLIVIA: It is a pretty spot, isn't it?

(*Marion throws her eyes up. Conroy is so white-hot with anger, however, that a question is unnecesssary*)

CONROY: My entire holiday is in fritters. My wife and I...

MARION: Oh.

CONROY: ...Saw a six-column-inch hotel advertisement, personal page of the *Irish Times*, no less. An oasis of calm; friendly, willing staff; all mod cons; superlative cuisine; relax and be pampered in de luxe tranquility.

MARION: (*Sympathetic*) Uh-oh.

CONROY: I suppose the hotel *was* an oasis, if that means a watering hole where the local animal life gathers at nightfall to drink and enshrine their patriot dead until dawn in ballad and bedlam. As for the staff, as far as willingness was concerned they were intestate. The all mod cons included a toilet that was unflushable and a hot water tap that haemorrhaged a cold viscous brown slime. As for the superlative cuisine, we should have known what lay ahead when I asked the waitress if the tomato soup was tinned and she said...

MARION: Tinned?

OLIVIA: He means canned.

CONROY: If it was tinned, and she assured us that no, it was thick. After that repast, my wife has been vomiting all night, and today she is in such a demoralized condition that either we return home or go where we can do our own cooking. So here I am.

MARION: You poor lambs.

CONROY: It's iniquitous. To serve food in this day and age that is uneatable is...

MARION: Unspeakable.

OLIVIA: You should try one of those self-catering cottages down the way. They're supposed to be...

MARION: Olly, hush up. Let's not lose him.

OLIVIA: Lose him? Marion, you wouldn't.

CONROY: Wouldn't what? *(To Olivia)* Is she with you?

MARION: Olly—Miss Olivia Gaynor—is my dear friend, confidante and indispensable personal assistant.

CONROY: Oh?

OLIVIA: Marion...please. *(To Conroy)* Don't let her.

MARION: *(To Olivia)* You're fired. *(To Conroy)* Your wife isn't here with you?

CONROY: She's resting.

MARION: In that place?

CONROY: *(To Olivia)* I told her to eat and drink nothing until I get back, and in particular not to think about the veal because it induces retching. Oh, a fine holiday, and a finer wedding anniv—...*(He stops, too late)*

MARION: Your anniversary? No!

CONROY: Oh, Christ.

MARION: But how lovely. And what a coincidence.

CONROY: Is it?

MARION: Most certainly. You're here and we're here, and it's your anniversary. Talk about a small world. *(He looks at her as if she were mad. He walks away, affecting to study the wall map)* Wood, tin or crystal? Or isn't it one of the specials? Whichever it is, I hope you're the kind of husband who sends flowers and says a thank-you for all the happy years. You should. Because, remember, we pass this way but once.

CONROY: Please God.

MARION: Amen. My own dear husband is no more. He passed over...or dropped dead, as we say back home. He was Irish, a professional man, that's why I live here: it helps me to feel that he's not really gone, but lurking. So often he would say to me, even when sober: "Marion, we should grasp each fleeting moment. One of us, you or I, might not see tomorrow." He was really taken aback when it turned out to be him. For all his faults, George was not a chauvinist: he believed in ladies first.

CONROY: Madam...

MARION: So how are you doing?

CONROY: Excuse me. I don't want to talk to you or to anyone. Or to be talked to or at.

MARION: Oh. You're mad at someone.

CONROY: Yes.

MARION: Don't be. She can't help being sick. Forgive.

(*Conroy goes to Olivia*)

CONROY: Can you stop her? Can anyone?

OLIVIA: Sorry.

CONROY: (*To Rooney*) Can you?

ROONEY: What?

MARION: Stop...hold everything! Son of a gun, I've got it. (*A happy smile of discovery*) You don't like Americans.

CONROY: Eh?

MARION: You devil, you.

CONROY: Please...*please*? I don't know you. I'm a man on holiday who's having a terrible time. Why are you picking on me?

MARION: Terrible time, huh?

CONROY: Yes!

MARION: So why do you let people kick you around? Quit being a fall guy. Get in there and come out with your dukes up. Give 'em the old one-two.

CONROY: (*Staring at her; then with quiet passion*) God, but I hate Americans.

MARION: You said it...oh, good.

CONROY: (*Regretting his rudeness*) I'm sorry.

MARION: Don't be. Everyone hates us. They envy us our know-how. They want our efficiency, our pizzazz, our orthodontists, our telephones that work and our get-up-and-go. What they don't want is *us*. Why is that?

(*A pause*)

CONROY: Deep down...

MARION: Shoot.

CONROY: ...And speaking for myself, what I abominate most of all is the pizzazz.

MARION: You're kidding.

CONROY: Truly. I don't mind the crassness or the vulgarity. Let's be fair: if we want to feel superior to Americans, that's the price we pay. No, what infests my brain with a desire to mutilate and maim is that blind, boundless energy of yours, that disgusting good humour that never lets up. Do you know what I'm saying? You have no seasons: with you, all the year round everything's coming up bloody roses. You're the voice in the back of the bus that wants a sing-song, the silver lining without a cloud in sight, the teetotaller on somebody else's morning after. You can't or won't understand that the rest of us need unhappiness and to have our lives go wrong: it's either that or the curse of perpetual motion, and we're your converts. Damn the lot of you: it's all sock-it-to-'em and wake-up-and-live. You'd organize a barbecue at a cremation. (*He pauses, exhausted by his outburst*)

MARION: Attaboy. Now don't you feel terrific?

CONROY: What?

MARION: I always say, letting it all hang out is good for what ails you.

CONROY: (*To Olivia*) Are you really her secretary?

OLIVIA: 'Fraid so.

CONROY: It's just that I saw a play once about three people locked in a room who were dead but didn't know they were dead. And they were in Hell, and each one was the other's tormentor. Do you think that's a possibility?

MARION: Aren't you curious to know what it is I do that I should have a secretary?

CONROY: No.

MARION: You're determined to worm it out of me, aren't you?

OLIVIA: The gentleman isn't interested.

MARION: What does it mean to you when I say (*Coyly*) "Mainly Marion"?

CONROY: Robin Hood?

MARION: Oh, boy.

OLIVIA: Marion writes a column.

MARION: Olly writes a column: all I do is kick a few thoughts around. Cracker-barrel stuff. Just for a hobby, but it's syndicated. I get fan mail.

OLIVIA: A letter a week.

MARION: When I remember to write it. It was a kind of therapy I took up when George handed in his dinner-pail.

CONROY: (*Apprehensive*) You write a gossip column.

MARION: Naw. I put a little zip into people's lives. You know, like the song says: "Get up, get out, and meet the sun halfway."

CONROY: I might have known. Well, I happen to believe that people can help themselves without self-help.

MARION: You do, huh?

CONROY: Now, if you'll excuse me...(*He brushes past her*)

MARION: Something else I did when George took that deep breath and forgot to exhale was, I went back to college.

CONROY: Interesting. (*To Rooney*) Excuse me, where is the nearest pub?

MARION: I said to myself: There's a new life out there and it's up for grabs. Go get it, girl.

CONROY: I said, can you direct me to the nearest public house.

ROONEY: It's...uh, if you cross the bridge and turn left at the... (*He sees that Marion has taken a pound note from her pocket and is shaking her head at him meaningfully*) There isn't one.

CONROY: Are you mad?

ROONEY: The owner died.

CONROY: Well, where's the next nearest?

ROONEY: There isn't one.

(*Conroy stomps away in disbelief. Following him, Marion gives the pound to Rooney*)

MARION: Bless you for that, he's an alcoholic. (*To Conroy*) I went back to college at the age of never-you-mind, and I majored in psycho-drama. You're a doctor. Don't you find psycho-drama invaluable in the areas of diagnosis and treatment?

CONROY: Not often. I'm a proctologist.

MARION: Oh. You mean you treat disorders of the...

CONROY: Yes. And allow me to tell you that you are the most acute pain in that part of the anatomy that I have ever encountered.

MARION: That's rude, but I forgive you. In psycho-drama, disturbed people act out their most intimate problems. It's a striptease of the human soul. (*As Conroy starts out, she interposes herself*) You don't want to go out there: you'll catch cold.

CONROY: There won't be time: I'm going to throw myself in the lake.

MARION: When a person acts out his inner tensions, he releases his hostilities...

CONROY: Excuse me. (*He tries to pass*)

MARION: ...The results can be a knockout. I have seen human lives transformed. I have seen marriages saved.

CONROY: Allow me. (*He gently moves her to one side and starts out*)

MARION: It could even save your marriage.

(*Conroy walks a few paces, then stops. He returns*)

CONROY: What did you say?

MARION: I said it could. No guarantees.

CONROY: (*To Rooney*) She's insane, isn't she?

ROONEY: 'Tis the gin.

CONROY: Ah?

ROONEY: They've been at it all day.

MARION: I bet you're one of those people who think their marriage is in pretty good shape.

CONROY: No, I don't. Being Irish and not American, I treat my marriage with decency. I don't think about it at all: I ignore it.

MARION: Your wife is sick, isn't she?

CONROY: What of it? That was rancid veal.

MARION: Uh-huh. And on your anniversary.

CONROY: Well?

MARION: You really don't see the significance?

CONROY: (*With elaborate sarcasm*) But of course! Her vomiting is psychosomatic. It is actually a cry for help and a symptom of her aversion towards me. Now you listen. I am waiting for a boat.

(*As Marion opens her mouth to correct him*)

ROONEY: Cruiser.

MARION: Thank you.

CONROY: I don't know you. Nonetheless, you have seen fit to accost, annoy and persecute me, and now, it seems, you want to pry into my private life. I pay my bills, I am eminent in my profession, and I've been contentedly married for twenty-five years...

MARION: A silver wedding, I knew it.

CONROY: We're total strangers, and in your case "strange" is an understatement. Why are you picking on me?

MARION: Easy. You're the only game in town.

(*He looks at her, unwilling to comprehend. A pause*)

OLIVIA: Marion is addicted to games.

MARION: Any time, any place.

OLIVIA: Two flies going up a window.

CONROY: I happen to think games are for idiots. And I never

gamble.

MARION: No? I'll lay you five to one you've got a mole under your left armpit.

CONROY: (*At once*) You lose!

(*She smirks. He scowls bad-temperedly*)

MARION: Oh, come on, we have time to kill. How's about it?

OLIVIA: (*To Conroy*) Don't play.

CONROY: I won't. (*Then*) Play what?

MARION: Happy Families. Or otherwise.

CONROY: You *are* mad.

MARION: Let me put it like this...

CONROY: (*To Olivia*) You're really her keeper.

MARION: This re-enactment of a marriage on the rocks could change your life. A scientific experiment, no horsing around. And if you won't buy that, let's say it's a load of baloney and we'll kid the hell out of it.

CONROY: Certifiable.

MARION: Now...you'll be you, of course, and I'll be—I don't think I know your wife's name.

CONROY: Her name? You know *nothing* about her.

MARION: I don't have to. All women are basically alike: noble, affectionate and married to bums. I could go overboard, but I want to stay impartial.

CONROY: Oh, good.

MARION: So...! You are you, I am Mrs. You, and Olly is the other woman.

CONROY: *What* other woman?

MARION: As well as our supporting cast.

CONROY: Damn your eyes, you meddlesome bag, I've never looked at another woman.

MARION: Maybe we could use a bit player as well. (*She eyes Rooney speculatively*) No, I guess not.

ROONEY: (*Suddenly*) Last year I was...(*He stops, shy*)

MARION: Pardon me.

ROONEY: When St. Kilda's Players put on *The Vice of a Fenian*, I was the English captain.

MARION: I'll be damned, a star is born.

ROONEY: (*Still in his rural accent*) "Rebel scum, you dare to bandy words with a kinsman of the Queen?"

MARION: I love it, don't change a thing. What was the Fenian's vice, by the way?

ROONEY: (*Simply*) The vice he talked with.

MARION: Oh. Forgive me, I get these blackouts. (*To Conroy*) Ready for Curtain Up?

CONROY: You're up to something. You know me, don't you, or you know of me?

MARION: (*Candidly*) Nope.

CONROY: (*Turning to Rooney*) You. These are business premises, and I'm a customer. Are you going to permit this lunacy or are you going to act?

MARION: He's going to act.

CONROY: God in heaven.

OLIVIA: (*To Conroy*) Excuse me, but why the fuss? A game needs players, doesn't it?

MARION: (*Warningly*) Olly...

OLIVIA: As long as you stay out of it and say nothing, what can she do?

MARION: Thanks, pal.

CONROY: You're right...thank you. (*To Marion, now good-humouredly*) You carry on. Play your game, and I'll sit here and watch you make more of a fool of yourself than you already are. I'll even give you a start. My name is G.P. Conroy. I specialize in medicine because I got tired of jokes about the G.P. I interned in Minneapolis, at the Mayo Clinic. I have a wife and two children: one daughter, one grown-up son.

ROONEY: (*Softly*) That'll be me.

CONROY: Now put up or shut up.

(*Conroy settles back comfortably, sure of himself. Marion looks at him with dislike. Then, without a change of expression*)

MARION: G.P., huh? What does the "G" stand for? (*He shakes his head smiling*) Gerald? Gareth? I think I'll call you George: it makes me feel all warm and connubial again, even though you aren't one teeny bit like him. (*She moves a small table up to the chair on which Conroy is sitting, then, during the following carries a chair over so that it is facing him across the table. Conroy picks up a brochure and affects to study it*) For one thing, he dressed better than you do. No offence, George, but you look like a proctologist on vacation. You aren't the anonymous sort, you know what I mean? What you'd really like is to wear your striped pants and white smock to let 'em all know you're you. I can understand your security. In your job, everybody bows to you, except that they do it in the wrong direction. But I mustn't be mean. I love you, and here it is, our fifth anniversary, (*Sitting*) and you've brought me to this lovely restaurant. (*Conroy blinks and looks about him*) Waitress! (*Olivia comes forward*) Waitress, my husband and I are five years married this very day. We want everything to be perfect.

OLIVIA: We'll do our best, madam. (*Conroy stares at her*) Are you and the gentleman ready to order?

MARION: (*Glancing at the brochure*) Why not? I think that seeing as how the occasion is so meaningful, I'll start with the oysters. (*She bats her eyes at Conroy*) Then the Châteaubriand, medium rare and rarin' to go.

OLIVIA: Thank you. And for the gentleman?

MARION: George, darling? (*No response*) He'll have exactly the same, except double up on the oysters. (*She looks at another brochure*) And for wine the Château-Latour seventy-nine.

OLIVIA: Thank you. *Bon appetit.*

MARION: You're welcome. (*To Conroy*) Five golden years... here's looking at you, kid.

CONROY: I'm not five years married, I'm...

OLIVIA: (*Warning him*) Ah!

MARION: Twenty-five...I know. This is a guided tour down Memory Lane. Yes, five happy gold-plated years. Do you remember the first meal I cooked for you, George? Or didn't cook...I got so excited that I forgot to light the oven. You were so sweet about it. You didn't utter one reproachful word, just looked at that raw leg of lamb and walked out of the house. I wonder why brides cry so much. Maybe it's for the same reason that babies cry: it strengthens their lungs for after. You've got to admit it, George, I do have strong lungs. (*He pays her no attention. She bellows*) GEORGE! (*He looks up, startled*) We're communicating, oh good. I shouldn't have let your impatience get to me, because that was a quality of yours I liked. You were in a hurry. And angry...you still are. You drive home from the clinic every day in the Mercedes, you put on those Gucci slippers you wouldn't be parted from, you pour yourself a Scotch, open a bottle of French wine for later on, check your Rolex, turn on the Sony, watch the BBC news and tell me what a mess Ireland is in. (*As he scowls*) Honey, it's a put-on, I'm kidding. You listening to me, sourpuss? You work too hard. It can't be for the money...it all goes to the Internal Revenue, except when your patients pay you in cash. (*He says nothing*) Do you think it's possible that in five years we have exhausted all our topics of conversation?

CONROY: (*Quietly*) You talked him to death, didn't you?
(*Olivia shakes her head despairingly*)
MARION: Who?
CONROY: George.
OLIVIA: (*Signalling*) Dr. Conroy...
CONROY: (*To Olivia*) Excuse me. (*To Marion*) You pizzazzed the poor bugger into the next world, didn't you?
MARION: No such thing. George was a born listener.
CONROY: I can see him now, coming home, opening his newspaper and wondering if today's the day he gets beyond Mutt and Jeff. (*During this, Olivia goes to Rooney and whispers to him urgently*) "George, why don't you ever talk to me, George? Do you know what I did today, George? I had the girls in for coffee, George, and I read *Anna Karenina*, landscaped the garden, wallpapered the living room and turned the attic into a padded cell. Don't you think that's cute, George?" (*Rooney has come over and is hovering*) What do you want?
ROONEY: I'm the waiter, and I've brung the oysters.
CONROY: (*Snarling*) Piss off. (*As Rooney retreats; to Marion*) Now I bet *he* had a girlfriend.
MARION: Who?
CONROY: Yes, I can see her, too...clear as day. No oil painting, couldn't boil an egg or darn a sock, but she was the woman of his dreams. A deaf mute.
MARION: (*Staying calm*) That's one quality I've never gotten used to in you, George: that destructive Irish sense of humour. In the five years of our togetherness...
CONROY: I am not playing this game...
MARION: (*Fondly*) Eat your oysters. (*Resuming*) I have noticed that you reserve the most cruel jokes for those you hold dearest. I heard you, George. We were at a party, and I was leaving early, and I called you. I said "I'm off now!" and I heard you say, corner of your mouth, to the man next to you: "She's been off for years."
CONROY: Did he say that?
MARION: Yes, George, you did. It was a cheap shot, not worthy of you, but that wasn't what got to me. The hell with it, any Irishman with a drink in his gut and another in his hand would set fire to his mother if it brought him a laugh. No, what riled me was your contempt.
CONROY: Contempt for you?
MARION: No, honey-bun: for you. You people are so screwed

up, you know that? To hear you tell it, Americans are a bunch of hicks, every Englishman is a no-chin punk, and the others don't count. You're the only real salt of the earth. So bully for you. Except that I've got a hunch that underneath all those flag-waving ego trips you don't go a bundle on yourselves. I mean, you don't like you, George.

CONROY: I curse the day Freud was born.

MARION: If somebody takes a shine to you, you can't for the life of you see why. And if somebody loves you...why that's so downright perverted that you pin their ears back for being a jerk. That was why you said "She's been off for years," wasn't it, George? To pin my ears back.

CONROY: Balls, if you'll pardon me.

MARION: I'll pardon you, but it's true. I swear it on a stack of...

CONROY: "Reader's Digests."

MARION: I wouldn't have brought it up on this...(*She stokes his hand tenderly*)...magical evening of ours, but what got under my skin was that smart-ass remark of yours about a deaf mute. Shame on you. When it came to other women, you had taste, George...don't knock it. Leastways, I always approved of Eleanor. (*She looks affectionately towards Olivia. Conroy follows her glance, as does the now avidly interested Rooney*) Nice kid.

CONROY: Who is? I'm getting confused. Are you talking about my marriage or yours?

MARION: (*A shrug in her voice*) Choose your partner.

CONROY: What?

MARION: Let's call it ours. Did you have fun, George, these past five years?

CONROY: (*Indicating Olivia*) What about Eleanor?

MARION: Later. What was it like starting out: Was the world all new and cool like lavender sheets? (*Conroy opens his mouth to reply, but clams up. Marion senses that she is making progress*) Hold it. (*To Rooney*) Waiter...you can serve the wine now. (*Rooney looks to Olivia for encouragement. He picks up a small flower-vase from his desk and comes forward, wary of Conroy. To Conroy*) In a minute you can open the conversational floodgates. (*To Rooney*) And there you are. That *is* the Château seventy-nine. (*She affects to inspect the label*) Attaboy...anchors aweigh! (*She watches as Rooney picks up an imaginary glass and pours from the vase, his elbows rising. To Conroy*) I ordered this claret because it's your... (*To Rooney*) Pardon me, I guess you're new around here. First, you pour just that teeny bit...for tasting?

ROONEY: Sorry.

MARION: Think nothing of it.

(*Rooney pours some of the wine back into the bottle, then himself tastes what is left*)

ROONEY: It's grand.

MARION: Terrific. (*To Conroy*) Do you get the impression that this place is going downhill?

ROONEY: (*Carried away; a hearty, unconvincing stage laugh*) Ah, sure it won't poison ye.

MARION: I think we've created a Frankenstein. (*To Rooney*) You can leave the vase. (*Rooney goes back to his desk, walking like Karloff's monster. Marion lifts an imaginary glass*) Here's to us, George.

CONROY: I wish this place *was* a restaurant.

MARION: Why? Are you hungry?

CONROY: The last meal I had was...(*He breaks off, too proud to unbend*)

MARION: But of course. That appalling dinner at the O'Borgias. Olly...

(*Olivia understands. She at once goes to where the cruise luggage is piled. She opens a hamper and through the following finds a paper plate, a serviette and sandwiches wrapped in cellophane*)

CONROY: Now what?

MARION: Never you mind. Why, you poor lamb, no wonder you haven't been the life of the party. You're starving.

CONROY: I'll survive.

MARION: My God, I can hear it. That rumbling...your stomach is like a bowling alley.

CONROY: It is nothing of the...

MARION: You should have had breakfast. There is no risk factor in bacon and eggs. Every Irish hotel ought to have a sign up: "It is safe to eat the breakfasts." Olly?

OLIVIA: Right here. (*She places the sandwiches in front of Conroy*)

CONROY: What's all this?

OLIVIA: Your Châteaubriand, sir. Medium rare.

CONROY: What? Now look here...

MARION: They were for the boat.

CONROY: The cruiser?

MARION: The ship. Don't worry about it, if we need more I've got the makings.

CONROY: I couldn't possibly. Are you sure?

MARION: Virginia ham and homemade preserves. This isn't just a pretty face, you know.

CONROY: (*Lusting*) If you're positive...

MARION: Enjoy!

CONROY: I'm starving...thank you.

(*Marion crooks a finger at Olivia, who is already pouring coffee from a thermos. Conroy attacks the sandwiches with a delight that is almost tearful. One can see his defences crumbling*)

MARION: Forgive me if I stare, but seeing a man enjoy his food always gets a woman where she lives. It's like watching Easter bunnies or the birth of a calf. (*Conroy, his mouth already full, pushes the plate at her and emits an incoherent sound of encouragement, not unlike "Uhnnf"*) No, thank you, George, I already ate. You were going to tell me about our first five years. Look... (*She rises, goes to the large relief map of the Shannon and indicates the spot where the river, flowing south, becomes Lough Derg*) This is where we are, right here and now, with that lake out there ahead of us. It's no rain puddle, that's for sure...you could get shipwrecked. All those deadly shoals, lying in wait.

ROONEY: Not at all...you just follow the markers.

MARION: Follow the markers! What symbolism...why, you're a poet without...

ROONEY: Otherwise, ye'll tear the arse out of her.

MARION: Without knowing it. (*To Conroy*) Our river, yours and mine. And up here is where we started out all these years ago. (*She indicates Lough Key in the extreme north*) How far would we have come in the first five of those years, do you think? (*Pointing to a spot on the map*) This far?

ROONEY: Them's the Inner Lakes...very flat country.

MARION: *Was* it flat, George? In the beginning.

CONROY: You're so damned curious, I'll...(*Swallowing*) ...excuse me, I'll tell you.

MARION: (*Happily*) You will?

CONROY: Why not? The time I interned at Mayo, they told me I had a talent for obstetrics. So I thought I'd specialize, come back home, put in my seven years. The joke was, the country had changed. Instead of having families of six or eight, the Irish were now having two or three of them and a motor car. Well, when women are no longer in labour...

MARION: Neither are the obstetricians.

CONROY: Right. There were other changes. According to statistics, the Irish were drinking more wines and spirits. Now wine, as you may know, when taken to excess, is conducive to haemorrhoids. So I switched to proctology.

MARION: Clever!

CONROY: From obstetrics.

MARION: Near enough.

CONROY: Excuse the subject while I'm eating.

MARION: Don't mention it.

CONROY: And my wife...(*Olivia puts coffee in front of him*) Oh, thanks.

MARION: (*Annoyed by the interruption*) Olly...! (*To Conroy*) Your wife?

CONROY: (*Still eating*) These are good. We weren't long married. I was still a house man at the Richmond, long hours and short pay...so she helped me. She had a few bob.

MARION: A few bob?

OLIVIA: (*Explaining*) *You* would say that she was loaded.

CONROY: No, no. She'd had a good job...managed to put a bit by. She encouraged me. It was a heavy responsibility, because when a woman like my wife is fond of a man, he is *ipso facto* a genius, otherwise it's a reflection on her good taste. I shouldn't have said that.

MARION: She's not here, George. *I'm* here.

CONROY: What was it you asked? Was the world all new then, and cool? I don't know...I was too scared to notice.

MARION: Scared?

CONROY: Of being no good. Of making mistakes. I couldn't talk to a patient.

MARION: You?

CONROY: What I mean is, I couldn't talk dishonestly: I had to learn. Now I'm the best there is. Watch. (*He goes to Olivia, his manner brimming with charm. He takes her hand*) My dear young woman, you are a flawless example of womanhood and almost a waste of my valuable time. Alas, Mother Nature—may I call you Dympna?—Mother Nature, Dympna, is forever jealous of perfection. She afflicts only the loveliest, and that is why you and I are destined to be friends. Yes?

OLIVIA: (*Demurely*) Yes, Doctor.

CONROY: So be off home with you, have nothing to eat, and be back here at seven sharp with two of your prettiest nighties.

OLIVIA: (*Tremulous*) Hospital...oh, no.

CONROY: Think of it as a holiday...five days of carefree idleness away from it all.

OLIVIA: But, Doctor...

CONROY: I must see you again. Go now...trust me. (*With his arm about her waist, he has been leading her towards an imaginary door*)

OLIVIA: But I can't...I...

CONROY: Do you like the theatre?

OLIVIA: Well, yes...

CONROY: We'll go, together. (*He ushers her through the "door," closes it behind her and turns to Marion*) Well?

MARION: Why, George, you're an old smoothie.

CONROY: Not at all. You should see Technique Number Two. Excuse me. (*He picks up another sandwich, then turns on Rooney, barking at him*) Young man! (*Rooney jumps to his feet, startled*) Look at you. Look at that stoop, that complexion, look at those eyes. Your sort will just not be told, will you? Why do you waste my time?

ROONEY: (*Petrified, not acting*) I don't know.

CONROY: *Don't know*?

ROONEY: ...Sir.

CONROY: (*Walking around him*) What a specimen. People tell bad jokes about the Irish, do you know that? They make us out to be stupid and slow-witted. Well, so we damn well are. It's the truth, and would you care to be told why?

ROONEY: (*Shaking*) Yessir.

CONROY: We're a race of thicks, because for generations we've been starving not only our bodies but our brains with a diet of carbohydrates. Potatoes and bread, bread and potatoes. And you still haven't changed your ways, except that you now eat pesticides and additives as well. Without protein, have you any idea of what your brain looks like? Eeugh! Dear God, it's a wonder you're still alive. My nurse will give you a diet sheet and a prescription for suppositories, and I don't want to see you in here again. Now get out.

ROONEY: Yessir. (*He flees from the room and out on to the jetty*)

CONROY: Well?

MARION: That was cruel.

CONROY: Yes, but it was accurate. And it works.

ROONEY: *(Looking about him)* Where's the nurse? *(He starts to take his own pulse, then reality dawns)*

CONROY: Twenty years ago, I couldn't have done that. I hemmed and hawed. They wanted God...any god, angry or merciful. Instead, I gave them a mendicant monk. How can you be Almighty God when your wife is paying the rent?

(Rooney marches back in angrily)

ROONEY: Making a fool out of a man! *(He resumes his place at the desk, snatching up his newspaper)*

CONROY: And on our anniversary there wasn't a restaurant or Châteaubriand or...*(Picking up the vase)*...whatever the year was. We were in a basement flat in Palmerston Park, and we had a row. *(Then) I* had a row.

MARION: I wouldn't fight with you?

CONROY: She wouldn't.

MARION: That's dirty.

CONROY: Right! I told her...*(He hesitates)*

MARION: Say it.

CONROY: I said: I'm jacking it in.

MARION: Are you, George?

CONROY: You heard me. I'm overworked. All I am is a dogsbody in that place, and even so, I'm no damn good at it. So I'm getting out. Done, over with.

MARION: Well, maybe you should.

CONROY: Get out. Quit.

CONROY: That's it, that's what she said! She had the nerve to agree with me.

MARION: If you're unhappy...

CONROY: I'm too miserable to be unhappy. I work twelve hours at a stretch, and when I get home it's textbooks until my brain is seized up. I have no life...where will it end?

MARION: If you get to be a specialist, I should say on a golf course.

CONROY: Is that meant to be funny?

MARION: I just want what you want.

CONROY: I'm telling you I'm exhausted. I get five hours sleep a night, and I'm fed up of being kept by you.

MARION: *(A smile)* Is this my anniversary present, George?

CONROY: That money was your savings, your nest egg. You're pouring it down the drain.

MARION: (*Shrugging*) It's my omelette.

CONROY: I have three more years to go. Let's say there's a miracle and I come out the other end. Then what? I'll be a brain-damaged proctologist without even the price of a light bulb for his proctoscope. How do I begin?

MARION: Others do.

CONROY: Oh, sure. The charmed circle who have money and pull, and the con men who wouldn't know a cyst from a sunburn. Or else they marry a woman whose father is an eminent quack, too old or too sick to practice. What chance do *I* have?

MARION: You tell me.

CONROY: I'm asking if you think I should bail out.

MARION: Yes, I do. I love you, George, but not enough to put my father through medical school.

CONROY: Fine. That's it, then.

MARION: You hungry? I'll fix dinner. He had a hard enough time learning to play the oboe.

CONROY: That is finally...it.

(*Marion affects to be busily cooking a meal. She mimes tying on her apron, breaking eggs, beating them*)

MARION: I never understood my father.

CONROY: The problem is...

MARION: Even on her death-bed, my mother didn't ask him about other women. She said: "Gilbert, why the oboe?"

CONROY: I say, the problem is...

MARION: I'm listening, hon.

CONROY: She...ah, called me "dear."

MARION: Who? Oh. Listening, dear.

CONROY: What do I do now?

MARION: Do?

CONROY: With my life.

MARION: Well, now that we've talked it over and you've been sweet enough to make me part of your decision, why not start up a nice family practice? We've got money enough for that.

CONROY: (*Heavily*) Where have you decided on?

MARION: Maybe some place where you can use what you've already learnt. No sense in letting four years be a total write-off. What about one of those cute villages in the west where people sit around a lot on stone walls?

(*Conroy looks at her, glowering*)

CONROY: You have it all cut and dried, haven't you?

MARION: Just quick on my feet, George.

CONROY: I mean, you were easily convinced.

MARION: Was I?

CONROY: I didn't have to twist your arm.

MARION: You're the head of the family, dear. I have faith in your lack of confidence.

CONROY: (*Getting steamed up*) You have, huh?

MARION: Yep. Hey, we have spinach. What do you say to eggs Florentine?

CONROY: I say, shag your eggs Florentine.

MARION: Is that the way you like them?

CONROY: I'm on to you.

MARION: Are you, George?

CONROY: If you want to crook me round your finger, try getting up early. You gave yourself away then, didn't you? Didn't you?

MARION: How do you shag eggs?

CONROY: (*Triumphantly*) You forgot to put on an act. You forgot to say: "Don't give up, pet…I know you can do it"! Because you don't think I've got the brains and you don't think I've got the guts.

MARION: There's no fooling you, George.

CONROY: I'm no idiot.

MARION: But darling, forgive me: you did display a certain lack of faith in yourself. You said you were no good.

CONROY: That was modesty.

MARION: Was it?

CONROY: I set a trap for you. (*Seizing on the inspiration*) That was it, a trap. And you walked right into it.

MARION: I agreed with you!

CONROY: Exactly…disloyalty. Well, now that our marriage is exposed as a mockery, do you know what I'm going to do?

MARION: Have dinner?

CONROY: Keep your dinner. I'm going to the Richmond, to help in Casualty. And I'll qualify, just to spite you. And not as a consultant…I'll set myself up in private practice, and in Fitzwilliam Square!

MARION: (*Suppressing a smile*) You wouldn't.

CONROY: That swept the ground from under you. You're not burying me in some Connemara kip. Good-night!

MARION: George, your shagged eggs… (*Conroy walks out of the playlet as if from a room. He stands, simmering down. Marion re-*

turns to the here and now and approaches him) That was pretty fancy footwork.

CONROY: What was?

MARION: You got my number, George. You put it to me in writing.

CONROY: Did I?

MARION: If that's really how it was.

CONROY: Near enough. You see, if a man's wife is afraid to take a chance in life, it's up to him to be strong for them both.

MARION: Absolutely.

CONROY: Except I think I may have got a bit carried away.

MARION: You were sensational. Tell him, Olly.

OLIVIA: I was spellbound.

CONROY: Honest?

OLIVIA: Riveted.

CONROY: (*Fatuously pleased*) Come off it. Mind you, I do have a natural flair for words.

MARION: Listen to me. I've been through this game with a paranoid schizophrenic, and you were *better*.

CONROY: Was I?

MARION: (*To Rooney*) Tell him.

ROONEY: (*Still sulking*) I'm not playing.

CONROY: Begrudger.

MARION: And you licked me. You won.

CONROY: Ha-ha.

MARION: You monster, you.

CONROY: No, no. I'm ashamed. My wife is the best woman in the world. Tales out of school...I was unchivalrous.

MARION: She was weak, George. What woman isn't?

CONROY: True.

MARION: So where does snitching come into it? And when you qualified and were a success, was she disappointed?

CONROY: No, she seemed to have gotten over it.

MARION: You see? You made her strong.

CONROY: (*Wanting to believe it*) No!

MARION: Yes, you did, too. Hey, you want to play some more?

CONROY: What? No, thank you.

MARION: It'll make you feel good.

CONROY: I feel superb.

MARION: Quitting while you're ahead, huh?

CONROY: I've already played.

MARION: You just got your feet wet.

CONROY: Look. You pestered me and you persecuted me, so I humoured you and I won, and that's it. Thank you for the sandwiches and the coffee. Much obliged, but I have a book I'm reading outside in the car, so if you don't... (*He breaks off. Her face is contorted with grief. Marion emits a great convulsive sob*) What is it? (*Marion opens her mouth, but no words come, just gasps*) What's up? What are you crying for? (*Marion points a finger at him, her mouth still opening and shutting. Conroy, to Olivia*) Good God, is this because I won't play with her?

MARION: (*Sobbing*) Errghh...errghh...

CONROY: Get a grip on yourself. How can you be so... (*He is about to say "childish" but she covers her mouth with her hand, goes to where her luggage and Olivia's is stacked and begins pulling bags this way and that*) What are you doing?

MARION: I'm...leaving.

CONROY: Why? What for? (*Marion picks up an overnight bag*) All this, because you want your own way and can't have it. (*As Marion starts towards the door*) And there's nothing out there. The boats haven't come in yet. (*Marion turns and fixes him with a long penetrating look filled with bitterness. Conroy, wilting*) I mean the cruisers.

MARION: I'm leaving you, George.

CONROY: Pardon?

MARION: And I'm taking the children.

CONROY: Oh, for God's sake!

MARION: Swear at me all you want...I'm through. Do you know what day today is? Our fifteenth anniversary.

CONROY: Let me out of here. (*He makes for the door, but Marion is there ahead of him, barring the way, her eyes blazing*)

MARION: Oh, no, George, I'm the one who's leaving. I've had fifteen years of you, and now it's over...*finito*, because I don't like you anymore. I've tried. Heaven will bear witness that I've tried. I've bruised the knuckles of my heart on you.

CONROY: Just get out of my...(*Then*) The what of your what?

MARION: You needn't worry, I don't want anything from you. You can keep the house...I'll send for the furniture. In the meantime, Mother will find room for us.

CONROY: (*Suddenly smiling*) My dear woman, it won't work. This is one game you can play all on your...(*A thought occurs*) Wait a minute. Gotcha!

MARION: Pardon me?

CONROY: And you can't even play it properly. So you're going home to mother! Your mother is dead. You said so.

MARION: Did I?

CONROY: (*Gloating, childlike*) Yah! Now who's clever-clogs?

MARION: It so happens, George...

CONROY: Breach of the rules...I win!

MARION: It so happens that it's your mother we're going home to.

CONROY: Eh?

MARION: You know she never liked you.

CONROY: Well, you lying...

MARION: Which is a gross understatement on account of I have no wish to hurt your feelings.

CONROY: You slanderous rip, my mother idolized me. She...

(*Mrs. Hand enters at this point by the door marked "Private." She wears a pinafore on which is the company logo and carries a pile of bed linen and towels. She is middle-aged, maternal, quick to sympathize. Her entrance is so unexpected that Marion, Conroy and Olivia stare at her*)

MRS. HAND: Fergal, have they come in yet?

ROONEY: (*Engrossed in the drama*) What? No.

MRS. HAND: (*Dismayed*) You're not in earnest, say they have. (*To the others*) Excuse me. (*To Rooney, lowering her voice*) I won't see my bed tonight. I have six change-overs to do, and there's a towel and a pillow-slip missing off the "Lady of Killaloe" and a teapot broke on the "Lady of Meelick." Be a good boy and call them in.

ROONEY: Can't.

MRS. HAND: Tell them the march is over...yes, you will. (*Seeing that Marion is looking at her*) Isn't it very changeable?

MARION: Sure is.

MRS. HAND: I'm the housekeeper. We'll have you snug as bugs in rugs the minute they come in. Any second now. (*Again in a low voice*) Fergal, the people are waiting.

ROONEY: Let them.

MRS. HAND: You're like the rest of them: You can't wait to be promoted to the dole. (*Making for a chair*) I'm staying here. 'Tis freezing inside in that hot press. (*She sinks into a chair with the glad sigh of one who has been a long time on her feet*)

CONROY: (*To Marion*) Well, that's put paid to you and your

game.

MARION: Has it?

OLIVIA: He's right, Marion. Call it a day.

(*Marion looks at both of them, then goes purposefully over to Mrs. Hand*)

MARION: Mom...

OLIVIA: Marion, no.

MRS. HAND: (*Pleasantly*) Yes, dear, can I help you?

MARION: I don't know how to tell you this...

MRS. HAND: (*Already sympathetic*) Oh?

MARION: ...Because it's going to come as a terrible shock. The fact is, I'm leaving George.

CONROY: (*Clutching his head*) Oh, God.

(*Mrs. Hand does not react. She looks at Marion, her face utterly devoid of expression*)

MARION: I'm leaving him for good because my life is meaningless. And please...don't talk. Hear my side of it. Don't condemn me, not just yet.

ROONEY: Mrs. Hand, ma'am...

(*Mrs. Hand, without otherwise moving or acknowledging his presence, raises a hand, bidding him to silence. Conroy looks on with a horrified fascination*)

MARION: (*On one knee, humbly*) Thank you. Forgive me for laying it on you like this, but there's no one else I can turn to. You're so kind and sympathetic. (*She places the other woman's hand to her own cheek, squinting as she does so at the ring on the wedding finger*) You are a good warm person, and above all else...(*Taking a chance*)...you are a *mother*.

MRS. HAND: Am I!

MARION: (*Anxiously*) Are you?

MRS. HAND: Don't talk to me.

MARION: (*Fondly*) Mom!

MRS. HAND: I'd five of them.

MARION: Five...how wonderful. (*She looks with sly malice at Conroy*) And yet one of them...am I opening an old wound?...one was a disappointment.

MRS. HAND: (*Amazed, clutching Marion's hand*) Yes!

MARION: The one you loved the best.

MRS. HAND: 'Tis true.

MARION: (*Smirking at Conroy*) And that child broke your heart.

MRS. HAND: She did, she did!

CONROY: (*A bellow of scorn*) Hah!

ROONEY: Mrs. Hand, ma'am, don't mind them...they're trick-acting.

MRS. HAND: Hold your tongue, child, this is grown-ups' talk. You have it all before ye. (*To Marion*) Talk to me, love, if you've no one else...sure 'twill be a gossip.

CONROY: (*To Marion*) You are an evil woman!

MRS. HAND: Is that him?

MARION: Sssh. (*She talks to Mrs. Hand as if to a confidante, but makes sure that Conroy hears*) I stood by him, Mom. All through the bad times, I was by his side, his tender comrade. When the going got tough, it didn't matter...we were together. I was his buddy.

CONROY: Oh, yuck.

MARION: Those were the happy years. Then he became successful. He's famous now. At first I was so proud of him...in his field he has treated the most eminent asses in this country.

MRS. HAND: Is he a vet?

MARION: Sort of. We have a nice house, we travel, we live high off the hog. I'm in the whisper-bracket. (*Whispering*) "That woman is Mrs. G.P. Conroy!" So bully for me. Except that I'm not important to him any more.

MRS. HAND: Ye creature.

MARION: What use am I? He's made it. Who needs a rickety ladder when they're on the roof? I feel old ahead of my time.

MRS. HAND: And tell, how long is it ye're married?

MARION: How long? Today is our fifteenth anniversary. I'm thirty-eight.

MRS. HAND: (*Shocked*) Oh, my God.

MARION: I look like I'm in "Lost Horizon."

CONROY: (*Half to himself*) I'll put a stop to this.

OLIVIA: Dr. Conroy...no.

CONROY: (*Addressing himself to Mrs. Hand*) Pardon me, Mrs....uh, madam. You are the victim of a stupid hoax. This woman is...

MARION: (*Getting in first*) Sometimes I think he'd like to disown me.

MRS. HAND: Not at all.

CONROY: This woman is not my wife.

MARION: (*Wailing*) You see?

MRS. HAND: Too true I see. (*Looking disgustedly at Conroy*) Oh,

CONROY: (*A bellow of scorn*) Hah!

ROONEY: Mrs. Hand, ma'am, don't mind them...they're trick-acting.

MRS. HAND: Hold your tongue, child, this is grown-ups' talk. You have it all before ye. (*To Marion*) Talk to me, love, if you've no one else...sure 'twill be a gossip.

CONROY: (*To Marion*) You are an evil woman!

MRS. HAND: Is that him?

MARION: Sssh. (*She talks to Mrs. Hand as if to a confidante, but makes sure that Conroy hears*) I stood by him, Mom. All through the bad times, I was by his side, his tender comrade. When the going got tough, it didn't matter...we were together. I was his buddy.

CONROY: Oh, yuck.

MARION: Those were the happy years. Then he became successful. He's famous now. At first I was so proud of him...in his field he has treated the most eminent asses in this country.

MRS. HAND: Is he a vet?

MARION: Sort of. We have a nice house, we travel, we live high off the hog. I'm in the whisper-bracket. (*Whispering*) "That woman is Mrs. G.P. Conroy!" So bully for me. Except that I'm not important to him any more.

MRS. HAND: Ye creature.

MARION: What use am I? He's made it. Who needs a rickety ladder when they're on the roof? I feel old ahead of my time.

MRS. HAND: And tell, how long is it ye're married?

MARION: How long? Today is our fifteenth anniversary. I'm thirty-eight.

MRS. HAND: (*Shocked*) Oh, my God.

MARION: I look like I'm in "Lost Horizon."

CONROY: (*Half to himself*) I'll put a stop to this.

OLIVIA: Dr. Conroy...no.

CONROY: (*Addressing himself to Mrs. Hand*) Pardon me, Mrs....uh, madam. You are the victim of a stupid hoax. This woman is...

MARION: (*Getting in first*) Sometimes I think he'd like to disown me.

MRS. HAND: Not at all.

CONROY: This woman is not my wife.

MARION: (*Wailing*) You see?

MRS. HAND: Too true I see. (*Looking disgustedly at Conroy*) Oh, 'tis an old saying and a true one: the browner the trout the thinner the thatch.

CONROY: Pardon?

MRS. HAND: And let him have me sacked out of this for saying it, but he wouldn't treat the sickest of his asses the way he's treated you.

MARION: No, you're wrong. George is not an evil person.

CONROY: (*Heavily*) Thank you.

MARION: (*Charmingly*) You're welcome, George. (*To Mrs. Hand*) I want to be fair to my husband. I felt I owed it to him to figure out what's gone wrong with our marriage, and that's what I sat down and did. He went Park Avenue.

CONROY: Where?

MARION: Big-headed, darling.

CONROY: Me?

MARION: (*To Mrs. Hand*) George and himself have always been the best of friends. But now it's got to the point where they're sleeping together.

(*Mrs. Hand takes a look at Conroy. She says nothing, but takes rosary beads from her pinafore pocket and sits with them entwined around her fist*)

CONROY: I think I'm beginning to cop on. It's not my marriage that's bothering you, it's *yours*. George...your George, he was the one with the smell of himself.

MARION: How many clubs do you belong to?

CONROY: Clubs?

MARION: The snooty kind...yacht club, golf club, tennis club, club-club. How many?

CONROY: None of your business.

MARION: Ten, George? A dozen?

CONROY: Find out. (*Then*) Yes, I'm a member of one or two...what of it? I meet other professional men. We relax, we exchange views...

MARION: And you drum up trade.

CONROY: We do what?

MARION: You advertise, baby, in neon lights.

CONROY: Liar...

MARION: I never saw a doctor who didn't. But you, George, you're the greatest. Put you in a club house, and you twinkle at every fat broad in sight, I've seen you charm them right out of their pants.

(*Mrs. Hand's eyes close. The beads and her lips begin to move*)

CONROY: (*To Mrs. Hand*) Yes? I can't hear.

MARION: She's taking inventory. They can't wait for the touch of those magical hands. George, why are women so crazy about doctors? (*Playfully*) Maybe because it's the only way they can have an intimate relationship with a man without worrying why he doesn't take his socks off. (*She looks at Conroy's scowling face*) Come on, smile at me, George...Smile charmingly. Or do I have to get a pain in my butt first?

CONROY: The kind of doctor you need will want to look higher up.

MARION: (*Mockingly*) At my heart? I used to keep your books; now you employ an accountant. I used to answer the door; now you have a receptionist. It's not that I mind being unused: what burns me up is feeling useless. (*To Mrs. Hand*) Mom, do you know how long it's been since I was utilized for *anything*? Three months.

MRS. HAND: (*Blankly*) Do you tell me?

MARION: I mean, since he's laid a finger on me.

CONROY: (*A yelp of outrage*) Have you no shame?

MRS. HAND: (*Getting the message*) You're never serious?

MARION: *Three months.*

MRS. HAND: Sacred Heart.

MARION: So how about that?

MRS. HAND: Well, maybe there's some good in him after all.

CONROY: (*To Marion*) Now you see here, Mrs. Whatever-your-name-is...

MARION: Conroy.

CONROY: If you persist in waging some insane vendetta against me, you might at least leave this woman out of it. She's done you no harm. She's a simple, good-natured...

MRS. HAND: (*Suddenly*) I wasn't wanted either.

MARION: Pardon me?

MRS. HAND: Himself...he'd no time for me. (*They stare at her. She continues as if in quiet contemplation*) Ah, he had at first... love and newness. Then it was off out with him and into a pub, or to a race meeting or a match. And if he hadn't money in his pocket, there was always a wall in the town that needed holding up. Any place but where myself was. He'd come home at night like a ticket-of-leave man back to jail...The ground pulling at his boots. Maybe we'd used up all the talk we'd in us, was that it? I was no more to him than a picture of someone dead...up on the wall that he never looked at. I stayed with him. I waited till the children were off and fending for themselves. Then I went.

MARION: You left him?

MRS. HAND: (*Again*) I went. If I wouldn't throw out an old dress for a skirt that could be made over, why would I throw away a life? And I always did a day's work, only now I'm paid for it.

MARION: (*Admiringly*) Mom, you're my kind of lady. Shake. (*She extends her hand. Mrs. Hand rises and moves away*)

MRS. HAND: Shake hands, how dare you?

MARION: Why not?

MRS. HAND: I have the leavings of my life all to myself now. A slave to no man and a fool to all of them.

MARION: A fool? Are you kidding?

MRS. HAND: A hard road is bad. No road is nothing.

MARION: You had the guts to walk out...

MRS. HAND: And I rue the day. Ah, the man was hopeless... fierce. But whatever the heartache, by yourself is the worst of all. I thrun away the one poor thing I had left. 'Tis gone, and now I have no one to turn his back on me. (*To Marion, with burning urgency*) That's why you won't leave him. You mustn't. Now say you won't.

MARION: (*Embarrassed, contrite*) Look, Mom...No, not Mom any more, I don't mean that...

MRS. HAND: You'll give him a second chance...yes, you will.

MARION: Please...

MRS. HAND: He'll make it up to you. Isn't he the best in the world?

MARION: Please listen to me. We owe you...no, goddammit, *I* owe you an apology.

MRS. HAND: (*Not heeding*) On my knees I beg you. You'll destroy yourself and for nothing. Stay with him.

MARION: I'm sorry, dear, I really honest-to-God am, but what this gentleman says is true. It's all been a stupid game that went wrong, and it's my fault.

MRS. HAND: A game?

MARION: He and I...I don't know how to explain this, but we...

(*Conroy is at Marion's side. He puts his arm around her shoulder*)

CONROY: What my wife is trying to say—and very badly—is that we're staying together. (*Marion glances at him, stunned. He is a new Conroy, solicitous, kindly*) And thank you, you've been very kind. If...uh, if Marion will overlook my behaviour and give me another chance, I'll do my best to make it up to her. I haven't been a considerate husband, but from now on I'll try.

MRS. HAND: (*Hardly believing*) You're saying it to please me.

CONROY: I mean it.

MRS. HAND: (*To Marion*) And yourself? Ye'll not leave him?

MARION: (*Nervously*) Leave George? That'll be the day.

MRS. HAND: Thanks be to God. Oh, 'tis what I always say and 'tis true: the longer the fast, the sweeter the thrush.

MARION: You said a...Could you repeat that?

(*Mrs. Hand is suddenly overcome by tears of sheer happiness*)

MRS. HAND: Will you look at me...making a show of myself. I need a breath of fresh air...I'll go back and sit in the hot press. (*As tears well up again*) God bless and keep the pair of ye. (*She takes a final look at Marion*) and may the saints pity her...only thirty-eight. (*She goes out*)

MARION: (*To Conroy*) You are a nice man.

CONROY: (*Not severely*) And you are an American idiot.

MARION: I'll drink to that. I am also a louse, a skunk and a rat fink. (*Extending her hand*) Now that we've cleared that up, I'm going to get my hand shook today if it kills me.

CONROY: (*Hesitating*) No more tricks?

MARION: Scout's honour.

CONROY: And no more games?

MARION: You got it. (*As Conroy makes to take her hand*) Except...

CONROY: (*Leaping back as if stung*) No! Except nothing. You keep away from me.

MARION: All I was going to...

CONROY: Get back!

(*The telephone on the desk rings. They all stare at it, including Rooney*)

ROONEY: (*Picking up the receiver*) Thanks be to Jasus. (*Into the phone*) Who's that?...Yes, yes, 'tis me. What...?

MARION: (*To Conroy*) Keep your hair on. Now that we're friends, I was only going to ask your advice. About Eleanor.

CONROY: About...?

(*Olivia rises and smiles at Conroy*)

ROONEY: (*Into the phone*) The corner of Kildare Street....I have ye. (*He looks at his watch*) Three minutes, so...Oh, I will, on the dot. (*As he drops his voice to a whisper, Conroy, bristling with im-*

patience, comes and stands over him) Listen, you won't credit it. I have a pair here forenenst me astray in the head. Loonies. I think they got over the shaggin' wall of some...(*He sees Conroy. Aloud*) I'll do that for ye, so. Sound man. God bless.

CONROY: (*Glaring*) Well?

ROONEY: Grand.

CONROY: Did that call have to do with us?

ROONEY: (*Flustered*) The...marchers are on time to the tick and they'll be handing in the petition at Leinster House at half-past three.

CONROY: It's nearly that now. Then what?

ROONEY: Nothing...the pubs'll be open. You'll want to fill in the form and pay your deposit. Wait, now. (*He finds a rental form and gives it to Conroy, who takes it to a table and sets about filling it in. Rooney waves a second form at Marion*) Missis...

MARION: (*Looking at Conroy*) We already filled ours in, didn't we, Olly?

OLIVIA: (*To Rooney, but looking at Conroy*) It's on your desk.

(*Rooney finds the completed form and stamps it, then again looks at his watch as if under starter's orders*)

MARION: (*To Conroy*) You're as sharp as a tack, you know that? You were right about George...*my* George. You were on the ball, because yes, he did have a lady fair.

CONROY: (*Mumbling*) "Previous experience..." None.

MARION: For all I know he may have played the field. But this was big league stuff...World Series. Name of Eleanor.

CONROY: "Probable destination..." Nowhere.

MARION: She scared me. Eleanor had the one quality that every married woman fears. She was single. (*As Conroy pays her no attention*) Hey, Doc...you with me?

CONROY: Sorry, but as soon as I get this filled in, I have to rescue my wife from that dosshouse that calls itself an hotel. So if you don't mind...

(*Marion goes to the relief map*)

MARION: Where were George and I then on life's river? Twenty years along it. (*Peering*) About here...Banagher. Say, Olly, doesn't that come into one of those cute Irish sayings of yours?

OLIVIA: Does it? Oh, yes..."That bangs Banagher."

MARION: That's the one. And George was banging Eleanor. Well, I knew there had to be another woman because he was putting on weight.

CONROY: "Four-berth or six-berth..." (*Then*) Putting on weight?

MARION: Sure. That's one of the drawbacks of adultery. It comes from eating two dinners. Well, it didn't take me long to find out who she was. Telephone calls...letters.

CONROY: Oh?

MARION: There weren't any.

CONROY: (*At sea*) Ah.

MARION: Want to know what I did? (*Conroy gives a quick empty smile and goes back to his form*) I thought about no telephone calls and no letters and what that meant, and one day I went downstairs, which was reserved for George's professional work, and I said: "I am Hercule Poirot, and someone in this house is a..."

CONROY: "Single screw..."

MARION: Right? Tell you the truth, that wasn't exactly what I said. What I did say was...(*Sweetly*) "Eleanor, honey..."

(*Olivia comes forward as Eleanor*)

OLIVIA: Yes, Marion?

MARION: Take a seat, dear. I thought we might have a chat.

OLIVIA: If you like.

MARION: Oh, I like. My, you're a pretty girl.

OLIVIA: Thank you.

MARION: And smart. And so trim and self-possessed...and single. Have you ever thought of marriage, Eleanor?

OLIVIA: Marriage?

MARION: You know...that thing where if you can hold on to your husband for twenty years, you get to keep him. Ever thought about it?

OLIVIA: Once or twice. But there's still plenty of time, and besides there's no one who's...

MARION: Single?

OLIVIA: Special, I was going to say.

MARION: (*Lazily*) Say it then, what the hell. What's important is, you're having a ball. You...uh, enjoy working under George? (*She stresses the "under" hardly noticeably*)

OLIVIA: Oh, I do. (*Gushing*) He's so...I suppose the word is "brilliant."

MARION: That's one of the words.

OLIVIA: To be part of his work, even the smallest, most unimportant part, makes me feel somehow...

MARION: Fulfilled?

OLIVIA: Yes!

MARION: Mm. Remind me...how long is it you've been with him?

OLIVIA: Four years.

MARION: No, I don't mean that. I don't mean as his secretary...I mean, how long have you been screwing him? (*This has the effect of causing Conroy and Rooney to look up sharply*) Or maybe it's *been* four years...what do I know? Maybe on that very first day he said: "Come in, Miss McNulty, and bring your notebook and a condom."

OLIVIA: (*Shocked*) Marion!

MARION: No, my guess is it began a year ago, around the time he stopped calling you "dear" and "darling" in front of me. (*Rooney picks up the telephone and starts dialing surreptitiously*) When people who like each other a lot start getting formal, I start wondering what else they're getting. Want to hear something else? George became a smiler. We'd be going to bed, and he'd stand there with one leg out of his shorts, and there was this...smile on his face. He's married and he's smiling. *Why?*

OLIVIA: Marion, this is ridiculous.

MARION: Is it?

OLIVIA: I don't want to be rude...

MARION: (*Hard*) Then don't be. Don't get up on that high horse with me, kiddo...it's a long way down. I'm telling you that I know about you and George. Now are you going to deny it or do I give you proof? Real proof.

(*Olivia is silent. Rooney gets his telephone connection*)

ROONEY: (*Into the phone, his voice low*) That you, Mossy?...Mossy, it's me...Fergal. What's a comdom? [*sic*]

OLIVIA: No, it's true. I don't want real proof.

MARION: That's good, because there isn't any. I wasn't sure.

OLIVIA: Oh.

ROONEY: (*Into the phone*) Well Jasus, find out. (*Hanging up*) Ignorance, ignorance.

MARION: (*Wryly, sing-song*) I fooled you!

OLIVIA: Yes, you did. Well, now that it's out in the open, I want to be honest.

MARION: You're a sweetheart.

OLIVIA: Neither of us ever intended it to happen. George and I...

MARION: I don't care. I don't care what George feels about you or what you feel about him. I don't care if you played the death scene from *Camille* in broad daylight and sold tickets. All I want is your can out of here.

OLIVIA: Well, if you're going to be vulgar...

MARION: You bet your sweet ass I'm going to be vulgar. Because if you are not out of here in twenty-four hours flat, you know what I'm going to do? I'm going to walk into George's waiting room with all those people sitting around, and I'm going to say: "Good morning, Eleanor baby, did you screw my husband again last night? How was it? Was it good for you? Did the earth move? Did you come?" I'm going to do that, and I'm going to keep on doing it.

OLIVIA: You wouldn't dare.

MARION: Me? Don't you know who I am? I am a vulgar, brash, loud American...a Catholic redneck from Detroit, Michigan. We don't have manners or refinement, we don't know from nothing. You think I'm going to fight you for my husband? By your rules...teacups at dawn? Crap, kiddo. I'm going to kick your tight little keester right out of here, starting now. So how do you like them apples?

OLIVIA: If I go, George will...

MARION: Stay right where he is and take it out on me. I'm not even going to tell him we had this conversation. You tell him.

OLIVIA: I will.

MARION: You do that.

OLIVIA: I mean it.

MARION: Fine! (*She steps out of the playlet and into the present*) Fine. That was just fine, Olly dear. Thank you. (*To Conroy*) Maybe she did tell him...I don't know. Eleanor went, and George and I never discussed it. Oh, I meant we should kick it around one day when we were old and folksy and too comfortable to care. Funny thing...that day never comes. Then George bought the farm.

CONROY: The farm?

MARION: (*Jabbing a thumb upwards*) Heavenly Acres. So I never did get to find out. (*Conroy looks at her quizzically*) What was it that made Eleanor so all-fired special? Why he went to her for the answers I thought I'd given him. I'd be obligated for your opinion.

CONROY: (*Again a quick, blank smile*) Don't have one. (*He signs his name with a flourish and rises from the table*)

MARION: (*Quietly*) Come on Doc, you're holding out.

CONROY: I never knew your late husband. I don't even know the sort of man he was.

MARION: You knew him.

CONROY: When?

MARION: You knew him like I know your wife...that little lady who's sitting on the edge of the bed right now waiting for you to come get her. I look inside of me and I find her. Part of her.

CONROY: I don't think George and I have that much in common.

MARION: Not even Eleanor?

CONROY: (*A moment's pause*) Never heard of her.

MARION: Don't get mad. I wasn't insinuating...school's out now. What I'm trying to say is, if there was an Eleanor in your life...*why*? Maybe because she's young and your wife isn't?

CONROY: (*Firmly*) No.

MARION: Why, then? Because she's pretty and smart and new, and her body is good?

CONROY: (*Stronger*) No.

MARION: What else is there? Maybe she's fantastic in the sack, is that it?

CONROY: Maybe George got tired.

MARION: Do you mean of me? (*Shrugging*) Sure. I'll buy that.

CONROY: No, not of you...of something that's so natural to you, to every damn one of you, that you don't even notice it. Of *scoring points*. You...you like to play games, right? Well, this knocks your kind of game into a cocked hat...only there isn't any winner, because it never stops.

MARION: Scoring...points?

CONROY: And we have to play it. George and I have to play it, because if we don't play, we go under. But we get tired: you have more stamina than we do. So maybe that's the reason for Eleanor. George just needed a rest.

MARION: Him? He never played a game in his life.

CONROY: No?

MARION: Who...George?

CONROY: (*Suddenly*) There's no salt on the table.

MARION: What?

CONROY: I said, Marion, you forgot the salt.

MARION: Did I? (*Then*) Wait a minute: sure. George says I forgot the salt, and I say..."Go get it yourself."

CONROY: No. You fetch the salt.

MARION: (*His pupil*) I fetch the salt.

CONROY: (*Prompting*) And later on...?

MARION: Later on I...(*She sees the pattern*) There's egg on your lip.

CONROY: (*Wiping it off*) Is there?

MARION: Yecch.

CONROY: All gone?

MARION: And you left the kitchen window open last night.

(*This last game begins casually, then escalates in speed and intensity to rage and mutual loathing. From his desk, Rooney looks on with mounting alarm*)

CONROY: Did I?

MARION: We could have been murdered in our sleep.

CONROY: Sorry.

MARION: Don't be. I forgot the salt and you forgot the kitchen window. Now we're quits.

CONROY: Even Steven.

MARION: Only we could have had our throats cut.

CONROY: I did apologize. I should have closed the window and I forgot. (*Fatally*) I was tired.

MARION: I get tired, too.

CONROY: I know.

MARION: I don't think you do know. Maybe in your book, in that encyclopaedia of yours, this house runs itself.

CONROY: You work hard, I agree.

MARION: That's damn white of you, George.

CONROY: And I do, too.

MARION: Sure you do...it accounts for your dishpan hands. Only I can't afford to take afternoons off.

CONROY: When do I ever take...

MARION: A week last Tuesday!

CONROY: Did I?

MARION: Three hours and...(*Being noble*) I'm not the sort of woman who counts minutes.

CONROY: Count them, count them. I had no appointments, so I went to play a few sets at Fitzwilliam.

MARION: If that's where you say you went.

CONROY: I'm telling you that's where I went.

MARION: Then I believe you.

CONROY: I was in...

MARION: Who cares!

CONROY: Fitzbloodywilliam! (*She shrugs, a woman wronged*) Come to that, you go out, too. You have your coffee mornings, you meet your friends...

MARION: Why shouldn't I go out? You want me to stay indoors?

CONROY: No, all I'm...

MARION: Cooped up in this Alcatraz?

CONROY: It happens to be our home.

MARION: It happens to be my prison. Christ, now he begrudges me one cup of stinking coffee.

CONROY: Since when?

MARION: One lousy cup.

CONROY: You can drink coffee until it...

MARION: And a Danish pastry. As for my seeing the very few friends that thanks to you I have left...well, that of course is what you cannot stand.

CONROY: Is that a fact?

MARION: That is a fact. You don't want me to have a life of my own. It burns you up. If you had any guts, it would stick in them. Well, I have news for you. From here on in, I go where I like.

CONROY: Go, then...go.

MARION: I see...now you want to be rid of me. Well, the Woman in the Iron Mask is free at last, you know that? Damn you, George, I've been the doormat in this house all my life. I waited on you, slaved for you, and I reared your children. You didn't rear 'em...I did. (*She goes to where Rooney is sitting and drags him upright from his chair by the collar. Shaking Rooney at George*) George, take a look at your son.

ROONEY: Easy...easy...

MARION: He's everything a father could dream of...upright, honest, cultivated.

ROONEY: Jasus, let go.

MARION: A young Adonis. Six foot two...an athlete, he can have any girl he likes. They grovel at his feet. As for brains, he is brilliant...and it's thanks to me, because you never cared about him, you were never here.

CONROY: That's a lie.

MARION: (*To Rooney*) Are you listening, darling? Your father never even liked you.

CONROY: You evil old bag.

MARION: He hated you.

ROONEY: Gerroff.

MARION: (*To Conroy*) Monster.

CONROY: Superbitch.

MARION: Psychopath.

CONROY: Cow.

MARION: Pig.

CONROY: American.

MARION: Ohhh!

(*In her revulsion, Marion lets go of Rooney, who goes fleeing from reception, pulling a whistle from his pocket. He reaches the jetty and blows three piercing blasts*)

ROONEY: Come on...for Chrissakes, will ye come in! (*Meanwhile, Conroy and Marion stand as if frozen, glaring with intense loathing at each other. Then their features slowly relax and soften until they are smiling. Rooney returns, panting*) They're on the way. (*To Conroy*) Excuse me...I say they're coming. Have you it filled in? I say, have you your form?

CONROY: (*To Marion*) Did you fill in a form?

MARION: Yes, we filled in a form.

CONROY: Do I need to fill in a form?

MARION: No, you don't need to fill in a form.

(*Conroy crushes his form into a ball and throws it away*)

ROONEY: Ye can't do that. If ye want to hire a boat.

CONROY AND MARION: (*Together, without looking at him*) Cruiser.

ROONEY: Ye have to fill a form in.

CONROY: Why don't we go out and see our ship come in?

MARION: Why don't we?

(*They go out on the jetty*)

ROONEY: (*Feebly*) 'Tis against the rules. (*To Olivia*) Where are they going? What are they at?

OLIVIA: I love them. Aren't they incredible? They do this every anniversary.

(*Marion and Conroy, his arm around her shoulder, stand looking off at the lake. The sound of a diesel engine is heard. A ship's hooter blows*)

The End

Katharine Houghton

BUDDHA

Katharine Houghton

In *Buddha*, Katharine Houghton weaves an enchanting tale of a mid-life encounter between a man and woman that tantalizingly combines a romantic flirtation with Zen philosophy. The play was first performed in January, 1987 at the West Bank Cafe in New York City, directed by Rand Foerster, with Miss Houghton playing The Woman and William Cain playing The Man. The play is the first of a trilogy of one-acts including *On The Shady Side* and *The Right Number*, all three under the collective title *The Hooded Eye*, and each produced at the West Bank Cafe.

Miss Houghton's career as an actress has received wide acclaim in New York, the regional theatres, television, and film. On Broadway Miss Houghton appeared in *A Very Rich Woman* and *The Front Page*. Off Broadway she won the Theatre World Award for her performance in James Saunders' *A Scent of Flowers*. She also authored and starred in her one-woman show *To Heaven in a Swing*, a portrayal of Louisa May Alcott, presented originally at the American Place Theatre. During the 1984-85 and 1985-86 seasons she was a member of the Off Broadway Mirror Repertory Company and played in their productions of *Vivat, Vivat Regina* as Mary Stuart, in *The Madwoman of Chaillot* as Gabrielle, in The *Time of Your Life* as Mary L., and in *Children of the Sun* as Avdotya.

Extensive acting experience in regional theaters, ranging from the Actors Theatre of Louisville to the Kennedy Center to the Hartford Stage Company, includes the roles of Portia in *The Merchant of Venice*, Kate in *The Taming of the Shrew*, Laura in *The Glass Menagerie*, Catherine in *Suddenly Last Summer*, Nina in *The Seagull*, Yelena in *Uncle Vanya*, Nora in *A Doll's House*, Hedda in *Hedda Gabler*, Hypatia in *Misalliance*, The Patient in *Too True to Be Good*, Louka in *Arms and the Man*, Leontine in 13 *Rue de L'Amour*, Isabel in *Ring Around the Moon*, Antigone in Anouilh's adaptation of Sophocles' classic, Kathleen in *Terra Nova*, and Deborah in *A Touch of the Poet*.

Her appearances on television include roles in "Judd for the Defense" and in the award-winning shows "The Color of Friendship" and "The Adams' Chronicles." In film she is best remembered for her role in "Guess Who's Coming to Dinner."

With fellow actor-playwright Ken Jenkins, Miss Houghton

founded the Pilgrim Repertory Company. Several of their productions have toured widely throughout the southern states. Among Miss Houghton's other plays are three dramas for children: *Merlin*, *The Wizard's Daughter*, and *The Thought Castle*.

Characters:

> A MAN, *about fifty*
> A WOMAN, *about forty*

At Curtain:

> *A Woman is sitting alone on a log on a narrow beach near a quarry. Bushes and trees are in the background. She is dressed in a long, pale pink gauze beach dress, plastic shoes, a large straw hat, and large sunglasses. She is looking out into the audience, which is also the quarry.*
>
> *A Man enters wearing a business suit and carrying a brief case and newspaper. He looks the Woman up and down.*

MAN: Hello.

WOMAN: (*Not averting her gaze from the water*) Hello.

MAN: I'm Fred Bishop. I'm on the board.

WOMAN: That's nice.

MAN: The board of this quarry.

WOMAN: Yes...I'm a guest. So's my son.

MAN: (*Looking around*) Who?

WOMAN: He's the one out there, floating about in the inner tube.

MAN: That's your son? Don't give me that!

WOMAN: What?

MAN: You're not old enough to have a son that...large.

WOMAN: He's big for his age.

MAN: Yeah, sure...You don't mind if I swim in the nude, do you?

WOMAN: No, go right ahead.

MAN: (*While taking off his jacket and tie*) We do that here, you know, this is a private place. Not a bad idea, really. I believe in privacy, escape from the masses...Aren't you going to swim?

WOMAN: I've been.

MAN: Don't you want to go again? (*He grabs an overhanging branch and breaks it off, and throws it into the bushes*)

WOMAN: You just threw my bathing suit into the bushes.

MAN: What?

WOMAN: My bathing suit was hanging to dry on that branch.

MAN: Oh, I'm sorry!...But that's sumac, poison sumac. I was

getting it out of the way. It will give you an awful itch...Now it's all over your swimsuit. I'm sorry, really...I guess I'm not thinking too clearly...I've had a few...drinks.

WOMAN: It's all right. Don't worry about it. (*The Woman rises and retrieves her suit gingerly out of the bushes, returns to the log, takes a baggie out of her beach bag and puts the suit inside*)

MAN: You don't want to put that swimsuit on, you know. You'll get itch all over you. You don't have to wear a suit here anyway; I never do. (*The Man takes off his shirt*)

WOMAN: I'm not going to swim again anyway, so it really doesn't matter.

MAN: Do I offend you? I don't mean to. Alluding to nudity, I mean.

(*The Man sits on the log near her and begins to remove his shoes. His left shoe, the one nearest the Woman, has a knot in the lace which he can't seem to untie*)

WOMAN: Not at all. You're a grown man. You can say and do as you please.

MAN: That's one of the things I like about this place...Damn this thing...I can always say what I want. At work...well. At home...well...

WOMAN: Here! Give me that shoe!

(*The Man puts his foot on her lap like a child, unselfconsciouly, and she unties the knot while he talks*)

MAN: The people here are different: Avery's friends. Sort of crazy, really, but they say what they want, do what they want...Perhaps it's this place...so pretty, don't you think? The dragonflies on the water...

WOMAN: Yes. I like the dragonflies.

MAN: And those slender white trees...

WOMAN: (*Smiling*) Birch trees. There. (*She releases the Man's foot and he takes off his shoe*)

MAN: Yes, birch trees, the way the sun comes through their branches and dapples the water, and those huge granite chunks projecting themselves up into the horizon...are you laughing at me?

WOMAN: No, of course not. I like the way the dragonflies skit along on top of the water. And their color. That blue.

MAN: (*Looking at the Woman thoughtfully*) I think I began this conversation all wrong. I really didn't mean to offend you. I was on my way home from work. I stopped and had a few drinks. And then I couldn't go home. I knew if I stopped here, I'd find some friends, or someone to talk to, someone who wouldn't...

WOMAN: What?

MAN: Never mind. It's not important... And there you were, sitting on this log, a pink, gauzy dryad...and I aggressed you like a common mortal, interrupted your train of thought, bullied into your space. I'm really not like that. Thank you for untying my shoe.

WOMAN: You're very welcome.

MAN: You're sure you don't mind if I swim in the nude? I won't, if it bothers you.

WOMAN: I don't know you, so you see it doesn't matter.

MAN: What does that mean?

WOMAN: It's not important. You should do what you always do, whatever makes you comfortable.

MAN: So...you're a guest.

(*The Man takes off his T-shirt and drawers. He is now stark naked. In a production that does not wish the Man to be totally naked, he should be in his drawers only at this point. He is really quite a beautiful man, well filled out and proportioned, but he is childlike in his unawareness of his beauty and grace.*

The Woman avoids looking directly at him in a discreet, matter-of-fact way. She is also trying to avoid the sun which is shining brightly from his direction. At various points throughout the rest of the scene, she hides her hands in her sleeves, puts handkerchieves over the tops of her feet, etc. The Man is never quite sure whether she is hiding from him or the sun)

WOMAN: That's right.

MAN: Never been here before?

WOMAN: Never.

MAN: The rocks from this quarry paved the streets of Utica and Schenectady.

WOMAN: Really.

MAN: That's right. There was a quarry like this back in Lancaster, Pennsylvania where I grew up. Used to swim there with my dog. Used to give him baths in that quarry. He was the cleanest dog east of the Pacific Ocean. He liked to jump from great heights, you see. He was always jumping out the second story windows of our house. At the quarry, I'd just throw a stick off a twenty foot drop, and down he'd go! Then he'd swim to shore, climb up to the rock, and give me the stick. I'd soap him up, throw the stick, and down he'd go again, and come up rinsed. Best dog I ever had.

WOMAN: What happened to him? Oh dear, I don't want you to tell me that he jumped off that rock one day and never came up.

MAN: No, that's not what got him. It was the doctor who lived next door. The dog dug holes in this doctor's woods, buried his bones and stuff, so the doctor poisoned him. Can you imagine a doctor doing a thing like that? Hippocratic oath and all?

WOMAN: That's terrible...I wonder if it's always been impossible to have trust in people, or if it's just a symptom of our time.

MAN: (*He looks at the Woman a moment*) ...I don't know...(*He senses a hidden sorrow*) So...where do you come from?

WOMAN: New York City.

MAN: Oh, yes. I've been there. I love that statue in front of the Plaza Hotel...at Fifty-ninth and Fifth.

WOMAN: Yes, she's lovely.

MAN: She's naked.

WOMAN: No, she's not.

MAN: Yes, she is.

WOMAN: No classical sculpture is ever really naked. It's too idealized to be that vulnerable.

MAN: (*Considering*) Perhaps.

WOMAN: In any case, there are too many people.

MAN: What?

WOMAN: In New York City, Fifth-ninth and Fifth is the mecca of pickpockets.

MAN: I've never had my pockets picked.

WOMAN: Well, that's one of the virtues of not wearing pants.

MAN: (*Looking at her sharply. She smiles*) You *are* laughing at me.

WOMAN: (*Smiling*) No.

MAN: (*After a small pause*) ...There are too many people here, too. I don't mean here, at this quarry, this is private, but in town! We never used to have so many people, but they're coming over the borders in droves, from Connecticut, and Massachusetts, and New York. There's hardly a secret place left, hardly a spot not swarming with invaders and their refuse.

WOMAN: Perhaps so, but it's nicer here. Peaceful. My time here has almost totally restored my faith in...

MAN: What? (*The Woman shakes her head and adjusts a small towel so that it covers her hat and shades her cheeks*) What is it?...What's the matter?...Are you scared of the sun, too?

WOMAN: Yes, the sun can be a killer. It can give you skin cancer.

MAN: You think so, huh?

WOMAN: I know so. My husband got skin cancer from lying out in the sun, year after year. If he'd had to work in the sun, then that's another matter. But he wore his tan as a status symbol. Don't ask me why, because I don't understand it. I've warned my son to be careful, but he doesn't listen to me either, as you can see, or he wouldn't be out there poaching himself in that inner tube.

MAN: That's not your son.

WOMAN: Yes, it is.

(*Pause*)

MAN: The sun's good for you. Vitamin D. Things can't grow without sun. I like to feel it all over my body.

WOMAN: It's good in small doses, yes, but people overdo it. White people sometimes consider themselves superior to Blacks, but they spend an awful lot of time and money trying to look just like them. "Look how black I am," they say. It doesn't make sense, does it? You, for instance, you're about as cooked as a white person can get without being hospitalized.

MAN: I didn't know you'd noticed.

WOMAN: I see more than you think.

MAN: You don't seem to be looking at me, though. The entire time we've been sitting here on this log, you haven't looked at me once. If you had, you would have seen that I'm not cooked, but...

WOMAN: My God, what's that?

MAN: What's what?

WOMAN: That!

MAN: Oh, that's Buddha.

WOMAN: Buddha?

MAN: Yeah, he's Avery's dog. You know Avery, who owns this place.

WOMAN: It looks like an hermaphrodite.

MAN: An what?

WOMAN: An hermaphrodite. Look at those teats!

MAN: Those what?

WOMAN: Teats! Look at its teats!

MAN: Tits! You mean tits!

WOMAN: No, I mean teats! They're so large, they look as though they've been suckled.

MAN: They're no more use than tits on a bull.

WOMAN: What?

MAN: Haven't you ever heard that expression? (*No answer*) Look at his balls! That's more to the point. Biggest balls I've ever seen on a dog.

WOMAN: Men have been known to employ their teats.

MAN: I beg your pardon?

WOMAN: I've read about cases, haven't you, where a woman dies and there's nothing to feed her baby, so the father puts the baby to his teat, and after awhile he begins to lactate, to produce milk, didn't you ever hear of that?

MAN: You're just as crazy as everyone else here at Avery's.

WOMAN: No, it's true. Stranger things than that have happened.

MAN: That's all right, remember this is the place where you can say what you like. (*He looks around to see if anyone is in earshot*) Did you know that a man's tits can be very sensitive, even like a woman's, that they can be an erogenous zone? (*She smiles*) Now, that's a fact! I know from my own experience...You think that's funny. Laughing at me again.

WOMAN: No.

MAN: Some men might not want to admit that, but I for one have felt...very sensitive...very pleasurable...about my tits...What are you looking at?

WOMAN: I'm...I'm looking at Buddha. He knows how to live...dozing in the water, half in, half out. An hermaphrodite crocodile.

MAN: Why don't we go for a swim?

WOMAN: I don't really want to now, and anyway you got poison sumac all over my suit.

MAN: You don't have to wear a suit here, remember? It's private. That's the point of the place. Avery lets just a few of us come here and nobody bothers about bathing suits. (*No answer*) You got something against nudity?

WOMAN: There was a woman here earlier.

MAN: Naked?

WOMAN: Yes.

MAN: Yeah, you see? Everyone's naked: decorously naked, men, women, children. I've noticed there're a lot of people around here who look better with their clothes off than on.

WOMAN: Buddha's not naked.

MAN: Well, you can see his balls, can't you, *and* his tits!

WOMAN: You wouldn't be able to see so much of them if he

hadn't been shaved.

MAN: Avery shaves him because of the ticks. That's another thing we never used to have so much of: TICKS! But they come over the borders too, from Massachusetts and Connecticut, and I suppose we even get them from New York.

WOMAN: She wasn't just naked.

MAN: Who?

WOMAN: That woman who was here earlier.

MAN: Yeah? What was she?

WOMAN: I think she was...I'm not sure what the word means...but I think she was...obscene.

MAN: No!...A woman on this beach?...One of Avery's friends? That's not possible!...What was she doing?

WOMAN: Sitting on a towel.

MAN: So?

WOMAN: Her legs were spread wide apart for all the world to see...Not just for a second or two, but relentlessly...(*Pause*) There were lots of people about. Lots of eyes. Looking. It was a sort of sacrilege...I felt sorry for her children.

MAN: Oh?

WOMAN: Her children were wearing bathing suits.

MAN: Children tend to be inhibited.

WOMAN: I don't know. They may know more than you think. I was glad that the parents let them wear suits, but I wondered if they mocked them for it in private.

MAN: I've never known a nudist who was a bigot, who *demanded* that others take their clothes *off*.

WOMAN: Certain things don't benefit from so much sun.

MAN: Don't you think that maybe you're a little old-fashioned?

WOMAN: Certain things prosper in the shade.

MAN: Or even Victorian?

WOMAN: Violets, trailing arbutus, lady slippers...If you transplant them into the sun, they wither and die.

MAN: Or just plain inhibited.

WOMAN: People wore clothes long before the Victorians.

MAN: People have been repressed for a long time. You take a society that abhors nudity, that demands full-dress uniforms and promotes cover-ups, and it's a fascist warlike society every time. Nudity makes you peaceable because you see very clearly that you're all brothers and sisters when it comes down to the skin.

WOMAN: People say the cave men wore clothes, tribes in Africa wear long robes, Islanders wear grass skirts, there must be a reason for it, and I don't mean just the weather. It's obvious why the Eskimo wear clothes.

MAN: The Eskimo! The Eskimo spend at least fifty percent of their time lying around naked in their igloos!

WOMAN: In the *privacy* of their igloos, yes! Covering our bodies, or parts of our bodies...may have...implications that we don't understand.

MAN: I grew up in the "privacy" of a household where nobody hugged and nobody kissed, and nobody went around without their clothes. For more years than I care to mention, I've been embarrassed about my body. I've even made love in the dark, by choice!...But now, since Avery started this little club, I've changed my mind about a lot of things. I've changed my mind about my body. I can come here and be free...and I'm no longer embarrassed to walk around in my skin, or to watch everyone else walk around in their skin, and I feel that this place here is the closest thing I'll ever know to Eden before the fall, and I say that that's good!

WOMAN: So, why are they called private parts?

MAN: What?

WOMAN: What that woman was showing to all the world.

MAN: Verbal repression. Part of the verbal repression that has swamped the species since time began...that has been laid on us by the priests, or the churches, or somebody...

WOMAN: Who? Who laid it on us?

MAN: Somebody long ago...I don't know when it started, somewhere back in the time of myth, I suppose. Perhaps it was even God, in the Bible! The God who kicked us out of Paradise, fig leaves and all.

WOMAN: I'm not at all sure that wearing clothes is a sign of repression.

MAN: So, what is it then?

WOMAN: Supposing, just for the sake of argument, that I was your lady, or even your wife...

MAN: (*Not hostile to the idea*) Yes...

WOMAN: And supposing at this moment this beach was crowded with people: men, women, and children, but especially men. Friends of Avery's, men with whom you compete in the world.

MAN: Yes...

WOMAN: Now, supposing you prided yourself on being...intimate with me, and supposing there was still an exciting and dynamic attraction between us...

MAN: (*Interested*) Yes...

WOMAN: Would you really be happy if I stood up and took off this dress, under which I have nothing on but my skin, my very white skin, and then sat down on this beach in front of everyone with my legs spread apart like an open scissors?...(*The Man doesn't answer*) Well?

MAN: Well...(*He thinks and then suddenly speaks*) So that's what you meant before!

WOMAN: What?

MAN: When you said it didn't matter to you if I took off my clothes...because you didn't know me!

WOMAN: Yes.

MAN: So, if you don't know me, and it doesn't matter to you if I'm naked, why have you spent this entire conversation not looking at me?

WOMAN: (*After a pause*)...I don't think that the first man and the first woman put on clothes to hide their shame.

MAN: No?...So, why did they do it?

WOMAN: They put on clothes to hide their beauty.

MAN: Now, what would they do a damn thing like that for?

WOMAN: Because they knew something more than the animals.

MAN: What?

WOMAN: Well...if Eden or Paradise is a symbol for an early state of consciousness, or really unconsciousness, and the expulsion from Eden was a result of eating from the tree of knowledge, and gaining a more self-aware complex sort of consciousness, one might say that we had to leave Eden because we weren't animals anymore. We knew something after we bit into that apple that separated us forever from our simple, unselfconscious animal state.

MAN: So, what did we know?

WOMAN: We knew mystery.

MAN: Mystery?...What kind of mystery?

WOMAN: I don't think that animals know mystery, do you?

MAN: Buddha! Hey! Do you know mystery?...He wagged his tail. What do you suppose that means?

WOMAN: You haven't answered my question...Do animals know mystery?

MAN: You haven't answered my question: why have you spent this entire conversation not looking at me?

WOMAN: (*After a pause*) You said earlier...about the land: "There's hardly a place left not swarming with invaders and their refuse." Couldn't that also be said about the body?

MAN: Are you talking about the proliferation of pornography?

WOMAN: Not necessarily...Do you, by any chance, have any thing, any feature about your body that you don't like?

MAN: ...Yes.

WOMAN: Do you want me to know about it?

MAN: ...No.

WOMAN: When you wear clothes...do you emphasize or minimize this...defect?

MAN: When I wear clothes! What is this? Some kind of survey? I wear clothes!...I minimize it, of course.

WOMAN: You see, you hide it, cover it up. You make it appear that you don't have this defect, and by hiding it, you free yourself to become something else, something not trapped by this defect...

MAN: (*Interrupting*) Don't keep calling it a defect! It's not that bad.

WOMAN: ...And then your spirit can become whatever it wants to become, whatever it fancies; it's not locked into the limitations of the body, even of a body that is modestly endowed.

MAN: Modestly endowed! (*He surveys himself*) Do you really consider me modestly endowed?

WOMAN: I wasn't referring to you in particular.

MAN: (*He is beginning to feel awkward*) I think it's going to rain.

WOMAN: (*Looking up at the sky*) Do you think so?

MAN: Yes, most definitely. (*He reaches for his T-shirt*) I can feel a chill in the air. The wind's rising. Don't you feel it? (*He puts on his T-shirt*)

WOMAN: (*Intimately*) May I tell you something?

MAN: Of course. (*He puts on his top shirt*)

WOMAN: My mother wasn't a beautiful woman...not really. Feature by feature, she would never have been called a beauty. But everyone said she was beautiful. She was given a body like a scrub pine and she transformed it into an elm.

MAN: (*Putting on his shorts and trousers*) She knew how to dress.

WOMAN: She did, yes. She knew how to dress...But it was more than that. She created the illusion of beauty by everything she did: the way she walked, her voice, her hair, her eyes, her smile, her laughter...her compassion. Men adored her. Women, too. The house was always full of people who wanted to be near her. But if from the beginning, she had been doomed to be naked, I wonder...I wonder if she would've ever had the chance to transform herself, to become the creation of her fantasy.

MAN: You are a beautiful woman. I don't know what your mother looked like, but I can see that you are a beautiful woman.

WOMAN: How do you know? What can you see? My entire body is covered up, even the tops of my feet...

MAN: I can tell. From the moment I saw you, I...I felt desire for you.

WOMAN: You can't see me. I could be a monster underneath all this—horribly scarred, or deformed.

MAN: I see you...I see the shape of you, the sound of you. You're no monster. That thing you're wearing is soft and gauzy like...feathers, like a bird, you are like a bird, a soft, downy little bird, and I want to touch you, catch you, you elude me, you won't look at me, and you won't tell me why, I want to take you home with me, I want to undress and caress you, you...What am I saying! You must forgive me. I have offended you. Please forget what I said. It *is* going to rain. (*The Man puts on his socks and shoes and loops his tie around his neck*)

WOMAN: (*In her own world*) Clothes may even be essential to our ability to evolve.

MAN: (*Relieved that she is not offended*) You must be freezing in that light gown. Would you like my jacket?

(*He picks up his jacket. She seems lost in thought, so he puts it gently around her shoulders. This next sequence of dialogue should build to a climax with the top of the build being "disrobes for the first time before the eyes of the beloved." They should both speak quickly*)

WOMAN: Clothes not only hide our bodily defects, but they reveal the substance of our spirits, our wild wingéd spirits that leap about in our poor bodies, like a bird trapped in a cage.

MAN: (*Still standing in back of her*) Like a bird, yes, I like it, I like your spirit, leaping about, more than I can say without even knowing your name.

WOMAN: There is a mystery...the first man and the first woman knew it. The angels, even, were jealous of them...I think.

MAN: Yes, a mystery...you are a mystery.

WOMAN: It's why I haven't looked at you...

MAN: Why?
WOMAN: Perhaps Eve knew it first.
MAN: This mystery?
WOMAN: Yes. She bit into the apple first, and then she held it out to Adam, and then they both became aware of the magic, the power, the exultation...
MAN: Yes, all that...
WOMAN: I don't know if it's a high mystery or a low mystery...
MAN: Perhaps it's both.
WOMAN: It has to do with the mystery of the hermaphrodite.
MAN: It does? You mean like Buddha?
WOMAN: The union of opposites...
MAN: The yin and the yang...
WOMAN: It is the mystery of the explosive moment...when one disrobes for the first time before the eyes of the beloved. (*Silence. The Man droops in dejection and sits back down on the log*) It's not too late, you know.
MAN: (*Looking up*) You mean...
WOMAN: That's right. I haven't seen you. I haven't the slightest idea what you look like, clothed or naked.
MAN: You don't? I thought you said you did?
WOMAN: No, that's why I haven't looked at you. I had a feeling it would come to this.
MAN: (*Pleased*) You did?
WOMAN: From the first, I recognized your voice, your hesitations, your silences...
MAN: Recognized? Did you know me before?
WOMAN: I've been waiting for you. I'd almost given up.
(*A brief silence as the Man looks at the Woman*)
MAN: Can I...can I see you sometime? I mean...You know what I mean.
WOMAN: Of course. I think it would be very nice.
MAN: Will you be back tomorrow, here at the quarry?
WOMAN: No, my son and I leave for New York tonight.
MAN: That's not your son.
WOMAN: (*Smiling*) Yes...it is.
MAN: He's your lover.
WOMAN: He's my son.
MAN: I have a strange feeling that nothing is what it really is...that you are really a spirit, a pink dryad disporting with a mortal. Even Buddha doesn't seem like just a dog today...

WOMAN: I'm real, and that is really my son, and Buddha is just a dog.

MAN: Shall I write to you? In New York?

WOMAN: If you like.

MAN: Your husband, he...

WOMAN: My husband is dead.

MAN: I'm sorry.

WOMAN: He got too much sun, and too little exercise, and knew very little about...

MAN: Mystery?

WOMAN: ...Yes.

MAN: Where do I write?

WOMAN: Phoebe Carleton, 342 East Seventy-ninth Street, N.Y., N.Y., 10021.

MAN: Phoebe...I like that name...it's, it's...

WOMAN: Victorian? (*She smiles. He smiles*)

MAN: No, it's romantic...a name of another time and place.

WOMAN: A place not swarming with invaders and their refuse?

MAN: Yes.

WOMAN: It was my mother's name.

MAN: My name is Frederick Bishop.

WOMAN: Yes, I know.

MAN: How do you know?

WOMAN: You told me at the beginning.

MAN: (*As if it were a long time ago*) Oh, yes...Frederick Archer Bishop. I was named for my mother's dad. Now, there was a fellow...but that's another story.

WOMAN: Tell me sometime.

MAN: I will. (*The Man gets up from the log*) Phoebe Carleton, 342 East Seventy-ninth Street, N.Y., N.Y., 10021...close your eyes and count to ten. Slowly.

WOMAN: One, two, three, four, five...(*While she's counting, the Man goes in back of her to take his jacket, but then decides to leave it on her shoulders. He vanishes through the bushes*)...six, seven, eight, nine, ten.

(*Blackout*)

The End

Deborah Pryor

THE LOVE TALKER

Deborah Pryor

Easily one of the most exciting plays in the 1987 Humana Festival of New American Plays at the Actors Theatre of Louisville, Deborah Pryor's *The Love Talker* makes its debut in this series. Miss Pryor's play was the single play in the Festival chosen to be directed by Artistic Director Jon Jory, who praised the writer's unique voice: "The thing that's always the most fun is when you find somebody who doesn't write like anybody else, and she definitely doesn't. She's fascinated with the folk tradition and with folk myth. And then she looks inside herself, finds the contemporary content of the traditional myth, the then she melds the two together." *Washington Times* reviewer Hap Erstein on its Louisville premiere cited *The Love Talker* as "a small gem that revealed a first-class writer emerging" and observed that the play "draws us so thoroughly into its mythic, folktale world that urban tourists should succumb to the spell of its nightmarish, unchartered land."

Born in Elizabeth City, North Carolina, Deborah Pryor grew up in various Virginia towns. She attended the College of William and Mary, where she studied playwriting with Louis Catron and had several of her plays produced in the theater department's playwrights' lab theater. After receiving her B.A. in English from William and Mary, Miss Pryor studied in the Playwrights Workshop at the University of Iowa, graduating with an M.F.A. in playwriting in 1980.

The New Playwrights Theatre in Washington, D.C. premiered her play *Burrhead* in 1983, which had a New York production in 1986 (and later won the 1987 Mary Roberts Rinehart Award). Another play, *Wetter Than Water*, was runner-up in the 1985 CBS-Dramatists Guild Playwriting Award, and was subsequently produced at the Virginia Stage Company.

Miss Pryor is currently writer-in-residence at the Arena Stage in Washington, D.C., under a grant from the National Endowment for the Arts. After writing plays for more than a decade, Deborah Pryor has been discovered by regional companies, who are certain to seek and produce more of the work of her unique talent.

Characters:

GOWDIE BLACKMUN, *a fourteen year old girl*
BUN BLACKMUN, *her sister, twenty years old*
THE RED HEAD
THE LOVE TALKER

Setting:

An old house in the Clinch Mountains, Virginia.

Time:

The present, the longest day of the year.

At Curtain:

The lights go up on a very old house surrounded by woods. Beyond the house is a ridge of mountains where the sky shows
through the trees. Woods close in on a small yard with a hollow
tree stump rooted near the house.

At the very edge of the yard, almost in the woods, stands the
Red Head. She is female, but her age is difficult to pin down.
She may look childish one moment, older the next. Her hair is
tangled and wild. She wears a long dark covering, a cloak or
blanket. She is compelling to look at, but not pretty. There are
things not quite human revealed in her body and mannerisms.
These things not quite human should be very subtle and not
dawn on us easily. From the first moment she's seen, she's
turned toward the house, pointing at it. She stands patiently a
moment. The light goes out on her.

The light in the yard goes up to the brightness of a midsum-
mer evening. The great room of the house is old and the walls
and floor have settled cockeyed. There's a big cupboard and a
little bed next to the wall. The front door is low, wide and deep.
Into the lintel wood above it are carved a row of crosses. The
door knob has been painted red. The windows all have red
thread or yarn tacked from top to bottom of the sills. There is
another door leading out to other rooms. This is not a cabin,
but a very old house. Some of its furnishings are heirlooms

gone to seed, mixed in with crude homemade pieces. There's a table, a half-churn, some chairs and a little stool. Nobody is in the house.

Gowdie Blackmun stumbles into the yard from the woods. She is a fourteen year old girl wearing a dirty work dress and boots. She drags an empty burlap sack after her and carries a short-handled mattock, half pick axe, half hoe, over her shoulder. She wanders through the yard disorientedly, dropping the sack and mattock behind her in a trail. She comes to a stop in front of the hollow stump, stands staring down into it and splashes the rainwater in her face. She squats on the ground beside it, reaches for a stick and starts drawing in the dirt.

Bun Blackmun enters the yard from a path. She is twenty years old, wears a work dress and is carrying a half-full milk pail. Gowdie stands up, staring at her drawing, drops her stick absently.

BUN: You just back? Looka this. One pail. Three cows and this is the grand prize. They all got blue tits, too. The old people used to say it means Something's been sucking them dry. Lucy and June both tried to kick me when I's milking but I ducked and they got each other. Now they're all mad. How 'bout that? A shed fulla steaming cows with blue tits and not enough milk to wash your foot in. (*Realizes Gowdie's not listening*) Gowdie?

(*Gowdie looks up at Bun for the first time*)

GOWDIE: Huh?

BUN: Gotta listen right the first time. Blink once and I'm gone, sugar. Got your work done?

GOWDIE: I guess.

BUN: Well, it's late to be just trailing back. Which field were you?

GOWDIE: Back digging them osh taters like you told me. (*They both look at the empty burlap sack*) I spilt 'em.

BUN: Uh huh.

GOWDIE: I had a dragging weight full, but coming back I tripped…and I spilt 'em. They all rolled down a hill.

BUN: All of them.

GOWDIE: (*Laughs despite herself*) Into gopher holes. Plugged 'em right up.

BUN: What are you snickling at? Have you lost your sense?

GOWDIE: (*Sober*) I'll pick them up tomorrow, Bun.

BUN: I reckon you will. I don't want you coming back so late again, you hear? I was starting to bother. The sun went from the ash to the poplar. If it wasn't St. John's you'da been walking in pitchy black.

GOWDIE: *How* long? From the ash...

BUN: To the poplar. (*She sees the drawing*) Is this yours? (*Gowdie tries to run away, but Bun makes her stand and look at it*) What do you call that? (*Bun grabs the drawing stick, switches Gowdie's legs*) Stand still. Stand still!

GOWDIE: Ow! God dang, Bun!

BUN: If you'da spoke something nasty as that, you'd had Boraxo bubbles coming outta your mouth a week. You know it? DO YOU KNOW IT?

GOWDIE: (*Overlapping*) I know it! (*Inspects her legs*) You nigh laid me open.

BUN: (*Scuffing drawing out*) I don't want no more art work on the yard. Where'd you get a low idea like that? Come on. Time to be inside. (*Bun picks up the sack and mattock. She looks at the clean blade*) Them's awful high-class potatoes you been digging that ain't touched dirt.

GOWDIE: (*Under her breath*) Maybe I licked it clean.

BUN: Don't give me sass. If you wasn't digging osh taters, what was you doing?

GOWDIE: I'll pick 'em up tomorrow.

BUN: I smell fish so bad they must be hanging in the trees. Go on, get. (*Gowdie goes in the house, toys with one of the red threads at a window*) Well. We ain't got no taters so we ain't got no mash so we ain't got no supper. Nothing but resurrection pie. (*Bun sets the mattock against the side of the house and brings the milk pail inside*)

GOWDIE: I ain't hungry.

BUN: You gonna break your health. Digging all them imaginary potatoes and not eating.

GOWDIE: I'll make you something. I'll make you sweet sop.

(*Gowdie takes a loaf of bread from the cupboard and cuts chunks off it. Bun dips a finger into the milk pail*)

BUN: If them cows get sick, won't that be a mess? I know what Grandaddy'd done if he'da seen them looking like that. Woulda set up all night in the shed with a rifle on his lap.

(*Gowdie pours syrup over Bun's plate of bread. She turns to put the bread and syrup up. Bun reaches out and grabs the tail of*

*Gowdie's dress. She picks burrs off the material, silently holds
up a palmful to Gowdie)*

GOWDIE: *(After a frozen hesitation)* Stickers?

BUN: Like hotel labels on a suitcase. Where you been, girl?

GOWDIE: No place.

BUN: It's written on you clear as paint. Them brambles and that
clean hoe. They're dancing around and singing a song to me. Did
you go off the road?

GOWDIE: Why would I?

BUN: Did you go off the road?

GOWDIE: It were just a rabbit. I don't reckon there's anything so
terrible following a rabbit a little ways.

BUN: I told you, don't go in them woods for nothing. Not a
rabbit, not a ladybug, not St. Joseph flying on a broomstick.

GOWDIE: I never meant it. I was just walking along to the patch.
And I seen this little brown rabbit run across the road in front of
me. And he stopped and turned his head like he was saying, come
on behind me.

BUN: So you followed this whitetail till almost sundown. That
what you want me to swallow?

GOWDIE: He went in the woods. I went in the woods. He'd hop a
step and I'd follow. Then we come to the edge of that old fallow
corn field. And I lost him.

BUN: Gowdie, do you get what I say when I talk or do you just
hear my teeth clacking? I mean it—keep outta them woods.

GOWDIE: When I looked up, in the middle of the field there was
this little springhouse sitting where I never seen one before. White
with a little pointy roof.

BUN: *(Deadly quiet)* Don't you make things up. Don't you dare
make things up.

GOWDIE: There wasn't no door at all but a board loose, so I
squeezed in. It was dark at first and all I could tell was water
bubbling from the spring in the very middle. Then my eyes
brighted and I could tell there was stuff on the walls.

BUN: Like what stuff?

GOWDIE: Pictures of men and women. Seemed like.

BUN: You ain't sure? It dark at noon or something?

GOWDIE: Men and women, certain. Drawed with something like
a piece of char from a fire. Covered ground to ceiling.

BUN: Were these ladies and gentlement doing anything like
what you was drawing in the yard?

(*Gowdie gives no answer for a moment*)

GOWDIE: At first they was hard to look at. It give me a funny feeling. Like a wet fish slipping down my back. I felt the air hugging me. And all them folks doing like barn animals up on the walls was winking and saying, come up here with us. I don't know how long I was sitting and I heard this plop in the spring so I looked down in it. And when I caught sight of myself, the me in the water looked like it knew more than I did and was waiting for me to catch up.

BUN: Hush!

GOWDIE: Then the springhouse just weren't there no more, and I was on my knees in the middle of the field and the sun going down.

BUN: (*Slaps Gowdie*) Hush! (*Bun goes to the front door, looks out of it suspiciously*) Don't talk no more. Forget it all, right down to the rabbit.

GOWDIE: How can I? It's in my head like a picture on the wall.

BUN: Right down to the *rabbit*. (*Bun goes down the passage to her room. Gowdie sits at the table alone*)

GOWDIE: (*Whispers*) It weren't so bad. (*Gowdie sulks a moment, dips her finger in a sugar bowl and eats sugar. She gets up, taking the sugar bowl and walks toward her bed. She looks up to see a man standing at the threshold of the open door—the Love Talker. He is barefooted and drenching wet, his hair matted in clumps. Long pond grasses hang from his clothes. He stands dripping, looking at her. She drops the sugar bowl and it spills across the floor. The Love Talker stoops down, reaches over the threshold and presses a finger in the sugar. He sucks it off his finger, smiling at her. Then he stands up and disappears from the door. Gowdie is frozen a moment, then runs to the door. She stoops and wipes at the drips. Glancing at Bun's door, she runs out in the yard, sees nothing, then runs a little ways into the woods. The man is nowhere. A strange, watery, rushing noise is heard. The Red Head appears suddenly before Gowdie*) Did you see...anybody? (*The Red Head smiles at Gowdie. She moves her mouth as though speaking, but all that's heard is the rushing, bubbly sound of water getting louder*) What? What?

(*The Red Head beckons Gowdie closer. Her voice is heard vaguely, getting louder while the watery sound fades*)

RED HEAD: Don't be afraid. Don't be afraid. The blood of fifty bulls, the sap of an old vine, the sharp edge of the new moon is in

you. Your enemy will crush like a brown leaf in your hand.
(*Gowdie comes slowly closer to the Red Head. She disappears. Bun comes back into the great room with an old cardboard box. She sees the mess of sugar, calls out the door*)

BUN: Girl! (*Gowdie runs back to the house. Bun catches her as she comes out*) I'll frail you till you look like a candy cane if I catch you going in them woods again. (*Bun pushes Gowdie inside. Gowdie stoops and tries to clean up the sugar*) What happened?

(*There is a long pause*)

GOWDIE: Nothing. I had a clumsy fit. (*Bun goes to the cardboard box, starts taking out ash wood crosses, red ribbons, bunches of dried yellow flowers. Gowdie inspects it all*) I never seen these.

BUN: Grandma's old charms. They was in the half-loft. (*Bun starts tacking up the ash crosses around the room*)

GOWDIE: You gonna hang the house with this mess?

BUN: (*Reciting as she places charms*)
Cold steel they cannot stand,
Crosses made of ash,
Rowan berry, red thread,
Nor knife in door may pass.

Grandma taught me that before I was three. Don't you undo a one of them. No telling what you been calling up. (*Gowdie finds a red ribbon and hangs it around her neck, laughs at herself, takes it off. Bun puts it firmly back on her*) You shouldn't a gone in. You understand me? Whatever your little white house looked like, it wasn't what it seemed. Just tricks and glamor. You shoulda stayed on the road like I said.

GOWDIE: It was such a calling thing.

BUN: I just bet it was. Calling, wiggling its hips and looking pretty. (*Gowdie angrily takes the ribbon off and throws it on the floor*) Come here. I'll comb your hair. I heard you could comb bad thoughts right out of a person's head. They come out in little blue crackles. I'll show you. Come on.

(*Bun pulls a chair into the open doorway and sets the little stool in front of it. Gowdie finally comes to sit on the stool. Bun sits behind her and combs her hair*)

GOWDIE: What do you reckon they're like? Them things made that little house?

BUN: The kinds of things that would wait all day for the chance to hurt you. It's jam on bread to 'em. Get you out in the woods to step on the stray sod so you couldn't find your way in bright sunlight three feet from your own house. But if you turn your clothes, sometimes that breaks it. There's the little girl without no clothes who walks beside you from that thorn tree down at the gate to the big oak and sinks in the ground...if she can't lead you off the side of the mountain in the dark before then. The thing in the orchard that you can't see, but you can feel it in the trees, hating you...up on the old cut where it goes through the hollow and it's always so dark you can't see daylight at noon on Easter, there's something like a old man, only brown-leathery and haired all over, following you ten paces behind and stopping when you stop. It got in Grandaddy's car oncet. He booted the thing out. That's what I say. Boot 'em all out.

GOWDIE: (*Under her breath*) I don't know if I would.

BUN: I beg your pardon?

GOWDIE: Said maybe I wouldn't boot 'em all out.

BUN: Your grandma woulda slapped you silly to hear that talk. She and her sister went to this granny that lived over the ridge to get their fates told. And the granny touched spit on Grandma's eyes and not on her sister's and they was walking home and sister looks off the road and says, "Ooooo, ain't it pretty?" And Grandma says, "What is, fool?" "That little chair, setting in the woods. I'm gonna go get it and take it home." So Grandma has to charge after her and gets there just in time to see her sister sitting down on a big nest of brownie spiders like it was the peartest little chair in the world. They had to hold her in bed for a month. That granny'd set your Grandma's eyes so she could see it was a trick. Them People couldn't never pull a thing over on her from that day on.

GOWDIE: I ain't a idiot. I ain't gonna sit down in a spider's nest.

BUN: Tricks and glamor. Food stealing, empty-handed-jealous, baby switchers. They can take one look at you and know what's written on your last page. (*Bun stops combing and stands suddenly*) It ain't good to even speak of them. (*She closes the door. The gloaming is almost over and the house is dark*)

GOWDIE: Did Mama ever see one?

BUN: God knows what she saw.

GOWDIE: Did she, yes or no?

BUN: There was something she called a love talker. No more talking now. (*Bun lights a kerosene lamp. She takes a big knife from the cupboard and lays it on the floor in front of the front door with the edge facing out*) Don't you worry. This is a safe house as long as you keep the door shut and your mind orderly. Time for bed. Don't open that door to nothing. Maybe you better come in with me.

GOWDIE: I ain't no baby.

BUN: Then wear this. (*She picks up the red ribbon and hands it toward Gowdie*)

GOWDIE: Did you ever see that springhouse?

BUN: Once.

GOWDIE: You never said!

BUN: There weren't nothing to say. I was twelve, I seen it in the woods and I said to Hell with it.

GOWDIE: How could you not go in? Bun—it wasn't so awful bad...

BUN: Don't mistake it, maidy! They are not your friends. Forget what you seen today and you'll be happy. And say your prayers so the light comes back quick.

GOWDIE: (*A revelation*) Bun's jealous.

BUN: Of what?

GOWDIE: Of what's in the springhouse.

BUN: (*Very quietly*) What is in it? (*Gowdie only smiles at her. Bun furiously pinches Gowdie's arm and hurls the red ribbon in her face*) WEAR IT!

(*Bun goes to her room and slams the door. Gowdie tries the charm on again. She takes off her dress and has on a home-made shift underneath it. She turns the lamp down dimly and sets it by her bed. She takes her boots off, gets into bed and closes her eyes. All during this process she recites over and over by rote*)

GOWDIE: Truly the light is sweet, and a pleasant thing it is for the eyes to behold the sun. Truly the light is sweet, and a pleasant thing it is for the eyes to behold the sun...

(*After a moment of silence, she sits up in bed. She gets up and hovers near Bun's door a moment, listening. She takes down the ash crosses. She gets scissors from the cupboard and cuts the red thread in the windows. She takes the knife away from the front of the door. She takes a chunk of bread and fills a basin with some milk and places it on the table. She opens the front door wide. Each of these steps is taken with trepidation. After each charm is taken down, each lure is set, she waits tensely for what might happen. Last, she takes the ribbon off her neck, slowly, fearfully. She gets in bed, lies shut-eyed and*) *listening. A whippoorwill calls close by. The Love Talker appears in the door. He enters, goes to the table, tips up the basin and drinks from it. He eats some of the bread. Then he climbs over the footboard of Gowdie's bed, and hunkering down, sits on her feet and watches her. She lies frozen, eyes closed. The Love Talker reaches out and touches Gowdie's forehead with his finger. She opens her eyes. He smiles at her)*

LOVE TALKER: I have good news for you, Gowdie Blackmun.

(He reaches to turn out the lamp. The lights go down. The lights come back up on the house, early the next morning. Gowdie is alone, asleep in her bed. She bolts upright, takes a moment to realize she's awake. She gets out of bed and stumbles sleepily outdoors. From behind the house she comes out with a washtub and some rags. The tub has some water in it. She takes the tub to the woods, sets it down and kneels to wash her face. She frowns at her face in the water. She stands in the basin and starts washing with the rag. She scrubs herself roughly, but then lets the rag glide up her leg. The Red Head has appeared from the woods behind her, wearing a wreath on her head made of flowering thorn. She watches unseen awhile)

RED HEAD: Caught you. *(Gowdie sees the Red Head, stands stock still in the wash basin)* Pretty stuff, lookie at it. All hunched up and grabbing the nightie. *(Holds out her hand in a friendly way)* All done? Come out of the little sea. *(Gowdie takes the Red Head's hand and steps out. The Red Head sniffs Gowdie's neck)* Good work. Very clean, so it is. Let's make friends, okay? *(She leans in close to Gowdie's face)* Don't you talk?

GOWDIE: Can you tell dreams?

RED HEAD: I'm very good at that. I'm good at just that very thing.

GOWDIE: It was last night. I'd lost it, after how you do when you wake up. But it been coming back to me.

RED HEAD: Like a fish flipping out of the pure air into your lap. Shh! I see it! I caught your dreamfish. There's you in bed, froze for listening. A bird called. And Something come in the door. This weight, heavy and warm as sun through a window pressed itself on you. He pushed gifts and riches into your hands you'd never seen before. He squeezed hot birthday present through your blood veins. He poured the running oil of gladness over your head, in your eyes, down your throat and between your breasts. And when the weight of all them presents was on you, he called you to come out of the old skin. And at first you wouldn't. You held onto the bedpost.

GOWDIE: It seemed it might be bad. Floating that way. I might not come back at all.

RED HEAD: But you let him drag your soul right up from the bed and when he dropped it, you fell for miles back onto the mattress. But not back into the little girl. She'd shrunk like a curl of ash. You were humming like something lightning'd struck alive. Lookie.

(*The Red Head motions Gowdie to look in the basin of water. Gowdie kneels and looks. She touches her face*)

GOWDIE: It won't stop shivering.

RED HEAD: Hit it pretty close?

GOWDIE: That was the dream.

RED HEAD: It wasn't no dream.

GOWDIE: (*After a moment*) Do you know him?

RED HEAD: (*Holds up two twined fingers*) That's us. Snug as a snake curled round an egg. He'll be back. He's got more for you. He'll put something in you like a hearbeat that'll make the trees try and touch you. He'll give you everything. Do you know what I mean?

GOWDIE: Sure.

RED HEAD: You opened the door. Your fortune was, you opened the door. There ain't no taking a welcome back. (*She kisses Gowdie on the cheek*) No taking back. (*The Red Head takes the thorn wreath off her head and shows it to Gowdie*) My present.

GOWDIE: White thorn.

RED HEAD: Yes. Pretty-pretty. Pleasure and pain twisted together.

(*The Red Head suddenly jams the wreath on Gowdie's head. Gowdie screams in pain. The Red Head watches her writhe a moment, then exits quickly*)

GOWDIE: Take it off! (*She stumbles blindly over branches and brush trying to pry the thing off*) Son of a bitch! (*She sits on the ground, wrestling with it. In the house, Bun enters the great room from her bedroom. She notices that things are not quite right about the room—it doesn't hit her all at once*)

BUN: Gowdie? (*Bun listens, hears something: the lowing of cows far off*) Them cows is out. Like they're way down the valley. It's all of them! Gowdie? (*Bun sees the cut threads, sees an ash cross thrown on the floor*) No. (*She feels a wall with the flat of her hand, as though sensing something from it. She feels more frantically: a door, the table top, the bed*)

No! Like the old days. The goddamn old days. (*Bun hurriedly leaves the house, finds Gowdie sitting in the woods with the wreath on, a little blood trickling on her face. Bun runs at her and knocks her over, sits on top of her*) Who give you the crown...Miss America?

GOWDIE: This lady. It won't come off. (*Bun tugs at it unsuccessfully*) OW!

BUN: Let me tell you 'bout my morning so far.

GOWDIE: Lemme go, Bun.

BUN: Someone's been rearranging the furniture and setting the cows loose.

GOWDIE: It weren't me.

BUN: Who was it then? What you done? What you let in?

GOWDIE: Don't sit on me, Bun. You scaring me.

(*Bun lets her up*)

BUN: Ain't no call to be scared of me, maidy. Just tell me.What did you let in our house?

GOWDIE: I thought it was a dream. There was this man. A real nice man.

BUN: Girl, you never let in no man. And he wasn't nice.

GOWDIE: He told me I was prettier than the apple tree in the west corner of the yard. He told me, I was grown and I'd be mistress of my own house.

BUN: You know how bad a thing it is you done?

GOWDIE: (*Whispers*) He climbed in my bed, he...

(*Bun pounces on her and shakes her*)

BUN: You ain't got no call opening our house like that! You ain't the only one living in it.

GOWDIE: He weren't bad. He talked pretty.

BUN: A pretty thing? Jumped down offa that springhouse wall?

GOWDIE: You never seen him, how do you know?

BUN: 'Cause I done heard him, sure enough!

GOWDIE: You never told me that.

BUN: When you was a baby. I kept singing and rocking you till it was over.

GOWDIE: Mama let him in?

BUN: I locked my door and sat up all night holding you in my lap, hearing her laugh, while something was trying to get in, pressing on my door like the wind bellying a sail. Last night after all them years I woke up and couldn't move. I thought it was a dream, but it weren't no dream. You put us in danger. You got to slam the door in his face.

GOWDIE: But I called him.

BUN: Come in the house.

(*Gowdie runs from her*)

GOWDIE: No!

BUN: Do you hear what I say?

GOWDIE: (*Flitting away from her, laughing*) No! Not today.

BUN: Where do you think you're going?

GOWDIE: Off the path.

(*Gowdie laughs, running off into the woods and off. Bun is left watching after her. The lights go down. The lights come back up on the house. Bun, wearing the red ribbon around her neck, sits alone, working the dasher in a little churn by her chair. After a moment the door to her room swings open a little. She gets up and shuts it. As she sits back down, the front door opens slowly, all the way. She closes it. After she sits down again, both doors slowly open. She sits still a moment, then slaps at something near her ankle, as though something were touching her. It goes farther up her legs. She jumps up from the chair*)

BUN: Stop it. (*Something touches her more and more intimately as she stands. It runs her onto Gowdie's bed*) STOP IT RIGHT NOW! (*She grabs a pair of big iron shears from a corner, opens them in the form of a cross and lays them under the mattress on Gowdie's bed and sits on it. Nothing happens*) I know you're still there. Waiting at the edges. (*The front door starts to open. She shuts it. It starts to open again*) I'll do it as many times as you want. (*She shuts it firmly, sits back down. The door opens again, this time Gowdie walks in. Her shift is weatherworn, muddy and torn. She has a dirty face, hands and feet and still has the wreath of white thorn in her hair*) Where you been? All day and all night and all day, driving me to death worrying. Where?

GOWDIE: I been here and I been there. (*She peeks in the churn*) Any butter yet? (*She dips a finger in, licks the cream*)

BUN: If you think real hard, you might remember that's your work. And catching in them damn cows scattered over three fields eating whatever they like. And digging the potatoes. I can't do all my work and yours too.

GOWDIE: I forgot.

BUN: What is it? Do you hate me? Is that it, is that what he tells you? Do you hate me, Gowdie?

(*The next five speeches are said all in a rush, one stepping on top of the next)*

GOWDIE: (*Covers her ears*) Don't speak that! I forgot my chores.

BUN: I ain't talking about chores.

GOWDIE: I don't hate you!

BUN: Shut him out. Tell him to leave us alone like we been.

GOWDIE: I forgot my chores. I FORGOT. (*There's a pause. Gowdie smiles to herself*) He makes it so I can stand in the middle of the woods and feel the roots of the trees growing down into the earth like it was a dark sky. Then he makes it all tilt so the earth, sky and the root trees are on top and the airy ones are below, and I can see both, tilting and twirling, dark sky chasing light sky, never catching each other. He lets me see this. He said he's gonna give me everything.

BUN: Like your mama?

GOWDIE: I don't even remember my mama.

BUN: I do. Real good. When Daddy died, her eyes got dark like she couldn't see us no more. She holed up sitting in the corner of the back room, rocking, facing the window, sputtering down like candle fat 'fore the light goes out. And she called Something. They had to come drag her down offa here. *I* was the one saved you and hid you up on the ridge in a log and whistled to you through a crack so you wouldn't cry.

GOWDIE: You making it up.

BUN: She drew things on the walls I had to scrub off every day, 'cause if you looked at them too long they turned you crazy. And went up on the ridge cutting stumps and branches into such god-awful shapes I couldn't even name 'em to you. I'd be walking down the road and there'd be one grinning through the leaves at me. Or sitting up where you can see the sunset, there'd be something funny about a branch over my head and it'd turn out to be something nasty she'd done to it. I hacked down every one I found and I burned it. You know what I think? I think you and Mama got you the same boyfriend. I recognize the goat smell.

(*Gowdie splashes the dasher down in the churn angrily*)

GOWDIE: Making it UP!

BUN: Then where's Mama? Don't you be going dark on me, too. Don't end up creeping through the woods at night and forgetting your own human name. What does he do that could make it worth that?

GOWDIE: (*Whispers, tantalizingly*) What's he do? What's he do?

BUN: I ain't sharing this house. I ain't waking up no more

shivering sweat. It tries to get in my room. It holds me so I can't move and it gives me dreams. Gowdie, please. I can't sleep here no more like that.

GOWDIE: Poor Bun. Her house got a hole knocked in it. The vines are slipping in, curling up the walls, strangling the cups and pitchers, squeezing the boards till they crack. What's she gonna do when she can't tell her house from the woods? Maybe it was the weight of something good buckling in your door and pressing you in the bed.

BUN: There's ways to drive them off. You can shut the door on him.

(*Gowdie takes Bun's hands and kisses each*)

GOWDIE: Bunny. Fall halfway down a well for me. Then I will.

(*Gowdie gives Bun a little slap. A noise has begun to stir outside. It goes around and around the house, making the walls creak as if they were being squeezed. It is a windy, rushing noise, getting louder. The cream in the little churn bubbles up and over the top onto the floor. Gowdie laughs delightedly and watches the walls of the house. Bun grabs a towel and tries to staunch the flow of cream from the churn. The front door bams open. Bun runs to her room and closes the door. It refuses to stay closed. She runs out again with a quilt from her room*)

BUN: I ain't staying where he is. (*Bun runs out of the house into the dark woods. Then, having to yell above the noise*) Father deliver against all wild things, all runners in darkness and tricking spirits, night whisperers, dream-pressers, things there but not to be seen...(*She can't go on. The noise is much louder—unbearable to her. She presses her hands to her ears and crouches down. The noise stops. Gowdie slowly walks toward the open front door*)

GOWDIE: (*Whispered*) Come in. Come in. Let me ride in your hand. Let one hand drop me and the other hand catch.

(*The lights go out on Gowdie as she stands in the doorway.*
The lights come up on the woods, dawn. Bun, camouflaged by her quilt and the underbrush, is asleep on the ground. The Red Head is wandering around slowly, bent close to the ground. She doesn't see Bun. Every once in a while she catches something and eats it)

RED HEAD: Squirm squirm. I gotcha. Ha! (*She slaps at something and swallows it. Bun wakes up, cautiously peeks out and watches*) Dig dig dig dig dig. Pop! (*Pops something in her mouth*) Ha!

(*Bun crouches motionless, then runs and tackles the Red Head. The Red Head screams with disappointment and struggles wildly to get free. Bun holds onto her and grabs a handful of the Red Head's hair*)

BUN: Ain't this interesting? Now what could this scrawny thing be? Not big enough for a human. Not pretty enough for a animal. You're slipping, Red, letting somebody sneak up on you like that.

RED HEAD: Lemme go. I just live down the mountain. My mama'll be looking for me.

BUN: They ain't a mama on earth looking for you. Yours probably stuffed you in a old log hoping somebody with a strong stomach'd take pity on you. Or does your kind even have mamas?

RED HEAD: I'll show you what I do got...! (*She tries to tear at Bun's face, but Bun holds her*)

BUN: Oh, don't leave now. Seems to me we got a little business to settle, me seeing one of you 'fore you seen me. I get a prize, don't I? I got to think. What's the worst hook I could stick into you night crawlers? It's names, ain't it? You got names you guard like stolen sin.

RED HEAD: No no no no no no! Nevernevernevernever names!

BUN: That's just what I want then. A name. I want that bastard's name. That love talker.

RED HEAD: Uh-uh! No!

(*The Red Head tries more wildly than ever to get away. Bun yanks her head back by the hair*)

BUN: You got to. I caught you and you got to give me what I want. Ain't it a shame? What is it?

RED HEAD: Got something better. Listen. I give you rich things. I give you sparkles. You want sparkles?

BUN: What, magnolia seeds for rubies? Godspeed petals for sapphires? Tricks and glamor, gone like pouring water on sugar.

(*The Red Head takes a ring off her finger and pushes it wildly at Bun*)

RED HEAD: Put this on! Never wrinkles, never old!

BUN: Tell me his NAME! (*Bun slams the Red Head's head on the ground. The Red Head shuts her eyes and mumbles something in Bun's ear*) Again. (*The Red Head whispers it again*) Better not be no trick.

RED HEAD: Done it, done it. Lemme go now.

BUN: Not till you tell me how it works. What happens if I say the name?

RED HEAD: Bad.

BUN: Bad enough to blow him outta these woods?

(*The Red Head doesn't respond. Bun starts to slam her head down again*)

RED HEAD: Yes, yes!

BUN: What else?

RED HEAD: Catch his eye unblinking and say the name to him in triple. In his ear.

BUN: And what's gonna keep him in whispering distance while all this is going on?

RED HEAD: If he comes near to you and you have his eye, he can't leave till you say it—or not.

BUN: Don't fret yourself. If he comes close enough, I'll say it. But if he's too scared to try his luck, he better stay away from me and my sister. Got it?

RED HEAD: Loose! (*Bun lets the Red Head up. She scrambles away*) Gonna get what you asking for, fool.

BUN: (*Laughs*) Oh I'm shaking! I'm peeing right down my leg! (*The Red Head furiously throws a pine cone at Bun. This only makes her laugh more. The Red Head disappears in the woods. Bun goes up to the house. Gowdie is asleep in her bed. Bun quietly puts the ash crosses back up, then sits down watching by Gowdie's bed. Bun makes a call like a whippoorwill. Gowdie wakes up, looks around immediately, sees only Bun*)

GOWDIE: You come back. Been sitting in that chair watching me all morning?

BUN: Oh, no, maidy.

GOWDIE: It's late. How come you not after me to do my work?

(*Bun says nothing. Gowdie starts to run for the front door*)

BUN: Going someplace? (*Gowdie stops at the door*) You won't find him.

GOWDIE: I reckon he finds me.

BUN: I think your loverboy's circuit ride's been cut.

GOWDIE: What you talking about?

BUN: Big sister knows his name and you ain't his girl no more.

GOWDIE: Liar.

BUN: Go and see. So gooey with love he nearly melts out on the floor for you. Where's it now?

GOWDIE: You're just dead green jealous. He don't leave just 'cause you flap your apron at him. (*Gowdie runs off into the woods. Bun just sits. In the woods, Gowdie flops down, stretches out on her back under the trees. She laughs*) Shoo you away with her apron! Maybe she been practicing. Scooping up storms in her tassie cup. Sopping up creeks with her mess rag. Pushing back the dark like a window curtain. (*Laughs at the idea*) You'll come. You'll bend down to me like a tree. You'll drag me up again. (*Still on the ground, she reaches her arms up. There is a long still silence. She sits up suddenly*) Won't you?

(*There is a distant rumbling of dry thunder. The lights go down on her. In the house, Bun has lain down on Gowdie's bed. The Love Talker appears at the open front door. He does not come in but stands outside, not clearly seen. His features are not visible. Bun sits up, alert*)

BUN: Ain't you got the word? I'm dangerous to be around.

LOVE TALKER: You ain't bound to use what you got. There's all kindsa possibilities.

BUN: Come here then. I'll give you one possibility you ain't gonna like.

LOVE TALKER: You wouldn't do it. You wouldn't be mean to me. Let me in. Find out what Mama was laughing about on the other side of the door.

BUN: Come close enough for me to tell the color of your tricking eyes.

LOVE TALKER: I know you. I know who you are. You hold your hands over your eyes when you dream.

BUN: Ask for it. Come on and ask for it, you bastard.

LOVE TALKER: Bun be nice. She wouldn't use the name. She grown up so pretty. If she was good to me, I'd do anything she wanted. I make her so happy she sprout leaves from her fingers.

BUN: Run and beg, boy.

(*The Love Talker starts to scratch on the door jamb, while his voice remains sweet*)

LOVE TALKER: Come on. Be nice. (*Motioning to her charms*) Look at all the magic you got. I must be all you think about. (*Bun angrily gets out of the bed, grabbing a salt shaker from the table and throws salt at him. His figure wavers back from the door but is still visible. Then, almost whispered*) Bunny bunny bunny. One way or the other.

(*The Love Talker vanishes from the door with a short, unearthly noise. Bun busts out the door and looks around. She exits into the woods, calling for Gowdie. Gowdie appears in the woods, much dirtier, torn. She looks sick*)

GOWDIE: (*Looking at the back of her hand*) So white. With little blue rivers. You won't come near to me. I tried and tried. I'm a leaf-slider. I'm a soft-flapper in the trees. I'm Nothing brushing by. (*Bun's voice is heard distantly calling Gowdie*) Gonna have your way. Gonna get your doors closed and have your way! (*She hears Bun call her name again. She covers her ears*) Stop it. STOP IT. I hate you. I do, I hate you!

(*At that moment, the Red Head appears somewhere in the woods. She smiles at Gowdie. A sound emanates from her, but is not her voice. It is a frightening noise. The Red Head holds her hand out to Gowdie but Gowdie backs away, scared. The Red Head says something, but the angry noise gets wilder and muffles it. Eventually her words weave out from the noise and the noise fades*)

RED HEAD: (*Simply, smiling*) All yours.

GOWDIE: (*Covering her ears*) NO!

(*The Red Head vanishes. Bun enters, rushes to Gowdie and hugs her*)

BUN: Come home now. Come back inside. It's all right. He's gonna leave you alone. I'll make you the best supper you ever had. Anything you want. Just tell me.

(*Gowdie walks weakly back to the house supported by Bun*)

GOWDIE: Feel how cold my toes and fingers. (*Touches Bun's face*) Feel.

BUN: Get you some food. Get you washed up. Then you sleep long and heavy and wake up tomorrow like my old girl.

(*Gowdie, siting at the table, violently knocks her plate off to the floor*)

GOWDIE: Ain't hungry. And I ain't your old girl.

BUN: He's not coming back to you.

GOWDIE: He is!

BUN: Well, let's see. Maybe he'll stand dying for you, think so? (*Bun opens the front door and dog whistles loudly*) Come on, boy! You were gonna knock my door in, don't be shy now. (*Gowdie starts to cry. Bun shuts the door and goes to comfort her*) You'll forget all about him.

GOWDIE: (*Tries to hit Bun*) Nunh!

BUN: Don't you strike at me.

GOWDIE: I won't. I won't hit. I won't do anything bad. Please. Let him in. I won't run away again. I promise. (*Whispers*) Listen—listen...I'd share. I would. You let him in, he forget every mean thing you done to him.

BUN: NO.

(*Gowdie suddenly flails out and beats on Bun in a rage, then stops, appalled*)

GOWDIE: I didn't mean it. I didn't mean it. Bun, don't be mad. (*Gowdie kneels and hugs Bun. Then she sings softly*)

Bun, Bun, I'm her slave,

She's the Queen and I'm her knave.

BUN: Will you stop wanting him? Will you stop looking for him?

GOWDIE: (*Starts to nod and say yes, then explodes*) NO!

(*Gowdie tries to run out the door but Bun holds her*)

BUN: You're staying in here. (*Bun drags and wrestles Gowdie over to the foot of the bed. She grabs a rope hanging on a peg on the wall and ties Gowdie standing up to the bed posts by her wrists. Gowdie bites and kicks her*) Cut out that kicking. I'm gonna find you out there. If you don't come, I'll know you for a coward. Then you watch out, slippery boy, I'll say your name so loud it'll blow you back to Hell butt forward. (*She lifts Gowdie's face up*) They switched on me. They stole my pretty little girl and stuck me with a monkey-face changeling with old eyes. I want my baby back.

GOWDIE: She ain't coming back. She's dead. (*Bun angrily grabs a rag off the table and blindfolds Gowdie. She starts out the door*) Sister. Be sure you don't take a wrong step.

(*Bun hesitates in the door, then goes out. Gowdie slowly, silently twists her wrists in the ropes. The lights dim on her. Bun makes her way through the woods and is not far from the house. She stops short, not quite like she's bumped into a wall, but more like an internal muscular jerk. She laughs uneasily at herself and starts off again. The same things stops her. She tries several directions, more and more panicked, but can't get farther than a few feet. The woods around her suddenly black out, leaving her in a small lit circle. She can't get past it*)

BUN: That's silly. There's the oak and the thorn where they always...(*She jerks around as though one tree had suddenly shown up in another spot*) I ain't fifty yards from the house. I know where I am. (*Whispered*) I know just where I am. (*She is totally disoriented; tries to find her way in many different directions but can't. She starts to sink down in panic. Then breathlessly fast, by rote*) Father-father-father, deliver against all wild things, all runners in darkness and tricking spirits, night whisperers, dream-pressers, visions that make your creatures mad, things there but not to be seen, crawlers in the leaf mold, hands that reach in the window, that touch the covers, that embrace, the rager with dark blood on its face, the love talker who touches the brain with cold and burns the body, from these deliver me. All creation is in your power and all these dangers you made too. (*She stops, frowns*) These you made...too.

(*In the house, Gowdie is still straining against the ropes. The Red Head stands at the door. She scratches a fingernail playfully down the wood of the door. Gowdie raises her head*)

RED HEAD: My, my. We doesn't look so good.

GOWDIE: She gone to get him. She got his name. She making me boil up. Looka me.

RED HEAD: (*Untying Gowdie's ropes*) He didn't promise pretty. He promised you everything. How can a little mind hold it? Like dipping a tea cup in the river, it'll knock it from your hands. Better not try and know it. Better step in and let it float you down. A darkness crackling with light and a brightness muffled up in a coat of dark. One hand drops, the other hand catches. One hand catches, the other hand drops. It's all for you.

GOWDIE: He said he had good news.

RED HEAD: That is the good news.

GOWDIE: I don't want all of it.

RED HEAD: Too late. Him or her? You have to choose.

GOWDIE: What if I can't?

RED HEAD: There's no such a thing.

GOWDIE: What if I choose against him?

(*The Red Head pushes Gowdie down on her back, folds her hands over her chest like a corpse and closes Gowdie's eyelids*)

RED HEAD: You wouldn't like it at all. (*The Red Head remains sitting crouched on top of Gowdie. She bends down close*) Let's make friends. Okay? (*The Red Head leads Gowdie by the hand to the hollow stump. She stands facing Gowdie across it. She dips her hand into the stump and it comes out dripping red. She presses her hand to Gowdie's chest, leaving a bloody hand print*) Do something about it.

(*The Red Head smiles, walking backwards until she's out of sight. The lights go down on Gowdie. Bun is still trapped in the stray sod. She looks up—sees the Love Talker who appears in the shadow past her circle of light*)

BUN: Come in. Come in. I have a word to say to you. I have

three words. (*The Love Talker doesn't move*) The leaves in the trees? Or the leaves on the ground? Which way am I? Up or down. It got to be one. Don't it? (*He just stands in the shadow*) Come closer. (*He moves into the circle of light very close to her. Gowdie is seen faintly at a distance, standing and watching*) Lemme see your eyes. (*The Love Talker raises his eyes to hers. Bun keeps her eyes on him always*)

LOVE TALKER: You turning your back to me so many times I know it better than your face. Holding your heart like a velvet jewelry box. Open it up and I'll cover you with all them dangerous pretties you never spent.

BUN: Once. (*Bun leans in and whispers his name in his ear, moves her head back swiftly to keep her eyes on his*)

LOVE TALKER: Back in the old days when you heard Mama singing and the window sash rumbled up, you laid the baby on the pillow and pressed your ear against the door so hard you could hear the swirls in the wood. You listened. And when Mama screamed, you screamed with her. I heard you. In that whispery little-girl voice...you screamed. Dirty girl. Bunching up the sheets and falling through the sky so fast your nerves got tails like comets. Come with me. I'll set you a dinner of smooth arms and round legs and wet hair at the back of the neck. I'll pour slow syrup on it all then throw in the match and make you dead and alive and nowhere.

BUN: (*Grimly*) Two times. (*She leans in and whispers the name in his ear, pulling back quick to keep eye contact with him*)

LOVE TALKER: Bunny. I'll give you joy and pain flipping like the sides of a penny. I'll take you off that straight path and set your feet dancing on a ground of witch burrs. All places will be yours. I'll make you someone you hardly know and when you catch sight of your dirty, smiling face in a still stream, you'll scare yourself. But it'll be all of you. Jump. It ain't the jaggedy end of the world. There's all sorts of possibilities.

BUN: Three times. (*Bun leans in to say his name the final time, but he kisses her before she does. Bun fights, starts to return the kiss, then hurtles back from him, breaking eye contact*) NO! (*The Love Talker quickly vanishes back into the shadows, gone. Bun runs back to the house, grabs the mattock leaning against the side of the house and slams it down before her as a protective charm*) I still know your name, you son of a salt bitch. Come court me now.

(*A rushing, keening, wind-like noise has begun to start up. Bun hurries apprehensively back into the house. The noise rises, going around and around the house.*

Gowdie walks slowly toward the house. The Red Head appears up on the ridge in her black cloak. She watches Gowdie, and as Gowdie passes by her, crouches and covers her face completely with her hood and lays her hands on her head. Bun inside the house runs for her bedroom door, but the noise seems to emanate from there; she looks, panicked, around the room.

Gowdie has reached the mattock in the yard. She stoops down and picks it up. Gowdie outside and Bun inside make momentary eye contact. Bun pushes the bed out and hides between it and the wall. Gowdie, carrying the mattock, walks into the house. She goes to the bed, kneels on it, swings the mattock up and brings it down in one hard stroke between the bed and the wall. There is no sound from Bun. The wailing noise stops and all that's heard are normal forest sounds. Gowdie watches a stream of blood run slowly out from under the bed. The Red Head stands up, uncovering her face. The Love Talker appears in the door. Gowdie turns to look at him. The lights fade quickly out)

The End

Paul Selig

TERMINAL BAR

Paul Selig

Paul Selig's *Terminal Bar* presents a futuristic view of the devastation inflicted on the country by an unspecified plague. Written as the public shows increasing concern with the AIDS epidemic, the play will prompt the observer to make a connection between the fictional plague and the actual menace. Despite the dire subject matter, Mr. Selig presents his moribund nightmare with generous touches of gallows humor, transforming the unbearable situation into a compelling, human drama. First presented at the acclaimed Edenburgh Festival Fringe in 1985, the play was described by reviewer Nicholas de Jongh of the *Guardian* as "an attempt to be a briefing for a descent into hell. I emerged in a cold sweat." And Raymond J. Ross of *The Scotsman* observed, "Despite bravado and pretense the characters' feet are still firmly on this earth and the bleakness of their situation (almost in the room of Sartre's *Huis Clos*) at times is lifted through the black humour and sharp irony." Subsequently the play was presented in London at the Man in the Moon Theater and in other productions throughout England. Such attention merited the inclusion of the play in the British anthology *Gay Plays III*.

The New York premiere in 1986 of *Terminal Bar*, presented by En Garde Arts, was cited by Mel Gussow of the *New York Times* as an outstanding example of a "site-specific" production—a play presented in a non-theater environment especially chosen and adapted for the locale of the play. Gussow further observes that to his credit the playwright "is less interested in making grandiose philosophical statements than in recording the life and life style of his particular survivors. The characterizations are acute..."

Other plays by Mr. Selig include: *Body Parts*, produced in New York at the Ohio Theater, *Long Island Dreamer*, a mini-musical written on commission for the New York Shakespeare Festival, *The Pompeii Travelling Show*, presented in workshop at the San Diego Repertory Theater, and *Moon City*.

Mr. Selig received his B.F.A. from New York University's Dramatic Writing Program, and he is a recent graduate of the Yale School of Drama. At present Mr. Selig is playwright-in-residence at The Poetry Center at the 92nd Street Y.M.C.A. in New York City.

Characters:

MARTINELLE, *twenty-five, a streetwalker*
HOLLY, *thirty, a runaway housewife*
DWAYNE, *seventeen, a schoolboy*
VOICE OF LENNIE
VOICE OF BERNICE

Scene:

The action of the play takes place in the Terminal Bar, an abandoned club in New York City's red-light district.

Time:
The season is winter. The time, the near future.

Prologue:
Music plays in the darkness. It is gentle, futuristic, slightly mournful. It continues quietly throughout the prologue.
Martinelle sits isolated in a pool of light. She is twenty-five years old and vaguely attractive. She wears a fake fur chubby, a mini-skirt, and sequined platform shoes. She holds a large portable radio in her lap. A price tag hangs from it. Martinelle fiddles with the radio. It broadcasts static.

MARTINELLE: *(To someone offstage)* So there I am, standin' in the ruins of the Crazy Eddie Christmas window holding on to this T.V. for dear life, an' I am dealing with this PERSON who is trying to pry it outa my arms. So I tell him, "What do I look like to you that allows for you to treat me in such a manner? I'm no refugee. You don't see me dragging my mattress along the highway." But he wasn't buying. So I say, "YOU take the radio an' give ME the damn T.V." ...Charlie? You get through to Staten Island or you still loving yourself in the mirror? Anyways, I told this guy he'd look real sharp walking around the streets with a radio. He said it was a basic look an' he was not a basic person. I told him to look on the positive. Fact that anybody's still walkin' the streets at all is cause for a party. "Radio'd add a bit of class," I said. "Like being in your own parade." Then he says to ME, "All's fair in love an' looting," an' he dances out the window with the freakin' tube...I'm not getting any stations on this. How's that for fun, huh Charlie? I spray painted lips on the hole in the wall. It's a big kiss from me to you...Charlie?

(Martinelle goes back to examining the radio. She remains dimly lit throughout the following. Lights up to reveal Holly on another part of the stage. She is thirty years old, southern, and very pregnant. She has an enormous teased hairdo. She packs a suitcase with miscellaneous items: baby bottles, a camera, etc. Dwayne, in darkness, is the voice of Lennie)

HOLLY: Lennie? I'm upstairs. Earth to Lennie.

LENNIE: What is it?

HOLLY: I feel like hell an' I ain't hung over. You doing somebody?

LENNIE: Yes.

HOLLY: I can sniff the formaldehyde all the way up here. Who you doing, Lennie?

LENNIE: Ricky Jordon.

HOLLY: Alice Jordon's son? He wasn't but a child. What happened to him?

LENNIE: Plague.

HOLLY: *(Excitedly waving an American flag from suitcase)* THAT'S THREE, LENNIE. THAT'S THREE FOR AURORA.

LENNIE: He'd been to Houston with the chorale from the high school.

HOLLY: I helped out at his party when he turned nine. I remember that day because people was actually saying it might snow. It didn't after all, but I remember wishing it had. Still, a fine time was had by all.

LENNIE: You frightened people.

HOLLY: *(Packing liquor)* I don't like kids. Kids don't drink. We never had any kids before 'cause they'd all suffocate.

LENNIE: What are you talking about now, Holly?

HOLLY: In the closet. You keep the cleaner's plastic in the closet. Folks know you use it for embalming?

LENNIE: Does it matter?

HOLLY: To me it does. It's distressing to get a dress back an' know the plastic's gonna be wrapping a cadaver. You get to my favorite part yet?

LENNIE: No.

HOLLY: Well, tell me when you do 'cause I don't wanna miss it. Tell me how it works, Lennie.

LENNIE: They let out a breath...

HOLLY: So you stick a feather on their lips so you can see when the time comes. (*Laughs*) That's my favorite part 'cause it's the most unnatural thing you do. I tell about it at parties. (*Pause*) Maybe I got the plague, Lennie.

LENNIE: Don't be a fool.

HOLLY: Maybe I do. TURN THE DISHWASHER TO BOIL. BURN THE SHEETS. HOLLY'S GOT THE PLAGUE.

LENNIE: You couldn't have it.

HOLLY: I most certainly could. I know what's going on in our country's urban centers. I read the magazines.

LENNIE: You couldn't have it. You're a Christian. Alice Jordon is very ashamed right now.

HOLLY: I don't believe it's true what they say. I think it's carried on the air. Like snowflakes, only invisible. (*Pauses, rubs belly*) Maybe it's just my condition. Lennie? I'm fine.

LENNIE: What are you talking about?

HOLLY: Jesus H. Christ. MY CONDITION. (*Pause*) I went down to the room yesterday.

LENNIE: Did you wear a mask?

HOLLY: I didn't know that was Ricky Jordon on the table. He developed just fine. Pretty as his mama. I went into the closet an' played with the plastic.

LENNIE: Did you wear a mask when you went into the room?

HOLLY: I shaped the plastic into a body. Do you know what that body turned out to be, Lennie? A woman. I thought that was sorta strange. I laid down next to it anyway.

LENNIE: Long as you wore a mask.

HOLLY: I THOUGHT about wrapping myself up in it. But I ain't lived yet.

LENNIE: Jordon boy used to come swim in our pool.

HOLLY: (*Closing suitcase*) I'm leaving you, Lennie. I'd rather be embalmed by a stranger.

LENNIE: Well, will you look at that. There it goes. There goes the feather. (Lennie laughs)

HOLLY: (*To herself*) I ain't even seen snow...

(*Lights dim on Holly. Martinelle still examines the radio. More static*)

MARTINELLE: Charlie? I stuck my head through the hole in the wall an' said our names together. They echoed around the entire room. Charlie an' Martinelle. Martinelle an' Charlie. (*Pause*)

Charlie? (*Lights up on Dwayne on another area of the stage. He is seventeen years old, homely, and wears a parochial school uniform. He is coatless and obviously freezing. Holly, in darkness, is the voice of Bernice*)

DWAYNE: HELLO? HELLO, MOM? I'M DOWNSTAIRS.

BERNICE: What?

DWAYNE: Under the window. Downstairs.

BERNICE: WHAT YOU WANT, WHITE BOY?

DWAYNE: Bernice?

BERNICE: DWAYNE? IS THAT YOU, DWAYNE? (*To someone inside*) It's the Copeland's boy, Dwayne. WHAT YOU WANT, DWAYNE?

DWAYNE: I can't get in the apartment.

BERNICE: I CHANGED THE LOCKS.

DWAYNE: What?

BERNICE: I CHANGED THE LOCKS.

DWAYNE: Where's my parents?

BERNICE: THEY'S EVACUATED.

DWAYNE: Can I have my coat?

BERNICE: (*Inside*) He wants his coat.

DWAYNE: I'M COLD.

BERNICE: YOU CRAZY, DWAYNE? YOU THINK I'M GONNA RUMMAGE THROUGH THAT FILTHY ROOM OF YOURS ON MY NEWLY FOUND LEISURE TIME? (*In*) Leave me be, Roscoe. Quit futzing with my hairpiece.

DWAYNE: I WANT MY COAT. I'M COLD.

BERNICE: YOU BRINGIN' ME DOWN, DWAYNE. YOU BRINGIN' ME DOWN AN' I'M HAVIN' A PARTY. WE'RE DRINKING THE NYQUIL OFFA YOUR BUREAU. (*In*) What? (*Out*) DWAYNE? ROSCOE WANTS TO KNOW DID YOU TAKE IT FROM THE LITTLE CUP THEY GIVE YOU OR PUT YOUR MOUTH ON THE BOTTLE?

DWAYNE: I…I don't remember.

BERNICE: WELL, THINK. THINK. 'CAUSE YOU'RE THAT WAY, AREN'T YOU, DWAYNE? YOU'RE THAT WAY. ROSCOE SAYS YOU TRIED TO TOUCH HIM THROUGH HIS PANTS WHEN HE WAS TAKING YOU UP IN THE ELEVATOR, AN' I FOUND MATCHBOOKS IN YOUR LAUNDRY. YOU'RE A CARRIER.

DWAYNE: GIVE ME MY COAT.

BERNICE: TELL BERNICE THE TRUTH, NOW. TELL ME

SO'S I'LL KNOW TO THROW MYSELF OUT THE WINDOW AFTER WE KILL OFF THE BOTTLE. (*In*) I know what floor we're on, Roscoe. It's the sentiment, that's all. The sentiment. (*Out*) TELL ME YOU'RE A BOIL ON THE MEMORY OF YOUR PARENTS AN' THE FAITHFUL MAID THEY LEFT BEHIND. YOUR MAMA LEFT BEHIND HER FURS. YOU THINK I LOOK PRETTY, DWAYNE? THEY LEFT A MESSAGE FOR YOU.

DWAYNE: What? What is it?

BERNICE: SAYS, "NURSE CALLED TO SAY YOUR ORTHODONTIST DIED." FROM STICKIN' HIS FINGERS IN YOUR MOUTH, I EXPECT. YOU AIN'T NEVER GONNA GET THOSE BRACES OFF NOW, DWAYNE, AN' YOU WAS UGLY TO BEGIN WITH. PREPARE YOURSELF FOR A LIFE OF MISERY. (*Dwayne begins to cry freely. Shrieking*) IT'S THE END OF THE WORLD. IT'S THE END OF THE WORLD. (*In*) What? How am I supposed to know where they kept any damn candles? They was all slobs. (*Out*) I NEVER LIKED ANY OF YOU, DWAYNE. DID YOU KNOW THAT? THIRTEEN YEARS AN' I NEVER LIKED ANY OF YOU. YOUR MAMA USED TO MEASURE THE LIQUOR. GO BACK TO THAT PLACE ON YOUR MATCHBOOKS IF THE NUN AIN'T BURNED IT YET. GO AWAY. (*Dwayne sobs*) Hey, Roscoe. Copeland boy's crying. No, it ain't. I take no responsibility. (*Out, concerned*) YOU CRYING, DWAYNE? YOU CRYING OUT THERE? (*Dwayne turns away from her*) WELL THAT'S JUST FINE. CRY ALL YOU WANT TO CRY. WE'RE ALL GONNA BE DEAD SOON ENOUGH ANYWAYS. SHED A FEW TEARS FOR BERNICE WHILE YOU'RE AT IT. BERNICE WHO'S GONNA BE LEFT ALONE AN' DEAD IN THE DARK. (*In*) Roscoe? Smile for Bernice so she can see where you are...

(*Lights fade from Dwayne. Prologue music fades. Martinelle rises. Thumps the radio*)

RADIO ANNOUNCER: ...REPEAT, THIS IS NOT A TEST...

(*Martinelle hurriedly switches stations. More static. Finally, music. Martinelle hugs the radio*)

MARTINELLE: CHARLIE. I THINK I GOT PENNSYLVANIA. LATER ON WE CAN DANCE. WE COULD DO IT IN FRONT OF THE MIRROR. PRETEND WE'RE IN A CROWD. Dance and not cope with anything...

(*Glass shatters offstage*)

MARTINELLE: (*Frightened*) CHARLIE?
(*Blackout. Music blares in the darkness*)

End of Prologue

Scene:
> *Lights up on the Terminal Bar, an abandoned club in New York's red-light district. A table, barstools, a bar. Also a huge hole in the plaster of one wall with red lips spray-painted around it.*
>
> *Holly stands, dripping wet from the rain. She has a Polaroid camera around her neck and clutches a soggy paper bag and an equally soggy map. Her suitcase sits open on a barstool, an "I Love New York" sticker peeling from it.*
>
> *Martinelle sits at the table. It is littered with cosmetics and she daintily paints her fingernails. A suitcase rests on the floor beside her. She is dressed as before, only her stockings are torn and her make-up is caked.*

MARTINELLE: …So I tell him, "Fine, Charlie. Fine. Get on the telephone. I'm happy to work. Fine. You do your business in there on the phone an' I'll do mine right here on my stool." That's it over there. Charlie carved my name in the seat with his knife. Stuffing pops out an' it's like I'm sitting on angel hair. Tammy an' Elvira used to work the all-night newsstand on Thirty-Ninth. Charlie sent 'em there 'cause they was both illiterate. That's what kind of man he is. Had them both stretch out on the sidewalk an' he spray-painted their outlines on the cement, an' then put in their names, the hours they worked, an' the number here at the bar in case of emergency. Tammy was just thrilled about the whole thing. Used to hang out on her paintmarks all the time. Off hours an' everything. Not working. Just lying there so's people'd know she belonged someplace. Used to go out in the blizzards and shovel snow from it. Charlie was touched. I thought she was being a deal.

HOLLY: I was worried you might be angry with me.

MARTINELLE: (*Ignoring her, with growing menace*) Tammy never did learn to read. Used to look at the pictures in *Good Housekeeping*. Elvira, on the other hand, got real hooked on *Ebony* an' changed her name to something African I can't pronounce right. So I used to call her Girlie. That's what Charlie called the ones whose names he couldn't remember. The lesser ones. Everything was,

"Hi, Girlie, how's your health?" or "Hi, Girlie, I hate your shoes."
New chick with a Jewish name was Girlieberg. She had only one
ear an' coveted my good pumps, but everybody's gotta be
someplace, right? Like, now you're here, an' a little while ago you
was irritating people somewhere else in our fair city. FINE.
Tammy an' Elvira evacuated a while ago to Pennsylvania where
the air's still good. Moved in with an Amish family. Sent Charlie a
snapshot of themselves both wearing bonnets. Just like you'd hope
to see in a margarine commercial, except they was black. Just like
both your eyes woulda been if you'd been five minutes longer
getting your ass back here, you bitch.

HOLLY: I...

MARTINELLE: You pregnant bitch. What is it makes you think
you can leave me alone for so long? You think I'm common or
something? You think I'm a common streetwalker? Well, maybe I
was, but I ain't anymore. I am the only one left an' I am
THRILLED about it. I am a harem unto myself.

HOLLY: I got lost.

MARTINELLE: I have been sitting here painting my fingernails
since three o'clock this afternoon.

HOLLY: An' they're very attractive.

MARTINELLE: They're like BRICKS. You could break every
damn window in New York with my fingernails.

HOLLY: Coulda started on your toes.

MARTINELLE: Hick.

HOLLY: I must say I'm flattered. I didn't think you'd miss me so
much.

MARTINELLE: I didn't miss you. I've been entertaining myself.

HOLLY: An' you got Charlie here.

MARTINELLE: HE'S ON THE TELEPHONE.

HOLLY: Still?

MARTINELLE: YES. STILL.

(*Holly puts paper bag on Martinelle's table*)

HOLLY: Must have the mint in quarters is all I can say.

MARTINELLE: I just got so shattered about your not showing up I
was getting ready to slit my wrists. (*Martinelle slashes her wrists
with nail polish. Holds them out*) An' what makes this REAL tragic
is I'm all outa red polish an' I gotta slit 'em in pink. I may be a
lotta things, but I ain't pink.

HOLLY: (*Drying herself off*) Well, I am very sorry, Martinelle. I
hope you know I wouldn't do nothing to upset you intentionally. I

plain got lost.

MARTINELLE: You don't get lost with a map.

HOLLY: It got soggy an' the streets started to run together. An' as I personally do not have the finest sense of direction in the world, I was using the Empire State Building as my point of reference. Then I looked up one second an' it just wasn't there no more.

MARTINELLE: What?

HOLLY: Lights went out. POOF.

MARTINELLE: We could be in Detroit for all we know.

HOLLY: I agree with you entirely. (*Wiping feet on map*) SO MUCH FOR NEW YORK. You know, I have this un-Christian part of me wants to get on the horn an' tell all the folks back home I finally been to see the lights of Fourteenth Street, only there wasn't any. (*Holly turns on the radio*)

RADIO: ...Symptoms which may include recently appearing or slowly enlarging purplish nodules on or beneath the skin, rapid and otherwise unexplained hair loss, a dry, persistent cough not caused by smoking, night sweats, weight loss of more than ten pounds in one month...

HOLLY: (*Blithely joining in*) Purplish nodules on or beneath the skin, rapid and otherwise unexplained hair loss, a dry, persistent cough not caused by...

MARTINELLE: I don't want to cope with the news.

HOLLY: What is it you expect of me, Martinelle?

MARTINELLE: CHANGE THE CHANNEL. (*Martinelle throws nail polish at Holly, streaking her dress*)

HOLLY: MARTINELLE. I AM SHOCKED.

MARTINELLE: (*Miserably*) So what. So what.

HOLLY: (*Turns off radio*) Now my dress reflects my bleeding heart. (*Goes to bar and pours herself the first of many huge drinks*) You'd think this rain'd turn to something more inspiring. I'm soaked clear through. (*Pause, seductive*) I could take off all my clothes, I guess. Put 'em by the radiator. If I had a hanger, I would do that.

MARTINELLE: You shoulda thought about the hanger nine months ago.

HOLLY: (*Giggling*) Stop that. Life's precious. (*Drinks*) Oh, I do enjoy retainin' fluids. Models sleep sittin' up. I read it in a magazine. Sleep sittin' up so's all the fluids'll drain from their heads an' they'll have cheekbones. What price beauty. I was to sleep sittin' up, I'd drown the kid.

MARTINELLE: You're such a deal.

HOLLY: I am not a deal.

MARTINELLE: Holly's a deal. Remind me later an' I'll spray paint it on the wall next to the lips.

HOLLY: A great big kiss from you to Charlie.

MARTINELLE: Hole looked naked. I got tired of staring at it.

HOLLY: Well, it's very attractive.

MARTINELLE: Don't try to be nice to me. I ain't forgiven you yet.

HOLLY: (*Exasperated*) I had to go all the way to the Indian Deli. Little Calcutta. They're foreigners an' don't know about the plague. I think it's what they're used to. Nasty boy in a turban kept trying to get me to buy coffee. I told him I didn't care to stay awake. I've SEEN just about everything. He wouldn't give me your boiled water for free. I had to buy a tea bag with it. I told him I don't drink tea. I told him my girl friend, who's an exotic named Martinelle, don't drink tea neither. What am I supposed to do with a tea bag?

MARTINELLE: Wait till the kid drops an' dangle it over the crib.

HOLLY: Well, I suppose. There was this old woman in the corner sitting on a milk crate. She had a dot on her forehead. It coulda been a lesion.

MARTINELLE: Did you get me a mirror?

HOLLY: (*Cheerfully*) You know the ones I passed was all broken?

MARTINELLE: Quit smiling.

HOLLY: I was voted most cheerful of my high school class.

MARTINELLE: You married a mortician.

HOLLY: Well, he had an above ground pool. (*Catches her reflection in drink*) OH, MY HAIR. MY HAIR. (*Takes camera from around her neck, smiles broadly, takes a flash picture of herself, then aims camera at stomach*) Smile, precious. (*Snaps picture of stomach*) Mommy loves you.

MARTINELLE: He's gonna be a poster child. I can feel it.

HOLLY: (*Removing hair spray from suitcase*) Your water's catching germs.

(*Martinelle dips a napkin in the coffee container, removing her make-up*)

MARTINELLE: I ain't had my face off in a week.

HOLLY: I fail to see what is so frightening about the ladies room.

MARTINELLE: Girlieberg's in there. She's been in there a month.

HOLLY: (*Fixing hair with snapshot as mirror*) Doing what?

MARTINELLE: Last I heard she wasn't feeling so hot.

HOLLY: I swear, if I was drunk I'd cry. (*Uncapping hair spray*) Hold your breath.

MARTINELLE: I hate that stuff.

HOLLY: Well, I hate things with moveable parts. One of the many reasons I left my husband. (*Sprays hair*) They say this stuff eats away at the ozone layer. Ozone's what stops the moon from falling down on us an' making us go squish. Neighbors back home had two teenagers used to come skinny-dip in our pool when Lennie an' me was sleeping. They kept threatening to picket my hair. (*Sprays room*) MY CONTRIBUTION TO THE WORLD OF TOMORROW. (*Laughs*)

MARTINELLE: You're such a tourist.

HOLLY: What of it. Maybe later you can show me some prostitution beauty tips. Maybe I can go to the bar next door an' practice soliciting in your shoes.

MARTINELLE: Charlie always said to be sure your shoes matched your make-up. That's 'cause johns always look at your feet first 'cause they're too embarrassed to look you in the face. Be sure they matched, so it don't come as such a shock going from foot to face.

HOLLY: I adore those shoes.

MARTINELLE: They're mine.

HOLLY: And you're the loveliest woman I've ever seen.

MARTINELLE: Yeah.

HOLLY: So maybe later you can show us how you do our national monuments.

MARTINELLE: I don't do that for fun.

HOLLY: Well, we're gettin' to be friends, an' there's no T.V.

MARTINELLE: I only do it for Mr. Greenberg.

HOLLY: Ain't the Statue of Liberty a sort of unnatural thing to desire?

MARTINELLE: It's a free country. He's a Russian Jew who landed on Ellis Island an' I remind him of his parents. He used to be in a wheelchair an' I'd just have to stand there with the torch while he rolled towards me an' rocked himself back an' forth to get that seasick feeling. Now he's bedridden, I go towards him an' he just rolls his eyes.

HOLLY: Sounds real patriotic.

MARTINELLE: Charlie wouldn't approve of my doing it for free.

HOLLY: You'd do it for a girl friend. We are girl friends.

MARTINELLE: Not quite.

HOLLY: Well, we're gettin' to be, an' I'm a laugh riot after I've had a few. Only reason Lennie an' me ever got invited out. I was the fun half of the couple.

MARTINELLE: Precious there, your first?

HOLLY: (*Proudly*) Yes. He's my one. (*Bellowing at stomach*) YOU'RE MY ONE. (*Waving flag from suitcase*) FIRST AURORA BABY TO BE CONCEIVED AFTER THE PLAGUE.

MARTINELLE: You got the plague in Aurora?

HOLLY: Yes, we do. Three cases documented. Lennie buried 'em all.

MARTINELLE: You never touched any of 'em?

HOLLY: Well...no. Why would I do that? I hardly even let Lennie touch me. He was about as much fun as pressin' fat into a half-slip. (*Sighs*) Maybe it's just men on the whole. First thing I said to him once we got married was, "Lennie, get me a vodka an' a single bed. I'm not sure I like you enough."

MARTINELLE: How do you account for precious?

HOLLY: I don't rightly know. (*To stomach*) YOU'RE AN ACCIDENT. YOU CAME FROM THE POOL. I'm convinced. It was one of them naked neighbor boys relieving himself of his male instincts into the chlorine. Picture me, if you would. Picture me floatin' flat on my back whilst I'm being attacked from all sides by these teenaged sperm cells. Like Jaws. Bouncing offa my artichoke bathing cap an' taking big hefty bites outa my private parts.

MARTINELLE: An' Lennie bought that?

HOLLY: He never was one to notice a person's appearance. Finally one day when I was stickin' out to here an' he still hadn't got the picture I figured it was time to go. An' here I arrive in the wicked city of steel an' glass just like Marlo Thomas in the opening of *That Girl*, only them folks I was hoping to sing my theme song's all dead.

MARTINELLE: Chill out.

HOLLY: Oh, quit being such an ostrich. How should I react? OH, NO. Cover my face? OH, NO. There ain't nothin' wrong out there. It's always five in the A.M. Stations are always signed off. Everybody's just in bed. In bed an' not living. We're making history, Martinelle. I got the Polaroids to prove it.

MARTINELLE: Who's gonna be around to look at 'em?

HOLLY: You an' me. Your friend Charlie if he ever gets off the phone. Baby when the time's right. THE PEOPLE NEXT DOOR. *(Holly goes to stool. Sits. Holds her breath and rotates herself to look through the hole in the wall. Rotates back. Exhales)* You gotta admire their determination even if you don't care much for their disease. Such endurance. Must be more men in there than's left on the entire Isle of Manhattan. *(Looks back in)* Can't tell if they're breathing or not, though. What's the name of that place?

MARTINELLE: It's the Epstein Bar. It gets boys.

HOLLY: It GOT boys. Looks like the waxworks in there. *(Sniffs)* Death and cologne.

MARTINELLE: It was always that way. Charlie kinda liked them. The way they looked at him.

HOLLY: What does Charlie look like?

MARTINELLE: *(Lighting cigarette, leaning back)* He's beautiful. He's the most beautiful man in New York. Even when there was more left, he was the most beautiful. When the Epstein closed at four, all the boys who hadn't gotten lucky used to crowd out on the sidewalk an' stare in at him.

HOLLY: *(Shaking head, pouring another drink)* My Lord. Hold your breath.

MARTINELLE: Wasn't so much like they wanted him. Charlie wouldn'ta stood for it. Least I don't think. More like they all had some idea in their heads about what pretty was, an' had to make sure it was still around someplace. Even if it wasn't available. Guy used to own this place'd sit right here until the last of the boys unglued his lips from the plate glass. Then he'd wipe it down with antiseptic.

HOLLY: I think I found a disease once floating in my drink. Rolled it on my tongue like a maraschino cherry. Didn't swallow it, though.

MARTINELLE: Charlie used to put his barstool right in the middle of the floor so's nobody'd have a bad view. Some nights the boys'd all hide their drinks in their coats an' it'd be like a block party out there, only everybody was depressed. When people started not feeling so hot it was pushing on Christmas an' too cold to hang out on the streets. That's when they carved the hole in the wall. With swizzle sticks. Took two months. Still, you wouldn'ta noticed the hole unless you watched it constant. Like a clock. Just another crack in the plaster getting bigger all the time. Then one night I look over an' see there's twenty faces sipping outa fairy straws an' staring in at Charlie. Not saying a word. Charlie knew they was there but pretended not to notice. Just moved his stool to where everybody could see. He said his being beautiful was the closest thing most people in this city ever got to having a religion.

HOLLY: Charlie had an awful lotta girl friends, huh?

MARTINELLE: Before. Now me. I'm Charlie's lump of pleasure.

(*Martinelle coughs suddenly, violently. There is a tense silence as Holly studies her*)

HOLLY: Smoke went down the wrong tube, huh?

MARTINELLE: (*Stubbing out cigarette*) I AM SICK TO DEATH OF DOING MY NAILS. I WANT TO DO MY FACE. I WANT A MIRROR.

HOLLY: I'll take a picture.

MARTINELLE: Don't you dare. I don't want a record of myself looking like this. Somebody might make copies an' post 'em. I'd never work again.

HOLLY: I'll do your make-up. It'd be a pleasure.

MARTINELLE: (*Knowingly*) I bet it would.

HOLLY: I hate to put a damper on your evening, Martinelle, but wake up an' smell the fucking roses. I am the only one here's looking at you. Anything you'd fix'd be for my benefit alone. An' I think you look just fine.

MARTINELLE: (*Glumly*) I don't feel like I'm in the room without a mirror. And there's Charlie...

HOLLY: Your Charlie's been on the pay phone an awful long time.

MARTINELLE: So? He's trying to get me some business.

HOLLY: Don't you think you should bring him a club soda or something? It's been two days.

MARTINELLE: Ain't no reflection on my being popular. All the conventions have been rerouted to healthier climates.

HOLLY: I'm runnin' kinda low on hair spray. Two days more an' you'll be embarrassed to have him meet me.

MARTINELLE: (*Indicating Holly's drink*) Two days more an' you're gonna have to get scraped up off the floor.

HOLLY: (*Primping hair*) No, no. I guess I'm fine. I'm enjoying my vacation. (*To stomach*) HOW YOU DOING IN THERE LITTLE PRECIOUS?

MARTINELLE: He's fermenting.

HOLLY: He's fine. He just kicked twice an' that means he's fine.

(To stomach) STOP KICKING YOUR MOMMY. MY INNARDS ARE NOT AN ESCALATOR. *(Laughs)* Yes, Lord, I am having fun. *(Martinelle glares at her)* Well, sweetheart, SOMEBODY'S got to.

MARTINELLE: Sure. You an' the nuns. They all escaped the convent. Last three months they been riding around the city in a yellow school bus, drunk outa their habits an' firebombing the neighborhood, so it'll be sterile for the Last Judgment. Hook up with them.

HOLLY: Nuns don't have hair.

MARTINELLE: Charlie says they live forever. They don't touch nobody but themselves.

HOLLY: I don't think that holds true anymore, dear. Now they're saying it travels on the air. Like radio waves.

MARTINELLE: Change the subject.

HOLLY: An' there was that entire high school in Lincoln, Nebraska that came down with it during a pep rally. I read it in a magazine.

MARTINELLE: Talk about something else.

HOLLY: *(Insulted)* I thought I was being topical. I'll get Charlie off the phone for you.

MARTINELLE: He's busy.

HOLLY: Give you someone else to interrupt.

MARTINELLE: He's doing business. He don't like to be bothered when he's doing business.

HOLLY: *(Arrogant, rising)* Well, he doesn't know me from Eve. I'd be a pregnant stranger.

MARTINELLE: *(Seductively)* Stick around. We can have some fun.

HOLLY: *(Flouncing away)* I need a little stretch. Get the alcohol circulating.

MARTINELLE: I'll do Miss Liberty. If you give me a quarter. It's gotta be official.

HOLLY: And do I get to wear your shoes?

MARTINELLE: I guess. An' find some music. I can't do it without music. *(Holly ambles over to Martinelle's table. Holds quarter out)* Put it on the table. I'm not an automat.

(Holly takes shoes. Sits on stool, puts them on. Holds radio on the shelf of her stomach searching for dance music. Gets dead air. Martinelle turns her back and begins to undress. Music plays. Holly stretches her feet out in front of her, pretending to

examine shoes, in fact staring hungrily at Martinelle)

HOLLY: Oh, I love these shoes. I want to be buried in these shoes. (*Martinelle has stripped to her bra and panties. She opens her suitcase and takes out large silver stars that she applies to strategic points of her anatomy, takes out crown, roller skates, puts them on, also a huge torch made of sparklers*) Does one dare to walk in these shoes? I mean, they are so very attractive, but you could fall an' break your hair.

MARTINELLE: (*Adjusting crown*) When I do this for the shut-in, Charlie spray paints me green. He leaves a patch clear on my back so the skin can ventilate. I look pretty authentic. I've been asked back forty-three times. (*Martinelle rises and rolls to the center of the room. She holds the unlit torch in one hand, a butane lighter in the other*)

HOLLY: (*Gasping, then bellowing*) LOOK AT YOU.

MARTINELLE: It helps if you pretend like waves.

(*Holly drunkenly slams down her drink, holds a hand to her heart*)

HOLLY: (*Holding back tears*) NOW WHO WOULDA THOUGHT? WHO WOULDA EVER? If it wasn't for all that looting, shaking me up so much the other day that I needed to duck in here for a snoot, we never woulda met. Never. Never ever. Every plague must have a silver lining, Martinelle, and the silver lining here is that we got to meet.

MARTINELLE: WOULD YOU KNOCK IT OFF WITH THE DISEASE ALL THE TIME?

HOLLY: (*Awed, a hand in her mouth*) OOOOOHHH.

MARTINELLE: You are the most gruesome person I ever met in my LIFE.

HOLLY: THANK YOU, LORD. SHE'S BEAUTIFUL.

MARTINELLE: An' I go through all the damn trouble of getting into my working gear for some GHOUL...

HOLLY: WHERE'S THE CAMERA? WHERE'S THE CAMERA? (*Holly takes a flash picture of Martinelle*)

MARTINELLE: I TOLD YOU NOT TO TAKE MY PICTURE. I DON'T WANNA BE REMEMBERED LIKE THIS.

HOLLY: I'D TOUCH YOU. I'D TOUCH YOU, BUT I KNOW I'D CRY.

MARTINELLE: GET WITHIN THREE FEET OF ME, AN' I'LL THROW YOU AN' PRECIOUS OUT THE FUCKING WINDOW.

(*Holly rises drunkenly from her stool, a finger outstretched*)
HOLLY: I'LL TAKE THE RISK. I'LL TAKE IT. ONE FINGER FOR ONE TEAR.

MARTINELLE: (*Skating away from her*) YOU DEMENTED? AIN'T YOU NEVER SEEN A WOMAN BEFORE? DIDN'T YOU NEVER TAKE A SHOWER AFTER PHYS. ED.? HOLLY. YOU'RE EXPECTING. (*Holly reaches for Martinelle. Martinelle swings the torch. Holly stumbles on the platform shoes and falls on her stomach. Holly's hands reach quickly for her belly. She lets out a quick gasp*) Holly? You okay? Is it the baby?

(*Holly rolls on her back, stares up at the ceiling in shock*)
HOLLY: (*After a long silence*) SQUISH. (*Roars with laughter*) Oh, squish, squish, squish. Wrap me in plastic an' take me away. (*Rubs stomach*) Hey, there inside, little precious. Mommy loves you.

(*Martinelle stares in disbelief. Skates around the room like a roller derby queen*)
MARTINELLE: B-I-I-TCH. GET OUTA MY SHOES. GET YOUR IDIOT FEET OUTA MY GOOD SHOES. THAT BABY'S GONNA POP OUTA YOU ANY SECOND LIKE A TOMATO BOIL AN' BAG DINNER, AN' THOSE SHOES COST ME FIFTY BUCKS.

(*Martinelle rolls to the bar and pours herself a drink. Downs it. Dwayne appears at the hole in the wall. He is dressed as before, but dirty and disheveled. He wears a name sticker which reads, "REMEMBER ME...DWAYNE...EPSTEIN BAR"*)
DWAYNE: (*Smiling, revealing a mouthful of braces*) PEOPLE. (*Martinelle gapes. Holly is oblivious*) You don't have to stare at me. I know what I look like.

MARTINELLE: Who are you?

DWAYNE: Possibly the ugliest boy left in New York. And what state are YOU representing?

MARTINELLE: I was just getting ready for the talent competition. The lush on the floor was gonna get Miss Congeniality, but the judges figured out at the last minute that she wasn't a virgin. (*Holly giggles from floor*) Shut up, you. She got disqualified.

DWAYNE: What's your talent?

(*Martinelle goes to her "working" barstool, seductive*)
MARTINELLE: I'm famous for my fingernails. They etch glass. I'm Martinelle. That's French for something. When I was younger people used to call me Marty. I've developed since. I got a friend

Charlie, tells me I sound like something you'd order after dinner in a fancy restaurant. You look like a tongue sitting there.

DWAYNE: (*Climbing through hole, going to bar*) Is there any food?

MARTINELLE: Garnishes. Cherries. I'll let you buy me a drink.

DWAYNE: Isn't it free?

MARTINELLE: Everything's on the house tonight. But it's the thought that counts.

DWAYNE: Anything special?

MARTINELLE: I'm extremely easy. You're a school kid, ain't you? I should make you show me your...identification. How old are you, anyways?

DWAYNE: I hope to be eighteen on my next birthday.

MARTINELLE: I won't tell a soul. Times like these you get the urge to rush things. This your first bar?

DWAYNE: Actually, I've been living in the men's room next door.

MARTINELLE: (*Disappointed*) Figures.

DWAYNE: I heard you screaming from in there. I thought, LIFE.

MARTINELLE: How come you live in the can?

DWAYNE: The bulb's been out for ages and people keep telling me I look better in the dark. It's the only way I can make contact.

MARTINELLE: (*To herself*) Everybody's a deal.

DWAYNE: I guess we always go back to the places we were most happy.

MARTINELLE: There a mirror in there?

DWAYNE: Somebody broke it while I was sleeping. I thought it was this one guy I'd been cruising for a while, but he turned out to be dead.

MARTINELLE: Bet you was never big on mirrors anyway.

HOLLY: (*Rising from floor*) HOLD YOUR BREATH, MARTINELLE.

DWAYNE: OH. SHE'S TERRIFIC.

MARTINELLE: No, she's not.

HOLLY: It's all your fault. All this pain. You an' your kind. YOU started this.

DWAYNE: Don't you read the magazines? We're just trendy.

HOLLY: HOLD YOUR BREATH.

DWAYNE: With my luck I'll live forever. Nobody wants me. (*Holly sits on barstool, puffing her cheeks and holding her breath. Sticks out her feet to examine shoes*) I KNOW THOSE SHOES.

MARTINELLE: They're mine.

DWAYNE: You used to work the corner of Thirty-Fourth and Eighth.

MARTINELLE: (*Pleased, but nonchalant*) And sometimes the highway, depending on the weather.

DWAYNE: I had a friend who was ready to kill for those shoes.

MARTINELLE: They're one of a kind.

DWAYNE: Iris Schoenberger. She was ready to cut your feet off.

MARTINELLE: Do I know this person?

DWAYNE: Iris was my best friend from Saint Hilda's. She was Jewish, but her parents sent her there so she'd have to wear a uniform. She had the wildest taste in clothes. All the girls used to have their heads covered for chapel in the morning and Iris used to wear this four foot tall thing made of real fruit. She'd wear it every day, till it got moldy or the insects started to bother her. We'd hang out at the Epstein together. Used to see you when we were coming out of the subway.

MARTINELLE: You two musta made quite a couple. She working the men's room too?

DWAYNE: She's institutionalized. Her mom was a shrink and pierced her ears when she was seven so she could express her individuality. By the time I met her she was wearing phone receivers off her earlobes. She caught them on the rings once in gym. Bounced on the cords for half an hour screaming how she wasn't in right now, while the nuns tried to pull her down. Her dad had her committed and her mom published an article on it.

MARTINELLE: Shame how things happen.

DWAYNE: I went to visit her once. She'd lost eighty pounds and was wearing a dozen hypo-allergenic pearls out of the one ear that wasn't ripped through. It was right after the first cases were reported. What the papers called "The Winter That No One Had Sex." Iris kept clippings. "What FUN," she said. "What FUN to die and be an event. If dying's on your dance card at least die of something mysterious. Get lots of attention."

MARTINELLE: They musta had her on something.

DWAYNE: Who knows? Maybe they let her out. It doesn't matter. Pretty soon people are gonna be floating out on the ocean. Living on barges. Not many places left.

(*Holly holds the radio in her lap. Dance Music plays. Gentle, futuristic*)

HOLLY: (*Dreamy, to herself*) Music...

DWAYNE: How come you stayed?

MARTINELLE: Lotsa reasons. I know who I am here.

DWAYNE: It used to be this city was the one place you could live in your head twenty-four hours a day and have it condoned by everybody. It's the only city in the world's got steam coming up from the streets. It's not that way anymore.

MARTINELLE: Who says? Things ain't different. Just deal with what you want to. Same as before. Like, I don't want to "deal" with you. I wanna dance. (*Leans over to read his name tag*) Come on, Dwayne. Dance with the national monument.

DWAYNE: (*Rising, spinning her on skates*) MISS LIBERTINE.

MARTINELLE: (*Laughing*) Yeah. If you was the only boy in the world and I was the only girl... (*Martinelle skates to the middle of the floor. Dwayne follows. She stands behind him, steadying herself, her hands around his waist. They dance. Then, dreamily*) This is what I needed. This is like real people. (*Holly ambles over. She cautiously places her hands on Martinelle's bare midriff*) You back?

HOLLY: (*With great longing*) Please. It's my first New York party.

(*They dance in their line, Martinelle dreamily running her hands over Dwayne's chest, Holly over Martinelle's stomach. The lighting should be quite dim at this point, dreamlike*)

MARTINELLE: This is good.

HOLLY: (*Trying to catch the mood*) Maybe Charlie'll get off the phone and join us. We could have a square dance.

DWAYNE: There's a man here?

HOLLY: Maybe shut-ins from all over New York will hear our music and join us. People'll keep adding on, an' we'll stretch clear out the bar, across the bridge to Jersey...

DWAYNE: You didn't tell me there was a man here.

HOLLY: ...All the way to Pennsylvania where the air's still good.

DWAYNE: Who is this man?

HOLLY: (*Romantically*) The most beautiful man in New York City.

DWAYNE: Really?

HOLLY: Even when there was more left, he was the most beautiful. He's Martinelle's beau. Ain't I right, Martinelle?

MARTINELLE: (*Eyes closed, to herself*) As long as Charlie's hanging out, there's still beauty.

DWAYNE: (*Breaking from line*) Opposites attract. Maybe I should meet him.

MARTINELLE: (*Waking up*) He's busy.

DWAYNE: I just want a peek.

HOLLY: (*Clinging to Martinelle*) They's gonna roll off together into the night an' leave poor old Holly alone. Leave her to limp away into these wicked streets an' drop her baby the natural way. Sure hope it learns to talk quick. I'm runnin' low on things to say to myself.

MARTINELLE: (*Breaking from Holly*) DON'T GO.

DWAYNE: (*Straightening tie*) Pickings are slim.

(*Martinelle skates to bar, retrieving torch and lighter*)

MARTINELLE: (*Reciting desperately, badly*)

GIVE ME YOUR TIRED, YOUR POOR,

YOUR HUDDLED MASSES YEARNING TO BREATHE FREE,

THE WRETCHED REFUSE OF YOUR TEEMING SHORE,

SEND THESE, THE HOMELESS, TEMPEST TOSSED TO ME.

(*Lights sparkler torch, holding it up*)

I LIFT MY LAMP BESIDE THE GOLDEN DOOR.

DWAYNE: (*Exiting off to pay phone*) Wish me luck.

MARTINELLE: (*Terrified, holding back tears*) WELL, IT HELPS IF YOU ROCK BACK AN' FORTH. SOME PEOPLE LIKE THAT. CHARLIE ALWAYS SAID I HAD A LOT OF TALENT. DWAYNE?? YOU HOMELY TEMPEST TOSSED FUCK!

HOLLY: (*Waving American flag*) Oh, that was wonderful. That was worth all the misery you put me through tonight. Better'n the real thing, I'll bet. Her stars don't twinkle when she moves.

(*The music ends. A news report comes on the radio. It is barely audible, occasional phrases picked up through the static*)

RADIO ANNOUNCER: Transmitted sexually, through bodily fluids...

MARTINELLE: (*Crying, holding torch*) Please, turn that off.

HOLLY: Radio's got moveable parts.

RADIO ANNOUNCER: ...Expected mortality rate of one hundred percent...

HOLLY: I don't think it's true what they say. I think it's carried on the air. Like snow. (*Martinelle watches helplessly as her sparklers fizzle out. Turns off the radio. Sits at table with her head in her hands, drunk, child-like*) Never snowed once back in Aurora. Did once before I was born but everybody called that a freak of nature. Used to have to decorate the tree with soap flakes. Spray the window an' carve out pictures with a razor blade.

(*Dwayne enters*)

DWAYNE: I used to watch him through the window.

MARTINELLE: Don't tell me how bad he looks. I don't want to cope.

HOLLY: He's the most beautiful man...

DWAYNE: He's decomposing.

HOLLY: (*Accusingly*) You said...

MARTINELLE: I said he was on the pay phone. I didn't say if he was breathing. Christ. Hell of a time to start taking me literal.

DWAYNE: (*Gently*) I'm real sorry.

MARTINELLE: (*Holding back tears, ashamed*) Yeah? Well, THANKS. THANKS A LOT. I mean, you wanna remember people when they look their best, right? Take baby pictures but not funeral shots, 'less you're real strange, right? Like, not going out anymore 'cause it doesn't feel the same. You know? You know what I'm talking about? First day I go in an' do his hair with the pick, way he liked it. Second day I go in, an' there's a FLY sittin' on one of his eyeballs. I screamed an' it flew away. I ain't been back. Holly shows up the next day with morning sickness. What a deal she is.

HOLLY: (*Self-righteous*) You must have loved him very much to deceive me in such a manner.

MARTINELLE: I WAS ONE GIRL OUT OF THIRTY. HE DIDN'T KNOW MY NAME HALF THE TIME. Hadda carve it on the fucking barstool. I was Girlie, the one with the shoes.

HOLLY: Deceitful, terrible thing to do.

MARTINELLE: Gets a lesion on his cheek an' runs around breaking all the mirrors. My compact even. I told him, I told him, "Charlie, I gotta face too. I gotta face too needs inspecting once in a while." He told me I didn't need no mirror. He's the best mirror a girl could ever have. I'm the only one who stayed. Don't matter none if he gives it to me too. I'm the only one left an' get to sleep on the mattress with him down in the beer room. I don't care. We could wake up in the middle of the night sweating an' coughing in harmony an' that'd be fine, 'cause it's Charlie an' pretty counts. FINE that he keeps me working to get his mind off his health. FINE that he calls me Girlie when we're making love. FINE. FINE.

HOLLY: Just who is it you think you're fooling, Miss Martinelle? I can just imagine where your thing has been to. You coulda picked up disease anywhere. Off the table like a half dollar.

MARTINELLE: After five drinks from a clean glass they all looked like Charlie. Charlie on a shitty day.

HOLLY: Oh, don't you just wish you'd DIED FIRST?

MARTINELLE: (*After a pause*) No.

HOLLY: (*Drinking from bottle*) I'd cry, but I'd run my liner.

DWAYNE: (*To Martinelle, comforting*) I was really in love once with this guy who used to hang out at the Epstein. I'd send him beers and he'd nod, and once I even smiled back. Figured we'd built up some kind of relationship and he wouldn't care that I had braces. I didn't know what color eyes he had.

HOLLY: (*Dryly*) You both just break my heart. My heart's just breaking. (*Holly removes a sheet of cleaner's plastic from her suitcase. Holds it over her mouth as if to protect herself from germs*)

DWAYNE: Dumb stuff like eye color gets important at night. When you're alone. One night when we were all crowded out on the street here, I sent Iris over to find out. She stood next to him for ten minutes. Finally she just yelled, "Shit if I can tell. Get this stud under the fluorescents at the all-night deli where EVERYBODY looks like they've been dead for a week." Then she handed him a banana off her hat and he walked away. I left Iris glued to the window, and I followed him. I followed him for miles and it was snowing. And when it snows, I always feel my age. I can date my life by snowstorms. He went into this place where there was this little blonde transvestite sitting in a booth, who directed me to a dark room full of stalls. He was standing in one. With the door closed. I waited for him to notice me...wishing he would come out or tell me to go away or invite me for coffee, so I could tell him that Iris was only looking at his eyes. Finally, I just went into the stall next to his where he couldn't see me and I could think. I put my hands out to brace myself, because it was dark and I was drunk, and I felt his penis coming through a hole in the wall. I knelt on the floor and he shot all over my braces and I stayed there, for what seemed like hours hoping for something. A kiss maybe. But he was long gone. And I never saw him again. Never. I went back to the holes a few times after that and got friendly with the transvestite, whose name was Bunny, who said to me, "Don't you just HATE it when people disappear like that? Don't you always think they're DEAD?" Which was sort of funny, because Bunny lived his life through the personal ads. Bunny came down with it, and I went to visit him in St. Vincents. Day before he died he said to me, "ENOUGH ALREADY. I RENOUNCE MY LIFESTYLE. MY NAME IS SHERMAN." And he ripped the wig off his head and pulled out a black leather motorcycle cap from under his bed that he'd been saving for just such an emergency.

HOLLY: Sick, unnatural, and unhealthy.

DWAYNE: There's lots of ways to embrace death.

HOLLY: If I had a son like you, I'd bury my head in the dirt. You'd embrace anything.

DWAYNE: (*Grinning*) Anything that'd embrace me back.

HOLLY: (*Abandoning plastic*) You know I ain't sure I feel like being in the room with either one of you at this point? I have to thank God that when MY life passes before my eyes, I'll be able to recognize all the faces pressin' down on top of ME. Martinelle, you may be the last woman left in New York, but I've got by long enough without you, an' I'll find in me the strength to do it again.

MARTINELLE: So go.

HOLLY: (*Losing conviction*) Cut the germs with a knife in here.

MARTINELLE: I ain't stopping you. I got company.

HOLLY: Maybe I'll just hold my breath. (*Holly sits on barstool holding hair spray. She defiantly puffs her cheeks. Her stomach has shifted noticeably*).

MARTINELLE: (*Confused*) Holly?

(*Dwayne advances on her grinning. Holly tries to press her stomach back into form*)

HOLLY: Stay away from me now. You hear? Stay away. (*Dwayne reaches up her dress. Holly screams. Dwayne spins her on her stool. Holly sprays him with hair spray*) OZONE. OZONE. STAY AWAY FROM ME. OZONE. STAY AWAY. I'M ENJOYING MY VACATION.

(*Dwayne removes a pillow in a Happy Face pillow case from beneath Holly's dress. It is leaking large amounts of feathers*)

DWAYNE: (*Shaking out feathers, laughing*) I hope you weren't expecting twins.

(*Dwayne and Martinelle howl with laughter. Holly grabs the pillow and attempts to stuff it back up her dress*)

HOLLY: DON'T YOU LOOK AT ME THAT WAY. BOTH OF YOU. BOTH OF YOU. I AM NOT WELL. I AM NOT A WELL LADY. DON'T YOU LAUGH AT ME, MARTINELLE. LIFE'S PRECIOUS. LIFE'S PRECIOUS.

(Holly reaches into her hair and effortlessly pulls out handfuls, holding it out to them, helpless. Martinelle and Dwayne stop laughing for a moment, then begin again. Their laughter continues throughout the remainder of the play)

DWAYNE: So what do we do now?

MARTINELLE: Paint my nails, I guess.

DWAYNE: Did you know your nails keep growing after you die? And your hair?

MARTINELLE: *(Her laughter mixed with coughing)* Say, Holly. You think your husband could exhume me once a month for a manicure and a perm? I'm going quick.

DWAYNE: We could turn on the lights and have Last Call. See what we really look like.

MARTINELLE: No. No, I never liked that part of the night. Not even in real time.

DWAYNE: I never saw a face once at the Glory Holes. Just cocks. Some nights they seemed to sprout from the walls. Like poison mushrooms.

MARTINELLE: Except you're too hungry to care. Too damn lonely.

DWAYNE: And it's too dark. Too dark to make any real distinction.

MARTINELLE: Can't tell always. Like fucking in the balcony of Loews. Like working.

DWAYNE: We could write our names on the bathroom wall. And the date.

MARTINELLE: *(Howling with laughter)* Somebody's in there. I think it's your friend Iris.

DWAYNE: We could save it for tomorrow.

HOLLY: *(Panicked)* ARE YOU ALL GOING SOMEWHERE?

MARTINELLE: Hey there, Little Mother.

HOLLY: ARE YOU LEAVING ME?

(Martinelle chuckles. Goes to Holly. Kneels on the floor and hugs her tightly)

MARTINELLE: No, honey. I think Martinelle's staying in tonight. She's already at the party.

HOLLY: I never will forget you, Martinelle. Even if you go first, I still got your picture. I'll put it under my pillow like wedding cake.

(Holly produces the Polaroid, looks momentarily lost, then happily stuffs it up her dress with the pillow. Martinelle laughs.

Dwayne turns on the radio)

RADIO ANNOUNCER: ...Several months ahead of schedule, estimating the population of New York City, to this date the most severely ravaged of this country's urban centers, at somewhere in the vicinity of zero.

HOLLY: *(Admonishing radio)* THREE AT LEAST. AT LEAST THREE.

RADIO: Evacuation procedures are currently in effect in:

Montgomery, Alabama
Little Rock, Arkansas
Phoenix, Arizona
San Francisco and Los
Angeles, California
Boulder, Colorado
Bridgeport, Connecticut
Tallahassee, Florida
Atlanta, Georgia
Chicago, Illinois
South Bend, Indiana
Des Moines, Iowa
New Orleans, Louisiana
Boston, Massachusetts
Bangor, Maine
Jefferson City, Missouri
Jackson, Mississippi
Billings, Montana
Lincoln, Nebraska
Concord, New Hampshire
Newark, New Jersey
Santa Fe, New Mexico
Raleigh, North Carolina
Salem, Oregon
Providence, Rhode Island...

MARTINELLE: *(Her ear to Holly's stomach)* I HEARD A KICK. I DID. DWAYNE.

HOLLY: *(Contentedly)* He kicked twice. That means he's happy.

DWAYNE: I fell asleep once in the Glory Holes and missed school. A porter woke me up in the morning and I thought he was God. *(Laughs wistfully)* Oh, it's too amazing. It was. Everything and all of it. Too amazing. Too much... *(Smiles, hugs himself)* freedom.

(Martinelle smiles warmly at Dwayne. ⟨. ⟩ ⊦ ɪck to embracing Holly. Prologue music begins to filter ɪᵣ Dwayne rises. He picks up handfuls of Holly's stray feathers. Dwayne blows the feathers around the room, keeping them aloft on the gentle wind of his breath. The effect is that of snow. Holly watches in wonder. She reaches out a hand to the vision of the blizzard surrounding her as the lights slowly dim to black. Music, the

constant drone of evacuating cities, and Martinelle's laughter mixed with coughing continue in the darkness)

The End

RAMON DELGADO, EDITOR

This publication is the eighth edition of *The Best Short Plays* edited by Ramon Delgado, who continues the series made famous by the late Stanley Richards, and established earlier by Margaret Mayorga.

An experienced literary advisor, Dr. Delgado has served as chairman for new plays at the Dallas Theater Center, as a literary advisor to The Whole Theatre Company in Montclair, New Jersey, and as theater consultant to Scholastic Magazine's *Literary Cavalcade*. Dr. Delgado has also been script judge for the Playwrights' Program of the American Theatre Association, the International Biennial Play Competition sponsored by Southern Illinois University at Carbondale, the Illinois Arts Council, and has adjudicated for the American College Theatre Festival.

Born in Tampa, Florida, and raised in nearby Winter Haven, Ramon Delgado started writing plays for marionette shows when he was eleven years old. By the time he had finished high school, he had written two full-length plays and several one-act plays. Recognition as a playwright has been received with honors in five regional and twelve national playwriting competitions, including those sponsored by Theta Alpha Phi, the University of Missouri, EARPLAY, and Samuel French. Three of his full-length plays, *Listen, My Children*, *A Little Holy Water*, and *The Fabulous Jeromes*, received honors in the David Library American Freedom division of the American College Theatre Festival. Seven of his short plays have been published, notably "Waiting for the Bus" in *Ten Great One Act Plays* and *Themes in the One Act Play*, and "Once Below A Lighthouse" in *The Best Short Plays 1972*. His full-length play *A Little Holy Water*, a Cuban-American romantic comedy, was published in 1983.

In 1978 Dr. Delgado's one-act play *The Jerusalem Thorn* was chosen for the Dale Wasserman Midwest Professional Playwrights Workshop, and after expansion into a full-length script, the play was produced Off-Off Broadway by the Acting Wing, Inc., at the Shandol Theatre. Two of his short plays have had Equity showcase productions at the No Smoking Playhouse and at The Glines. The New York Hispanic theatre INTAR selected him as a Playwright-in-Residence in 1980. Three of his short television plays have been aired over PBS, Channel WSIU, Carbondale, Illinois.

Dr. Delgado began his education at Stetson University in Deland, Florida, then studied with Paul Baker and Eugene

McKinney at the Dallas Theatre Center. He received an M.F.A. in 1967 from the Yale School of Drama, studying playwriting there with the late John Gassner, and later with Christian H. Moe at Southern Illinois University at Carbondale, where he received his Ph.D. in 1976.

Cited twice by Outstanding Educators of America, Dr. Delgado has taught acting, directing, playwriting, and dramatic literature at Kentucky Wesleyan College; Hardin-Simmons University in Abilene, Texas; St. Cloud State University, Minnesota; and Montclair State College, New Jersey, where he is presently Professor of Theatre. Dr. Delgado holds memberships in The Association for Theatre in Higher Education, The Dramatists Guild, and the Nashville Songwriters Association.

Dr. Delgado's full-length play, *Stones*, produced at Montclair State College in December of 1983, stimulated discussion on the toxic waste problems of the environment. His acting textbook, *Acting with Both Sides of Your Brain*, published in 1986, has been adopted by colleges nationwide, and he is working on an acting styles book, an introductory text for theater appreciation, and is compiling *The Best Short Plays of the 1980's* and *The Best Short Plays 1989*.